New Critical Perspectives on Martin Walser

NEW CRITICAL PERSPECTIVES ON MARTIN WALSER

EDITED

BY

FRANK PILIPP

CAMDEN HOUSE

Published by Camden House, Inc.
Drawer 2025
Columbia, SC 29202 USA

Printed on acid-free paper.
Binding materials are chosen for strength and durability.

Printed in the United States of America
First Edition

ISBN:1-879751-67-4

LIBRARY OF CONGRESS CATALOGING-IN-PUBLICATION DATA

New critical perspectives on Martin Walser / edited by Frank Pilipp. -- 1st ed.
p. cm. -- (Studies in German literature, linguistics, and culture)
Includes bibliographical references and index.
ISBN 1-879751-67-4 (alk. paper)
1. Walser, Martin, 1927- --Criticism and interpretation.
I. Pilipp, Frank, 1961- . II. Series: Studies in German literature, linguistics, and culture (Unnumbered)
PT2685.A48Z79 1994
838'.91409--dc20 94-1979
CIP

Acknowledgment

Publication of this book was made possible
by grants from
Lynchburg College.

Contents

Preface

INTRODUCING A VOLUME ON Martin Walser with yet another astute preamble presents, admittedly, an exacting task, for, especially in recent publications, others have submitted eloquent models. In addition to two perceptive and comprehensive essays that have appeared in such authoritative reference works as the *Dictionary of Literary Biography* (vol. 75, 1988) and the latest revised edition of the *Kritisches Lexikon zur deutschsprachigen Gegenwartsliteratur* (1992), the editors of the bilingual volume *Martin Walser: International Perspectives* (1987) have provided as succinct an introduction as the author of *The Novels of Martin Walser: A Critical Introduction* (1991).[1] This seeming richness of recent studies on a variety of aspects of Walser's works, some of which address specifically the English-speaking readership, is complemented with this volume which focuses exclusively on Walser's prose works.

As Wulf Koepke points out in his essay on *Ehen in Philippsburg* (1957; *Marriage in Philippsburg*, 1961) and *Halbzeit* (1960; Half Time), there is no need to belabor the legitimacy of Walser's social criticism. After almost four decades it may be said beyond a reasonable doubt that Walser has emerged as one of the most prolific German novelists. His oeuvre provides an astute and satirical commentary on the development and affairs of the Federal Republic. Since the late fifties the author has observed the social and political evolution of postwar Germany, consistently engaging in a critical dialogue with the prevailing winds in that country. In his fictions Walser has always devoted his attention to those whom he considers the underprivileged; those who, forever spurred by the materialistic amenities promised by social advancement, have climbed the social ladder from proletarian to middle class, but who cannot acclimate themselves psychologically in their new social environment.

Although he and his characters frequently cross national boundaries, Walser must be considered a singularly German writer; not only primarily on the basis of such a specifically German theme as is reflected in his novella

[1]For complete references of these works see the bibliography at the end of this volume.

Dorle und Wolf of 1987 (*No Man's Land*, 1988), but also, and more important, on account of the individual traits of his characters. Walser consistently portrays his protagonists as malcontent, middle-class intellectuals who find themselves in a world ruled by unfairness and hypocrisy. Walser creates external reality from the inner point of view of his characters, a perspective that is fleshed out and transcended subtly with a sophisticated measure of irony tinged with humor. The troubled psyche of the main character grants insight into social discrepancies. Walser's fictions evoke an unmistakable and rather subtle sense of nostalgia for a time before the growing preoccupation with materialism took over in the mid-fifties. What is most striking though is the author's preoccupation with the present, and not the past. Especially in Walser's later novels, those from *Runaway Horse* (1978), *The Inner Man* (1979), *The Swan Villa* (1980), *Letter to Lord Liszt* (1982) until *No Man's Land* (1987), the reader, witnessing the protagonists' agonizing self-withdrawal from impinging public demands and dictates, cannot help experiencing the author's own peculiar mixture of woeful resignation to, muted opposition to, and indignant lamentation about social power games.

In German literature of the last twenty years, Walser has taken a unique path. Unlike other authors in the early seventies, he was never tempted to escape external reality and lose himself in the ivory tower of unconditional subjectivity. It is also obvious that he believes reality no longer to be reproducible in its totality, and therefore he presents the reader with fragmented and subjective, that is, character-bound impressions of its threatening presence. He continually articulates the gap between reality and ideality, between an imperfect present and a more perfect future. He considers his writing a response to actually existing conditions. Although an ideal state is unachievable, Walser nevertheless lets us know that we do not even live in the best of all *possible* societies. While he does not formulate or propagate a clear-cut ideology, the vital thrust of Walser's criticism becomes manifest through his unrelenting attempts at probing into the underlying social causes of the delusions and disillusionment of his characters. In his recent novels, especially *Jagd* (1988; On the Prowl), *Die Verteidigung der Kindheit* (1991; In Defense of Childhood), and particularly *Ohne einander* (1993; Separate Lives), there emerge more distinctly gender issues such as discourses of sexuality or the clash of male and female voices in general that have yet to be investigated in more detail.

The prime asset of this book is undoubtedly that the contributors, most of whom have previously published on Walser, have expert opinions to offer. Interestingly, many of the essays here take a contrastive approach. Together they create both a synchronic and diachronic context: they illuminate thematic parallels between Walser and other contemporary authors (Mews, Pilipp), draw connections and analogies to earlier literary periods (Wagner-Egelhaaf,

Mathäs), and discuss genre issues from a historical perspective (Lawson). Especially welcome are the contributions that discuss Walser's recent novel *Die Verteidigung der Kindheit* (Doane, Pickar), as well as the author's approach to literary interpretation as evidenced both in his essays (Dowden) and in *Breakers* (Fischer), indisputably one of his most scintillating novels. A critical reevaluation of two of his early novels (Koepke) and a comprehensive discussion of Walser's heroes' torment under capitalist conditions (Bullivant) aptly complement the new critical perspectives on the writer in context.

To date, nine of Walser's fifteen novels have been translated into English. Unfortunately, not all translations are readily available; but the contributors consistently quote the primary texts in translation to reach especially the readership in this country. In addition to his fiction, Walser has published ten volumes of essays and speeches on social, political, cultural, and literary topics, as well as countless essays in newspapers and books. This book serves to accentuate the continued critical interest in one of the most prolific and critically acclaimed German authors and, not least, aims, as much as it can be in the power of critical scholarship to do so, to call attention to and, if not to revise, then at least to lament the deplorable state of affairs of the gradually diminishing number of Walser's novels available in English translation. This collection originated in the conviction that Walser is worth reading and merits renewed and continuing critical interest.

F. P.
January 1994

The following abbreviations are used for parenthetical documentation of Walser's texts:

The Translations:

B	—	*Breakers*
BAL	—	*Beyond All Love*
IM	—	*The Inner Man*
LL	—	*Letter to Lord Liszt*
MP	—	*Marriage in Philippsburg*
NL	—	*No Man's Land*
RH	—	*Runaway Horse*
SV	—	*The Swan Villa*
U	—	*The Unicorn*

The German texts:

Br	—	*Brandung*
BL	—	*Brief an Lord Liszt*
DW	—	*Dorle und Wolf*
E	—	*Das Einhorn*
EP	—	*Ehen in Philippsburg*
FP	—	*Ein fliehendes Pferd*
GK	—	*Die Gallistl'sche Krankheit*
H	—	*Halbzeit*
JL	—	*Jenseits der Liebe*
MG	—	*Meßmers Gedanken*
S	—	*Der Sturz*
SA	—	*Seelenarbeit*
SH	—	*Das Schwanenhaus*
VK	—	*Die Verteidigung der Kindheit*

1

The Reestablishment of the German Class Society: *Ehen in Philippsburg* and *Halbzeit*

Wulf Koepke

THERE IS NO NEED TO belabor two essential points in Walser's early novels: his social criticism (*Gesellschaftskritik*) and his possibly excessive love of details, defining his brand of "realism." The German critics noted these points when the novels appeared, and the scholars have followed their lead and systematized their suggestions.[1] What is still in need of some elucidation, however, is the question to which degree the reestablishment of a capitalistic class society was in need of public relations through the mass media, how and why Walser focuses primarily on this aspect, and what it means for his characters.

It should be remembered that the inflation after World War I led to a widespread impoverishment of the traditional bourgeoisie, the *Bürgertum*, and a concomitant fear of loss of social status. Also during that same period of the Weimar Republic, an enormous increase in the number and kinds of white-collar workers, the *Angestellten*, took place, requiring a comprehensive new social legislation and creating a group with a new social consciousness described by Siegfried Kracauer in his classical study of 1930. The white-

[1]Some of the critics who have dealt with these problems: Klaus Pezold, *Martin Walser: Seine schriftstellerische Entwicklung* (Berlin: Rütten & Loening, 1971); Thomas Beckermann, *Martin Walser oder die Zerstörung eines Musters: Literatursoziologischer Versuch über "Halbzeit"* (Bonn: Bouvier, 1972); Heike Doane, *Gesellschaftspolitische Aspekte in Martin Walsers Kristlein-Trilogie* (Bonn: Bouvier, 1978); Georges Hartmeier, *Die Wunsch- und Erzählströme in Martin Walsers Kristlein-Trilogie: Nöte und Utopien des Mannes* (Bern, Frankfurt, New York: Peter Lang, 1983); Ulrike Hick, *Martin Walsers Prosa: Möglichkeiten des zeitgenössischen Romans unter Berücksichtigung des Realismusanspruchs* (Stuttgart: Hans-Dieter Heinz, 1983). See the bibliographies of these books for further references.

collar workers were among the most defenseless victims of the great depression exemplified by the bestseller novel of Hans Fallada, *Kleiner Mann — Was nun?* (1932), a novel with such a universal appeal that its translation, *Little Man — What Now?* (1933), topped the bestseller lists in the United States. Both the traditional *Bürgertum*, relying in part on inherited wealth, and the new employee groups (such as office workers, salesmen, lower echelon government bureaucrats, advertising and leisure industry agents), living solely on their current income, were most vulnerable to economic crises and social change, and the unemployed *Angestellten* were among the first who listened to the promises of National Socialism. With the new full employment after 1933, an apparent stabilization of the economy, and new opportunities for the entrepreneurial groups, there seemed to be no fundamental reason to quarrel with the new regime, in spite of mutual reservations of the middle class and the party leadership. Contrary to its campaign rhetoric of egalitarianism, National Socialism protected the privileges of the moneyed classes, provided they offered their technical and administrative know-how for the stabilization of the regime. Since this silent pact excluded Jews, and the rearmament and war policies necessitated an encroachment of the state on private enterprise and business, the coalition was beset with conflicts on account of state-owned enterprises, regulations, and restrictions.

Nevertheless, when it all came to a catastrophic end and a crashing halt in 1945, it was undeniable that private industry and the professional classes had overwhelmingly collaborated with the regime, and that white-collar workers had been loyal followers. It seemed obvious that the people who had held leading positions before 1945 should not be the leaders in a transformation to a new democratic society. This could have touched the very foundations of the German social hierarchy, if the Western Allies had not decided to establish or reestablish a free-market economy and rely heavily on the established technical and administrative elite as well as on the industrial companies already in place, with largely token gestures toward punishing war criminals, for example the management of Krupp. For a short moment, however, everything seemed open and possible, even socialism, and since most Germans lived under the same conditions of scarcity, a new value system seemed to be at hand. This did not last long, and the mood of guilt and defeat changed quickly into one of resentment. People tended to forget what Germans had done to others and saw themselves as victims of the Allies, especially the Soviet Union. The introduction of the D-Mark in 1948 and the liberalization of the markets unleashed an enormous outburst of energy which, in social terms, reestablished the social hierarchies, fusing old established families and powers with the groups of new opportunists and new money.

The war and postwar years from 1939 to 1948 had taught the German population to recognize not only life's essentials and necessities but also that, in the face of pervasive death and destruction, inner values were crucial, and life after the war should be meaningful for the survivors and should contribute to a betterment of humankind. However, the new miraculous market economy could only succeed if people could be persuaded that the quality of life consisted in material goods far beyond the necessities of life. The public had to be convinced, step by step, that what was regarded as luxuries and mere status symbols was in reality necessary for a decent life-style. The Third Reich had developed an unprecedented propaganda machine for political purposes, and it had been singularly effective; the Federal Republic thrived on the wings of an advertising campaign for boundless consumption and for a decent middle-class appearance and behavior. People were enticed to feel good about buying furniture, clothes, cars, spending money on pleasures, and, most of all, keeping up with their peers.

It would be trivial and superfluous to describe such ubiquitous practices and mentalities, were it not for the fact that their onslaught in Germany after 1948 represented a sudden and radical change in lifestyle and mentality. At first sight, the new wealth and the abundance of goods seemed as unreal as the huge sums of inflationary money that the black marketeers had shuffled around before 1948. The unexpected successes of the new free-market system brought at first a giddy feeling together with nagging doubts about the moral degradation and corruption associated with this economic recovery and expansion, and the distinct conviction that this windfall could not last, that it would definitely end with another disastrous crash. The economic miracle, praised in official publications of the Federal Republic as the basis for a stabilization of society and a *new* democracy, seemed to perpetuate on a psychological level the existing existential insecurity of people who had grown accustomed to live and survive day by day. They were ready to enjoy whatever there was to be enjoyed, while the better or ideal society could wait for later.

During the war human relations had progressively adjusted to the day-by-day survival mentality. In the absence of many men during the war, with the constant reminders of imminent death, sexual morals were bound to change to those of instant gratification. Many of the quick marriages were dissolved after 1945 when divorce rates were high, but with the reaffirmation of the middle class after 1948, the bourgeois conventions of marriage reemerged as well, except that it may have been more facade than reality in many quarters. With a distinct disproportion of the number of men and women in certain years, like those born between 1915 and 1925, the sexual mores and extra-marital affairs may have been not too far from the picture Walser presents in his early novels. The view of post-1948 West German society that he shares with most other writers is that of a breakdown of values rather than a reestablishment of them. The conventional bourgeois view could hold that the stealing of food and heating material, prostitution for survival, and illegal black-market deals had all been immoral and were now a thing of the past. Law and order and respect for institutions, government and the churches in particular, had finally returned. The other side of the coin was that such elementary human values as decency, friendship, solidarity, mutual assistance, honesty, concern for the community, that had been considered essential, were now hardly in demand except for public relations. The transformation from the society of scarcity and black-market survival to the new law and order and prosperity had its victims: the *Aussteiger*, social drop-outs of sorts — often encountered in the novels of Heinrich Böll — whereas the majority of the population tried to forget the past and profit from the present as well as they could. While there were enough wholesale enthusiasts and opportunists for the new kind of life, many of the participants harbored their mental reservations while participating in the gold rush and hoped for a more decent society later. Just as Adenauer and Erhard profited from this prevailing mood of participation in the new prosperity and social advancement, Willy Brandt would be able to tap into the reservoir of frustrated hopes and ideals when he emerged in the sixties.

Walser offers classical portrayals of characters who might have been *Aussteiger*, but who allow themselves to be carried away by the dynamics of this new social restoration. His protagonists are in the position of dependent white-collar workers with the consciousness of intellectuals, intent at a certain point to make it to the top in order to decrease the indignities of their dependence. Walser uses in *Ehen in Philippsburg* (1957) the time-honored novelistic approach of the protagonist as the newcomer, the outsider who sees the establishment with fresh eyes, whereas in *Halbzeit* (1960) he allows his alter ego Anselm Kristlein the luxury of returning from a hospital stay and a trip to the United States to gain some distance from his environment. In order to maximize the impact of the new order of the Federal Republic on his characters (and readers), Walser stays as close as possible to the stream of consciousness of the respective protagonist, so that in *Halbzeit* it becomes almost impossible to distinguish the narrator's voice from that of Anselm.

These would-be intellectuals who are not real professionals are the ideal helpers to advertise the new system and its values. They are the agents of culture industry, of public relations, and of advertising. Walser focuses on the new mass media, especially the emerging television potential. Advertising and public relations create their own fictitious world in which the characters are arrested: a world of illusion and disillusionment, fraud, lies, breach of trust, and generally hypocritical behavior. There is no trust among these characters, only suspicion and the constant attempt to manipulate, to calculate, to observe. Everybody has something to hide, be it an unsavory political past, homosexuality (then illegal), cheating on a wife or husband, fraudulent business deals, even diseases that could render someone unfit for this fight for survival. Walser therefore constructs two parallel contrasts: the contrast between the appearance of prosperity, respectability, and order as opposed to the chaotic and dubious state of the economy and society; and the contrast between the public appearance and actual status of individual people and their intimate lives.

If appearances, public relations, creating one's own image of reality can be kept up long enough, appearances may actually change into reality. All of these characters are drifting, trying not to drown until they reach the point where they may have solid ground under their feet. Their notions of happiness beyond the daily and nightly enjoyments are not quite apparent, and the stories have no real beginnings or endings, not even in *Ehen in Philippsburg* where the episodes could be multiplied. The fundamental difference between *Halbzeit*, for example, and the epic narratives of Joyce and Proust with which it has been compared is that Walser does not create a new mythology; there is no quest, society does not appear as a whole, in spite of a multitude of events, details, and characters. In fact, Walser undermines the attempts of the official public relations for the Federal Republic to create legends and a self-legitimizing mythology of the new Germany that rose like a phoenix from the ashes. While this self-image of the Federal Republic insists on its economic, moral, and political solidity and reliability, it stresses its peacefulness and vows it will only fight against the evil enemy in the East. While it insists it has already shaken off an ugly past and is willing to assume new responsibilities, the lives of Walser's characters are presented as a chaotic mosaic of unconnected moments reflecting in a broken mirror fragments of the present and flashes of the past.

The "message" is thus cumulative; it consists of bits and pieces filtered through the ironic skepticism of the protagonists, demanding a constant watchfulness from the reader: a valid "message" of the narrator may come from the most untrustworthy messengers — in fact, some of the most acceptable statements in these constant monologues and dialogues come from characters the reader is invited to reject. The reader will have a difficult time formulating a final verdict; at least it will have to be revised several times in the course of the reading. The narrator, no less than the protagonists, is no real outsider, but a participant. The people he portrays are his people, and they appear in a much more negative light when analyzed than at first glance when, in fact, they seem rather amiable, even "fun to know" and by no means dwellers of a sinister underworld. Many episodes may sound satirical, even grotesque, but a comprehensive look at the complete picture, as it were, is not a condemnation of society out of righteous moral indignation. For all the fundamental doubts about this life-style and the direction society has taken, no real alternatives exist or are presented here. The protagonists have their moments when they feel like alienated outsiders and consider getting off this train, but they never do. With a good dose of cynicism they stay on board and try to enjoy whatever there is to be enjoyed. One of their saving graces is exactly their lack of illusions. They are honest with themselves, far from pretending to be the saviors of the Occident. Disillusioned, they see through any phony pathos and are ready to pour their sarcasm on everybody who "believes." In order not to appear naive they keep to themselves whatever secret hopes and desires they may have. However, they only *play* the roles of "tough guys" in the business world where one fights without gloves. In reality, the men are a traumatized, defeated crowd, who try their best to hide their real feelings. Anselm Kristlein's illness which has to be hidden from his customers is symptomatic.

Both *Ehen in Philippsburg* and *Halbzeit* reflect a specific moment in the postwar development, the earlier and later fifties, respectively. In each case, the outsider and would-be social climber is from a rural and lower-class milieu, especially Hans Beumann, the illegitimate son of a waitress, whose background could present a very serious handicap for his career. They enter an already reestablished upper class that is still vulnerable and thus ready to coopt new forces, but is firmly in charge of the country's destiny. Hans Beumann's career is more conventional and sounds like a parody of a cheap novel: he meets and marries the rich Anne Volkmann, who sees to it that he finds the right job and is properly introduced into society. However, that is where the similarities end. While in his heart Beumann knows from the beginning that he does not want to marry Anne, he feels much more justified in his job, providing public relations for the corporation of Anne's father. Still, he will finally acquiesce. Anselm Kristlein, on the other hand, considers his wife's background — her father is a university professor — rather a drawback and a source of constant pressure on him to perform and become "respectable." Out of opposition to this pressure he had dropped out of university and begun a "career" as a traveling salesman, gaining his knowledge of the real business world the hard way, and losing all inhibitions, moral and otherwise, on the way. It is only as an advertising writer and executive that Anselm can climb the social ladder, helped by a network of so-called friends. Both Beumann and Kristlein gain entrance to the higher society and the amenities of that lifestyle through enhancing the image of that society, the products it sells, and its leaders. The affirmation of the system is the price for upward mobility.

It might be asked why this is in any way unusual or even reprehensible. The answer is not quite as ready in the German context of the fifties as it is in the American context of today. Socialism, had it been of the humanistic, of the democratic variety, and not brutal and dictatorial, seemed to be a desirable system to many, and in a way morally superior to capitalism with its accompanying symptoms of corruption and exploitation. Even the German constitution of 1949, the *Grundgesetz*, sanctioned by the Western Allies, contained a section about expropriation of private property. The lingering doubts about this economic miracle are scattered all over these books and the rest of German literature of the fifties, until turning into more concrete efforts for reforms in the literature and real life of the subsequent decade, or, in some quarters, for a real revolution. *Ehen in Philippsburg* and *Halbzeit* still reflect a period of getting accustomed to a new way of life and some uneasiness over missed opportunities to move in other directions.

Shreds of this moral malaise are spliced as satirical vignettes into the fabric of the narration, specifically in *Halbzeit*. During the long and momentous session with Frantzke about the advertising campaign, Dieckow, the writer, voices his disgust with cheating the customers with mere repackaging. A corporation like this, he affirms with some moral pathos and correct political arguments, should improve products, not advertising. After all, business has considerable "responsibility toward society." "Our" Western world is locked in a deadly struggle with a society that concentrates its resources on essentials, while "we" are solely concerned with the "superfluous," and actually "abuse liberty" (H 424-25). Anselm Kristlein, one of the silent participants, thinks to himself that this fixation on the enemy in the East is anachronistic; it is more characteristic of the old generation (that of Adenauer, the eighty-year-old Chancellor). Lambert, designated to reply to Dieckow, can easily expose Dieckow's phony position. Dieckow's social criticism is part of legitimizing the system: a system that allows opposing views is really democratic. Dieckow himself lives off the rich, and his poetic warning about the nuclear holocaust is ludicrous. In other words, Dieckow is merely another pawn in the games of the culture industry.

That Dieckow is easily discredited does not necessarily invalidate his arguments, although they are off the agenda for the present purpose. Anselm's sarcastic account of the scene does not gloss over the unwelcome aspects of capitalism, it rather adds one more dimension to the picture. However, revolutionaries are absent from this text; Edmund's eventual move to the GDR is motivated by very personal considerations, and if there is any ideal that these characters carry in their innermost selves, it would have to be that of a "third path" between East and West. In political terms, therefore, *Halbzeit* may indeed be defined as a satire, since it hints at the desirable state of its society only *ex negativo*.

The murky and uneasy atmosphere of the present in the Federal Republic is most clearly seen in the recurring confrontations with the Nazi past. There is simply no coming to terms with the Nazi past, and even less with the war experience. Anselm has flashbacks to his traumatic years as a prisoner of war in the Soviet Union; Josef-Heinrich cannot come to grips with his victories and defeats as a much-decorated flyer-ace; a corporation, such as that of Frantzke, is full of people like Dr. Fuchs who have a despicable past in the higher ranks of the SD, the security service of the Nazis. Society has agreed to forgive and forget the Nazi past and wants to ignore war and postwar traumas. Now Dr. Fuchs sits at the same table with the son of a victim of 20 July 1944. The one real crisis that almost throws Anselm off this moving train not by accident involves the only Jewish character in *Halbzeit:* Susanne, a survivor without a home, drifting like the others, involved in image-making in a different way (a travel agent), used and rejected in Germany. Anselm's love relationship with her threatens to tear his supporting network apart, but he is rescued, thanks to his chronic ambivalence and his American sojourn and training. She leaves, and all he can do, as Edmund says, is to make more money.

America is the magic word. *Halbzeit* contains numerous references to American music, providing more than just a contemporary atmosphere for bar hoppers. It is punctuated by the rhythms of American jazz, both disturbing and soothing. America is the wonderland where Anselm receives his higher initiation into the secrets of advertising. America is a valid pretext for everything one wants to do. When Anselm finally succeeds with Susanne, he follows an American-type manual on selling; but at the same time it is programming the failure of their relationship in advance.

Ehen in Philippsburg, as the title suggests, focuses primarily on male-female relationships, distinctly from the male perspective, and questions both the institution of marriage and the societal constraints on individuals, as well as the indecisiveness and lack of courage of men. If this (and *Halbzeit* as well) is a "male" novel, it is also a serious indictment of men, and the only intact persons are women — not all of them, by any means. While women are seen as the "other," and often enough as mere objects (mostly objects of desire), it is the gaze of the men that is criticized or at least questioned. When it comes to commitment, the men are compromising opportunists, never reliable, who shy away from any relationship if it interferes with their social status and comfort. *Ehen in Philippsburg* still dramatizes this point as something lamentable, steering the different episodes to catastrophic climaxes. The suicide of a wife or a car accident shatter the false feeling of security and throw the men back into a void. In *Halbzeit*, such potential crises and breakdowns are averted, life goes on, and everything is well. While presented in *Halbzeit* as more resigned and therefore ready for imperfect relationships rather than none at all, the female characters continue to be more demanding in their nature: they want commitments, and they can be absolute. They are described as unfulfilled, lonely, in search of an impossible ideal of a relationship. On an individual level, therefore, the women still preserve the pre-1949 ideals of "true" love and partnership, whereas the men are generally seen as incapable of transcending the mediocrity of their environment: they are broken and anxiously avoid dramatic conflicts, preferring little white lies and a pseudo-idyllic family setting.

The drama in *Ehen in Philippsburg* arises from the premise that true relationships and the lifestyle of the new society are irreconcilable. Sooner or later, one has to make a choice for one or the other. Again, Walser agrees on this point with writers like Heinrich Böll, Günter Grass, Ingeborg Bachmann, or Hans Erich Nossack. The major difference, however, between him and most others is that he adopts the point of view of the opportunists and not of the *Aussteiger*, albeit in a decidedly ironical manner. All male characters are ill at ease, and ultimately their opportunism is ambivalent. Despite a clear lack of compelling arguments against joining the establishment, they would still like to live in another, better world. Essentially the men in Walser's stories know that they are defeated, and their moneymaking and professional success are no compensation for a wasted life. While the women still seem to demand more than they can get, they tend to become embittered and disillusioned about the men in their own way.

All of this suggests that the institutions of marriage and the family — the latter being the most stable social institution in times of such crises as the Germans had experienced — become a mere facade needed for the self-image of the new society but do not correspond or cater to real needs of real people. The fundamental paradox of the new respectability of the Federal Republic, that the urgent need for a clean-looking facade goes hand in hand with a state of utter disorientation at the individual and psychological level, is brought out in these novels from a different point of view. *Ehen in Philippsburg* contrasts the surface appearance with the real truth in a straightforward manner and points directly to the parallelism between human hypocrisy and the divergence of product and advertising with regard to public relations. Instead of the honest truth of much confusion, unsolved problems, ugliness, and unhealed wounds, all the unpleasantness is repressed and covered up, and varnish is applied to the image of the whole society.

Ehen in Philippsburg offers examples of two men whose lives of respectability become derailed: the one, Klaff, a real *Aussteiger* and would-be writer, who is dismissed from his job for his "evil" gaze and subsequently abandoned by his wife; the other, Hans Beumann, who ends up accepting what is offered to him. His life is also beset by "accidents" such as the need for an abortion for Anne, but they are soon forgotten. A symptomatic scene is the engagement party which is, literally, almost destroyed by a violent storm reminiscent of the final scene in Heinrich Mann's *Der Untertan* (1918; *Man of Straw*, 1946). However, in contrast to Heinrich Mann, the tempest passes in Walser's novel, the villa is not seriously damaged, and the guests turn to gambling, where Hans Beumann wins while seeming to lose. Beumann's attitude and point of view are carried over into *Halbzeit*, where no melodramatic apparatus is needed any more, and where the crises pass, as mutual interest ensures that life shall go on as usual. In other words, in *Ehen in Philippsburg* Walser still dramatizes the human costs of this new social system, similar to Gerd Gaiser in *Schlußball* (1958; *The Final Ball*, 1960), the novels of Wolfgang Koeppen or Heinrich Böll, but in *Halbzeit*, as it were, they have been paid already, and the loss of integrity is a fait accompli. Anybody who nurses scruples except for his own pleasure is fighting windmills.

Ehen in Philippsburg focuses primarily on the need of the new society to polish its image and keep it shining. *Halbzeit* looks at the same society a few years later, but more from an inside perspective. Now the double standards appear transparent and are generally accepted, while everybody tries to profit from the system. There seems to be much less need to listen to moral scruples. Church and state have been solidly reestablished; no need to praise or even mention them, but they are good for snide remarks. There are no dark secrets any more, only open secrets. It is a matter of skill and the right manner of presentation to turn a disadvantage into an advantage. Thus, Dr. Fuchs, the prime example of failure and hubris, is banished from society not for what he did before 1945, but for the clumsiness with which he tried to hide it. He could have been denazified when the opportunity was conveniently available. The facts, like time, are in a continual flux, they are movable and depend on the spin one gives them. In this manner, the second level of reality, the interpretation given to facts, becomes reality.

The art of Walser in *Halbzeit* is that Kristlein's consciousness encompasses both levels, the unpleasant side and the means to make it look good, as well as the knowledge of what this process really entails. Many scenes, therefore, seem grotesque or repulsively funny, and we empathize with Anselm's constant need for overcoming his inner resistance and repulsion. He dreams about being left alone, not having to talk people into something they do not want, much less need. The narrator, as far as one is discernible, enhances the ironic contrasts, especially by pointing out some truths through the questionable medium of a negative character. Surely most characters know who they are and what they are doing, and they periodically burst out into some expression of what ought to be. Dieckow, who is an "official" agent of bad conscience, mixes disturbing clichés with real concerns. Hence he can state that the so-called high society is nothing but the crest of seafoam on the infinite surface of the water, and often enough not even foam but scum (*Abschaum* instead of *Schaum*).[2] When, on the other hand, Anselm hears other people getting morally indignant about fraud and deceit (*Betrug*), all he can do after so many years as a traveling salesman and as an advertising writer is smile. Here the "message" would have to be deduced by the reader, by penetrating beyond the intrinsic irony of the narration.

The inevitable major metaphor of *Halbzeit* is that of the stage, although this may already be somewhat dated in terms of technological development. Just as in the famous story *Bahnwärter Thiel* (1888; *Flagman Thiel*, 1933) by Gerhart Hauptmann, where the sound of the approaching train is compared to that of galloping horses replaced by modern means of transportation, Walser keeps referring to the theater while talking about radio and television. The characters of *Halbzeit*, in any event, are seen and feel themselves as actors in a strange play. They (or at least Anselm) assume that there must be some director in charge. Although, or perhaps because, it is incomprehensible to the participants, Anselm and the narrator do not really expect logical, causal connections or meanings, and are certainly not surprised by the accidental and arbitrary nature of this narrative. If "absurd" designates an absence of meaning where meaning and causality are expected, this is not absurd, but one might call it a theater of disconnectedness. It is on one level an unending monologue in the manner of Proust and Joyce, and we may assume that all characters in *Halbzeit* are engaged in a similar monologue. There is a purpose to this chaotic game without beginning or end: everybody tries to sell something, including themselves. Theater as the making of a self-image turns into a mode of advertising that reveals just enough of the acting character to make the partner and the audience want to accept the character's proposition.

The inner monologue, the isolation of individuals, the world of mere appearances, the fundamental estrangement from life, from society, and from oneself, all of this is reminiscent in a more than casual way of the epic search of time lost in Marcel Proust.[3] However, Walser applies Proustian features to a very different society and for very different purposes. There is no equivalent of a time regained in *Halbzeit*; it ends where it began. Anselm

[2]*Halbzeit*, p. 418; in association with *Schaumkrone* and *Abschaum*, the moral judgment is much less dominant than the idea of drifting and being determined by exterior forces, or the idea of a short-lived reality. Foam as a very short appearance has neither duration nor substance, yet repeats itself all the time.

[3]See also Martin Walser, "Leseerfahrungen mit Marcel Proust" (1958), *Erfahrungen und Leseerfahrungen* (Frankfurt/M.: Suhrkamp, 1963) 124-42; much more research and analysis of this connection would be needed.

is back with his family, would like to stay in bed and float with his dreams, but is called back to "reality."

Ehen in Philippsburg presents us with the parody of a "new" political party embracing most major ideological positions (except communism), where success will sweep away all inherent contradictions, as in the case of the conservative party, the CDU. *Halbzeit* reduces politics to snide remarks. Whereas in the first novel, the entrepreneurial class is still concerned about creating a government willing and able to support its expansion, *Halbzeit* takes this role of government for granted. Political persuasion is superfluous, for advertising concentrates on products. This is not a society that wants to change and be changed — it wants to consume and enjoy. With a general cynicism about politics and the political process, these characters support the political *status quo*. Far be it from them to disagree with the CDU's most successful slogan, "No Experiments."

Walser presents his own version of what sociologists have called the "skeptical generation." Anselm Kristlein typifies the returning POW who faces an emerging or already established new system. Being one of the latecomers, he cannot flatter himself that he can prevent the continuing restoration: the power structures and the leaders are already in place. Like countless others he now discards his humanitarian and humanistic baggage of dreams, plans, and hopes for a better life — in a moral sense — and exchanges his dream for what he can get: a decent and improving living standard. He simply forgets about war trauma, guilt feelings, and the idea of renewal. Lacking any particular respect for the new leaders in politics and industry, he nevertheless adjusts to the system that enables him to launch a career, maximize profit, and does not ask for any real commitment. For him, "skeptical" means holding back, rolling along, though without real conviction, always afraid of getting trapped in a real commitment. Josef-Heinrich's eleven or twelve engagements are not merely funny, but they describe precisely his human position. If he enters into a steadfast relationship at the end, without engagement, it will also mean a real departure.

The half-serious character of this wait-and-see skepticism is also exemplified in the question of national identity. This question finds its outlet in the argument between Edmund and Dieckow about World War II and what constitutes *typisch deutsch*.[4] Anselm notices sarcastically that nowadays "typically German" is that style or trait which everybody dislikes in others;

[4]*Halbzeit*, pp. 605-09; the text also contains countless casual remarks pertaining to latent national pride and resentments. Walser is definitely a keen observer of underground currents in the collective German psyche, certainly in the social strata that he describes. There are, of course, no true representatives of the working class in *Halbzeit*.

it is *de rigueur* to appear as "un-German" as possible, preferably American or French in certain aspects. The debate on the German responsibility for the last war and its meaning or absurdity, however, degenerates into a mere party game trying to knock out one's opponent, in the course of which the opponents defend positions that they would normally attack. As this is done in front of a "chorus" of partygoers, it is nothing but a show and a match, as it turns out, with no real winner and no message, as far as the reader is concerned. After reading Anselm's sarcastic account of this verbal boxing match, one arrives at the conviction that the two opponents might have debated any point in the same acrimonious manner; and that the aftermath of World War II and what it entailed, not least for Anselm, has been degraded to a mere party game. This is true on one level; yet, on another level, the choice of the topic was anything but arbitrary, for that is precisely what is constantly and painfully on their minds. They are indeed deeply hurt in their national as well as in their individual pride. But in order to shrug it off and go on living, they pretend that the idea of a German Nation is an obsolete concept. In their view, it is poor manners to have strong convictions and to fight over real moral and political issues; only in the form of a party game can Edmund and Dieckow give vent to their innermost convictions, and even then only in an ironical manner.

The community in *Halbzeit* is also quite different from a genuine democracy, where opponents respect different views and convictions and try to find common ground where practical needs dictate it. German postwar society is still ruled by very authoritarian old men who selfishly insist on their ways. If they and their aides tolerate others, they do not act out of democratic principles, but rather to keep up appearances of a tolerant and open society. Anselm's crowd, on the other hand, does not believe in convictions at all, or at least pretends not to believe in them. They tolerate everything and declare every conviction to be phony, especially when it serves social advancement. This general agreement in cynicism keeps society open and humors the arbitrary and authoritarian decrees of the old men in power (who will not last long anyway). As with the wounded pride, fighting for a cause cannot be admitted, for it would appear utterly naive and disqualify the individual from any serious "business."

An analysis of the characters and events Walser portrays, especially in *Halbzeit*, must necessarily assume the appearance of a totally pessimistic and satirical picture; yet Walser is no Swift. While *Ehen in Philippsburg* still contains its measure of moral indignation, not least in the character of Klaff and in the account of the demise of Benrath and Alwin, *Halbzeit* moves along gaily, with much irony, sarcasm, and cynicism, but with no thundering judgment. While the story abounds with grotesqueness, there is a limit to its repulsive aspects: on the outside everything remains nice, friendly, and "normal." While Anselm's secret fear and nightmare is that this may all be a mere soap bubble bound to burst, and that he will be thrown back into his former misery, be it in the Soviet Union or as a salesman on the road, this new reality which seems in constant flux gains its own kind of solidity and maintains its dominance, silencing all moralistic doomsayers.

While much of the earlier postwar literature in Germany resounds with moral indignation, Walser hits on the *Wirtschaftswunderton*, the tone of the economic miracle that Grass captured to a degree in his *Blechtrommel* (1959; *The Tin Drum*, 1962) and that Böll was able to express in such stories as *Doktor Murkes gesammeltes Schweigen* (1958; *Dr. Murke's Collected Silence*, 1963) and in several of his later novels. Walser is ahead of most others in his comprehensive view of the techniques of image-making and advertising by means of which the new postwar miracle became reality. Walser makes us aware how pervasive the role of this image-making was, and how the professional intelligentsia conformed to a power structure it in fact disliked. *Halbzeit* describes this process as a matter of course, and the concomitant phenomena of alienation and degradation are mentioned rather casually. Society operates entirely on expediency and on casuistic decision-making. As a routine, relationships are dominated in a matter-of-fact fashion by calculation, salesmanship, image-making, deceit, lies, and suspicion. While the women may occasionally break out of this consensus, the men generally do not possess the strength to do so. In a society operating on the basis of this tacit understanding of duplicity, any harsh decisions and principled actions can only be disturbing.

We are not concerned here with Anselm's future problems and conflicts in *Das Einhorn* (1966; *The Unicorn*, 1971) and his demise in *Der Sturz* (1973; The Fall). The second and third part of the trilogy move the action forward to later stages in the development of the economic giant, the Federal Republic, and Walser begins to affront the sixties. In *Halbzeit*, however, he captures a moment in German postwar history (1957) which could be called a climax in economic terms (before the first recession in the sixties) and a nadir in moral terms. This is achieved with uncommon authenticity, as the novel describes the malaise as well as the brilliant facade of the German miraculous economy. While *Ehen in Philippsburg* still communicates some of the shock over the nonchalant reinstatement of the old/new power structure, *Halbzeit* tells us how it affects the willing or unwilling participants who have no choice but to survive in this environment. Obviously Walser does not *accept* this new society, and although any revolutionary indignation and energy seems to be virtually absent from the portrayal of its institutions, the cumulative message for the reader is clearly not to lose time in fighting a seemingly immutable system. Readers on their part will be amused, and, ill-inclined to condone what Walser presents, will begin to question the picture he draws. The somewhat baffled reactions from the first reviewers to the novel's subversive potential, its subtle and ironic debunking of unreflecting social conformism shows that they were not used to this degree of sophistication and multiple layers of meaning. Even in later years, critics found it hard to cope with the novel's rich and often seemingly contradictory mosaic. As fiction *and* document, *Halbzeit* remains a singular success, providing insight into a very troubled and insecure society and its ambivalent attitude toward change.

2

Working Heroes in the Novels of Martin Walser

Keith Bullivant

THE NOVELS OF MARTIN WALSER are usually understood as breaking down into three, or even four groups: *Marriage in Philippsburg* (1957, trans. 1961) was a relatively conventional social novel set at a time of social mobility that had more in common with, e.g., John Braine's British novel *Room at the Top* (1957) than with the then contemporary West German novel. *Halbzeit* (1960; Half Time) and *The Unicorn* (1966; 1971), the first two parts of the Anselm Kristlein trilogy, were strikingly more modern in the somewhat rambling form, in the innovative use of language, and in the central thematic concern with identity and role-playing in modern society. As such they were seen as belonging to the same sort of category as Grass's *Die Blechtrommel* (1959; *The Tin Drum*, 1962) and Uwe Johnson's *Mutmaßungen über Jakob* (1959; *Speculations About Jakob*, 1963), with these novels in turn being understood to constitute a breakthrough of the West German novel into the company of international modernity. The final part of the trilogy, *Der Sturz* (1973; The Fall), was in many ways closer to the style of the earlier part than to Walser's writing of the early seventies and can justifiably be seen as the summation of Walser's novels of the sixties. However, as early as 1964 it was clear that Walser was becoming highly critical of the major tendencies of "bourgeois literature," which for him had lost its initial emancipatory impetus and had by now become merely affirmative, its main characteristics being

> the leeway granted, the precisely delimited fool's license, the boldly undertaken linguistic expeditions into elegant or attractively wicked

dead ends ... into the modern supernatural. Into nothing but language games.[1]

This disquiet, closely linked to Walser's growing political awareness in the turbulent sixties, reached its zenith towards the end of the decade when, taking a break from writing himself, he championed the publication of the life stories of people outside the middle class[2] and became involved in the work of the cooperative of worker-writers, the *Werkkreis Literatur der Arbeitswelt*. To this phase also belonged Walser's *Die Gallistl'sche Krankheit* (1972; Gallistl's Disease), his attempt "to write a socialist novel from the point of view of a petty-bourgeois intellectual";[3] the experimental prose piece *Fiction* (1970); and the completion of the Kristlein trilogy. The next — and, it would appear, final — phase of Walser's fictional prose-writing was ushered in by the highly criticized novel *Beyond All Love* (1976; 1981) and in 1993 consists of eight novels and two novellas. The works are linked back to the trilogy, in that, like *Der Sturz*, they are all concerned with individual failure in modern competitive society. They are seen, however, as forming a discrete unit insofar as they are all far more conventional and readable and, above all, are marked by an extensive use of free indirect speech that produces an intensively subjective form of realist writing having much in common with the "New Subjectivity" of the seventies.[4]

There is much to this reading of the progress of Walser's career as a novelist; it certainly addresses the major stylistic changes in his craft over the last twenty-six years. Walser, however, has argued that while "the finer spirits really don't want to see occupations of any sort in today's novel," every one of his own novels and novellas features a central character with a clearly defined job: Hans Beumann (*Marriage in Philippsburg*) is a journalist, Anselm Kristlein is a sales representative, a writer, and the administrator of a rest home; Josef Gallistl has various jobs and ends up as a writer; Franz Horn (*Beyond All Love* and *Letter to Lord Liszt*, 1982; 1985) is a sales

[1]Walser, "Freiübungen," *Erfahrungen und Leseerfahrungen* (Frankfurt/M.: Suhrkamp) 97.

[2]Cf. here Erika Runge, *Bottroper Protokolle* (1968), Ursula Trauberg, *Vorleben* (1968), and Wolfgang Werner, *Vom Waisenhaus ins Zuchthaus* (1969).

[3]Anthony Waine, *Martin Walser* (Munich: Text + Kritik, 1980) 102.

[4]Cf. here Frank Pilipp, *The Novels of Martin Walser: A Critical Introduction*, Studies in German Literature, Linguistics, and Culture 64 (Columbia SC: Camden House, 1991) 32-35, and Keith Bullivant, *Realism Today* (Leamington Spa, Hamburg, New York: Berg, 1977) 213-20.

executive; Helmut Halm (*Runaway Horse*, 1978; 1980 and *Breakers*, 1985; 1987) a schoolteacher; Klaus Buch, his alter ego in *Runaway Horse*, a journalist; Xaver Zürn (*The Inner Man*, 1979; 1984) a chauffeur; Gottlieb Zürn (*The Swan Villa*, 1980; 1982 and *Jagd*, 1988; On the Prowl) a realtor; Wolf Zieger (*No Man's Land*, 1987; 1988) is a local government official and GDR spy; and Alfred Dorn (*Die Verteidigung der Kindheit*, 1991; In Defense of Childhood) is a lawyer employed as a civil servant.[5]

Walser's career as a novelist began in the late fifties, at a time when a number of writers and critics, notably Alfred Andersch, Walter Jens, and Wolfgang Rothe, were complaining that, despite the urging of Julian Schmidt and Karl Gutzkow a hundred years earlier, the German novel continued to focus on the world of leisure rather than the workplace as the determinant of modern existence. While it can be argued that such a view ignored certain of Böll's shorter prose works of the time, Walser's first novel, *Marriage in Philippsburg*, was a truly isolated work in the context of the German novel of the fifties. In his case — although the possible influence of Andersch, a colleague at the Südwestfunk, cannot be excluded — the strong evidence is that Walser's concern with the pressures on the individual working within modern competitive society can be traced back to his doctoral work on Kafka and to his interest in the work of Robert Walser (no relation), especially his novel *Der Gehülfe* (1907; The Servant), which thematically anticipates *The Inner Man*. Only as a result of his politicization in the sixties does the sympathy for, and support of, working-class efforts for self-expression in writing emerge, a concern that continues into the eighties.

The apparent emphasis in Walser's first three novels was on the price paid by the individual for success (or merely survival) in modern society. Hans Beumann, much like Joe Lampton in *Room at the Top*, succeeds in his new social milieu by squashing the noble ideals of his student days. His finer feelings are suppressed in favor of a dog-eat-dog attitude that enables the quick-witted protagonist to succeed in the marketplace of Philippsburg. The price of success is, though, betrayal of people like himself (climaxing in the scene when he forcibly evicts a proletarian gate-crasher from the exclusive Sebastian Club), suppression of true feelings (he really prefers the humbler Marge to Anne Volkmann, marriage with whom is, though, his entrance card to the higher society of Philippsburg), and, ultimately, deformation of character.

[5]Walser, "Brauchen Romanhelden Berufe?" *Frankfurter Allgemeine Zeitung* (Literary Supplement) 11 Jan. 1992: 1-2. It should be stated here that, notwithstanding the point Walser makes, the emphases in *No Man's Land* and *Die Verteidigung der Kindheit* are different from those of the other later novels and will not be examined here.

Although marking a radical stylistic breakaway from the relatively traditional first novel to an aggressive avantgardism, *Halbzeit* continues the concern with modern pressures on the individual. Walser's protagonist this time is a sales representative, a figure of particular significance for Walser:

> It has struck me how awful it is if someone constantly has to sell things when those around him don't really need anything. Or, at least, they can just as easily buy or order what they've bought or ordered from this sales representative from any of his competitors. There is, therefore, no other job that could so forcefully make a person aware of his or her own superfluity as that of the commercial traveler.[6]

We are confronted with the impact of such problems on the individual at the very beginning of the novel, when we learn that Anselm Kristlein has recently returned home from hospital, a stay brought on by job pressures. But, trapped in the system though he is, Anselm is clearly a survivor, able to achieve some degree of independence through his chameleon-like mastery of role-playing and, at the same time, indulging himself in his weakness for the opposite sex. In *The Unicorn*, the second part of the trilogy, Anselm has become a free-lance writer, but the social game remains the same — indeed, he has now become even more expert as a player of social roles. This talent enables him not only to survive in the competitive world but also (unlike Hans Beumann) to maintain his identity:

> His identity is never seriously endangered. He is chained to it as to nothing else. That is to say, he is in no sense a pathological case, he is absolutely not schizophrenic; his roles are simply his attempt — through masterly conformism towards those stronger than himself — to make himself appear a strong person.[7]

The final volume of the trilogy marked a decisive turning point in Walser's portrayal of Anselm Kristlein. By the time he came to write this novel, Walser had moved farther to the Left politically, strongly supporting efforts by groups within the DKP (the German Communist Party) and by the

[6]In an interview with Horst Bienek in the latter's *Werkstattgespräche mit Schriftstellern* (Munich: Hanser, 1962) 195.

[7]Walser in a letter of 27 July 1967 to Melvyn Dorman, a graduate student at the University of Birmingham (UK). Quoted in R. Hinton Thomas and W. van der Will, *Der deutsche Roman und die Wohlstandsgesellschaft* (Stuttgart: Kohlhammer, 1969) 124 (my translation).

Werkkreis Literatur der Arbeitswelt to articulate in literature the price paid by those working in capitalist society. His *Die Gallistl'sche Krankheit* focuses — in a way that takes us back to Hans Beumann — on the deformation of character as an integral part of the work process; Gallistl works

> in order to earn the money that I need to be Josef Georg Gallistl. But by having to work so much, I never get to being Josef Georg Gallistl. Up to now I have never been anything more than the person who works for the Josef Georg Gallistl who doesn't yet exist. (GK 22-23)

Gallistl is weary of the hard and lonely struggle, dreams of escape into the world of manual labor and considers joining "the Party" (presumably the DKP) in order to end his isolation. The Anselm Kristlein we meet in *Der Sturz* is a not dissimilar figure. The (now) fifty-year-old is exhausted by the "pressure to earn money" (S 25), longs to experience life without that pressure, but — having known no other life — is afraid "that my life would at once cease to have any meaning at all if the pressure to earn money were removed. Up to now it has had no other meaning than earning money" (S 26). In a desperate attempt to make money he has risked and lost all of his wife's inheritance, 72,000 marks, walked and worked his way south from Munich in his quest to rejoin his family, and been arrested and tried on suspicion of murder (being freed only after the intervention and detective work of his wife, Alissa). Traumatized by these experiences, which culminate in his being attacked by persons unknown after his release, and as a result more or less incapable of communication with the members of his family, Kristlein now runs a rest home for the entrepreneur Blomich and finds himself surrounded by fellow victims: the worker Berthold Traub, unable to face the thought of returning to work in the Blomich works, commits suicide, as does the ex-gardener Michel Enziger, while Kristlein's wife has a nervous breakdown. The final disaster comes when Blomich sells out to the American competition and all of the employees are dismissed. Kristlein's sovereign "counter-type" has now made himself completely independent of the world of commercial competition, while the isolated Anselm, turning too late to Alissa for support and comfort and lacking the political support enjoyed by those who are politically organized, can envisage only further catastrophe. The final section of the novel, "With the sailing boat across the Alps," Anselm's dream (narrated in the future tense) of what might now happen, is a bizarre act of individual rebellion, in that he fantasizes about running off with Blomich's treasured possession, an episode which ends, significantly enough, with boat and trailer causing an accident in the Alps and the line: "It's downhill all the way for us" (S 352).

The central thematic concerns of *Der Sturz* — the increasing inability of the middle-aged male to cope with the pressures of the rat race, with those problems exacerbated by the inability of Walser's protagonist to break out of neurotic individualism and take advantage of the support offered by a loving wife or political organizations — are at the heart of most of Walser's subsequent prose fiction. These works differ stylistically from their predecessors in their intense focus on the inner life of the antihero, achieved by the extensive use of free indirect speech. The prototype of the protagonist in this sequence of works is Franz Horn, a sales executive with a firm of denture manufacturers. He has obviously enjoyed a good measure of success in former years but now finds himself increasingly incapable of coping with the intense competition coming from younger colleagues. He has been making a series of more or less unconscious protest gestures against the diminution of his standing within the firm, through heavy drinking, weight gain, and involvement in trade-union activities directed against the management. However, it is only during the course of a business trip to England that he becomes truly aware of the depth of his dissatisfaction when confronted with his alter ego Keith Heath. He crowns the failure of his business trip by taking a (nonfatal) overdose of sleeping pills, having found a sort of contentment in having exited the rat race by embracing failure: "All he wanted was to be left alone with his own worthlessness, which he no longer disputed" (BAL 66; JL 112).

This survival tactic is continued by Horn in the epistolary *Letter to Lord Liszt* and is adopted too by the failed realtor Gottlieb Zürn and Helmut Halm, during his visiting semester in the U.S.A. in *Breakers*, as a means of coping with the pressures brought out so forcefully (and economically) in *Runaway Horse*. In the figure of the seemingly Peter Pan-like Klaus Buch we appear to have the successful embodiment of the ethos of competitive society. He regards every sphere of his life — work, sex, sport — in an incredibly competitive light and appears to enjoy success in all these areas. Only when he is swept overboard while sailing with Helmut Halm on Lake Constance does his young wife reveal the implosive effect of his lifestyle on her and, too, the true misery of Klaus's life:

> "He didn't have much of a life," Hella said. "It was just one long grind. Every day ten, twelve hours at the typewriter. Even when he couldn't write, he still sat at the typewriter. 'I must be at the ready,' he would say then. Everything he did was a terrible effort.... He often used to cry out, at night. And more and more often he would break out into a sweat, in the middle of the night...." (RH 98; FP 136-37)

While Klaus embodies the attempt to cope with societal pressures through total conformism to the norms of competitive society, Helmut Halm adopts a radically different strategy. In a form of controlled schizophrenia (living *doppelt*), he safeguards his true self by superficial conformism at school and withdrawal into an internalized existence in his private life.

This is the "inward path," the "subordination of the external world to that of the soul," as Walser calls it, that in his view has made an artistic virtue out of historical necessity within the history of the German novel of the nineteenth and twentieth centuries.[8] The irritant source of this "petty-bourgeois tendency" (*Kleinbürgertendenz*) is the "violation of human dignity brought about by dependency," i.e., wage labor of all kinds,[9] the means of coping with it in literature the depiction of the withdrawal into an inner life in which the true self can be just that. In Walser's work this is seen with particular force in the figure of Helmut Halm in *Runaway Horse*. While, however, this latter work would seem to fit beautifully into the scheme of Walser's ideas and be supported by, e.g., *Der Sturz*, a number of other works in the last phase of Walser's career raise problems. The figure of Gottlieb Zürn embodies all the features of the Walser antihero that characterize the novels since 1976. He dreams of finding peace by making his fortune — "Money would mean living without stop-watch and whip" (SV 86; SH 87) — but, like Franz Horn, lacks the dynamism and courage of his competitors and comes to enjoy the various defeats that he suffers as realtor, husband, and father. His final defeat, the demolition of the Swan Villa for which he has failed to get the listing rights, induces a rapprochement with his wife, Anna, that gives him the strength to fall asleep (a recurrent motif of survival in these works). However, even though all the constituent parts are there, it is difficult to consider Zürn in any way as victim; indeed, the self-indulgence that characterizes his behavior throughout is based on the fact that, whatever financial insecurity he may claim to suffer from, he is exceedingly comfortably off. By the time we get to *Jagd*, the sequel to *The Swan Villa*, Zürn has been able to take early retirement, thanks to his competent wife's taking over the running of the business. As a result he can, he says, indulge himself in idling and writing (although the bulk of the novel is concerned with his efforts to achieve sexual fulfillment). The self-indulgence of the protagonist and the ultimate slightness of these works

[8]Walser, "Goethe hat ein Programm, Jean Paul eine Existenz," *Literaturmagazin* 2 (1974): 108-09.

[9]Walser, "Die Literatur der gewöhnlichen Verletzungen," *Die Würde am Werktag: Literatur der Arbeiter und Angestellten*, ed. Martin Walser (Frankfurt/M.: Fischer, 1980) 7.

makes it difficult to read them as substantial workings out of Walser's theme, but rather they come over as — in the German marketplace — commercially successful novels for a middle-class readership that could recognize its own foibles and problems presented in ironic form.

The same playing with Walserian leitmotifs, by now lacking real provenance in the structure of modern capitalist society, marks *Breakers*, which sees Helmut Halm on sabbatical in California. While the central thrust of the novel is to push the theme of midlife crisis from *Runaway Horse* into the realms of the absurd, much of its bulk is made up of sometimes elegant, often funny sketches that have little or nothing to do with the theme Walser claims to be addressing. And Halm, the German schoolteacher with all the rights, privileges, and complete security afforded by the civil service status of such a position, can — despite the way in which he otherwise exemplifies the Walser protagonist since 1976 — no more be considered a "petty bourgeois," in any societally significant sense of the term, than Dr. Gottlieb Zürn, the failed but comfortably-off realtor.

Many of the experiences of Helmut Halm at the "University of Oakland" are, as is widely known, based on Walser's stay in the German Department of the University of California at Berkeley; perhaps less well known is how much of *Beyond All Love*, which seems to be set in the world of commerce, is based on Walser's experiences during his time as Writer in Residence at the University of Warwick.[10] This knowledge, together with input from what others know or have learned from conversation with the ever candid Walser, suggests that there is a close link between the fiction and the life and times of Walser himself. And indeed, if we look back over the range of his novels, it is clear that there are close parallels between the author and his protagonists over and beyond those written since 1976 — in the figures of the women, some of whom bear the names of members of the Walser family; in the sense of financial insecurity (Walser has often stressed that it was not until the success of *Runaway Horse*, published when he was fifty, that he attained financial security and was freed from the burden of an enormous mortgage); in the age of Helmut Halm as well as of other protagonists and the experience of midlife crisis. Above all, it is the social background of the protagonists, successful though they now are in real terms, that is strikingly similar: Hans Beumann and Franz Horn are the illegitimate sons of waitresses, while Helmut Halm is the son of a waiter; Anselm Kristlein and Gottlieb Zürn grew up in impoverished circumstances after the business failures and subsequent suicides of their fathers. Walser's father ran a small *Gasthaus* and a small coal business on the side, but was a poor businessman

[10]Cf. Keith Bullivant (ed.), *Englische Lektionen* (Munich: iudicium, 1990) 80.

and, when he died of diabetes at the age of forty-nine, Walser's mother was left to bring up her family burdened with debt; the father, like a number of Walser's antiheroes, sought solace in attempting to write.[11] It could, thus, be argued that the Walser novels dealt with here constitute to some considerable extent a constant working over in fictional terms of problems and neuroses that are those of an author who claims to be, like his protagonists, "deformed by my petty-bourgeois background," but who has, in real terms, long since left this behind him.[12] Those main characters, like the author himself, are parvenus (*Aufsteiger*), typical products of a West German society marked, at least in its first few decades, by a remarkable social mobility that soon produced a "leveled-in middle-class society" (*nivellierte Mittelstandsgesellschaft*), in Helmut Schelsky's term, full of arrivistes like Walser and his antiheroes coping, with varying degrees of success, with the psychological baggage of their petty-bourgeois past. There is another, final way in which the likes of Kristlein, Franz Horn, Klaus Buch, and Gottlieb Zürn — all those, in fact, involved in selling in one form or another — embody to some extent Walser's own preoccupation with his position and activity as a writer in modern society (as influenced by his social origins): in an interview with Horst Bienek, quoted in part earlier, he stressed the impact on the consciousness of the sales representative Anselm Kristlein of his quintessential superfluity. This, Walser went on, "is what has made me sympathetic towards this profession: it reminds me of that of the writer."[13]

There is one of the post-1973 works, however, which cannot be read as yet another variant on Walser's highly individualistic and to some extent autobiographical working out of the *Kleinbürgertendenz*. It admittedly contains a number of the key motifs of the other works; its protagonist is, moreover, a member of the Swabian clan that we know from them, and his grandfather had committed suicide in the face of bankruptcy; but Xaver Zürn (*The Inner Man*) is the only true petty bourgeois amongst them.

Whereas the other members of the extended family that we know have all gone through higher education and subsequently "made something of themselves," as the phrase goes (whatever mixed blessings they may feel that process has brought), Xaver has been able only to move up from forklift-truck driver to the position of chauffeur. Unlike his relatives, he has been

[11]On Walser's childhood cf. Waine, pp. 7-11.

[12]In an interview with Donna L. Hoffmeister, *Vertrauter Alltag, gemischte Gefühle. Gespräche mit Schriftstellern über Arbeit in der Literatur* (Bonn: Bouvier, 1989) 170.

[13]Cf. Bienek, p. 195.

frustrated in his hopes of social advancement: the Mercedes he drives, normally a potent symbol of "having made it" in West German society, is for him the badge of his servitude. Even in the case of this remarkably precise analysis of the consequences of "functional specificity,"[14] Peter Hamm claimed "of course this driver isn't really a driver" but, as with the other novels discussed here, "the author."[15] We would, however, argue that the personal problems inherent in the extreme form of master-servant relationship embodied in that between chauffeur and employer-as-passenger in no way correspond to the anxieties that characterize the rather privileged existence of both Walser as free-lance writer and of his troop of antiheroes. What he is doing here is drawing on a long-term preoccupation with the implications of such a position through literature, on the one hand (that tradition embracing Robert Walser's *Der Gehülfe* and Brecht's *Herr Puntila und sein Knecht Matti* [1948; *Puntila and Matti, His Hired Hand*, 1972]),[16] and through personal observation, on the other. Walser's second prose manuscript (of 1951, unpublished), entitled "Memoirs of a Chauffeur," was based on his early experiences as a radio journalist traveling around for months with a sound engineer and a chauffeur.[17] Chauffeurs also crop up in both *Halbzeit* and *The Unicorn* and are thus further testimony to the author's long preoccupation with what he sees as the social significance of the figure.

The Inner Man has the same sort of dramatic structure as the post-1973 novels, beginning just before a major crisis in Xaver Zürn's life. A long drive undertaken in the first part of the novel ("May"), from Lake Constance to Düsseldorf, Cologne, Giessen, Heidelberg, and Munich, confronts us with the total exclusion zone between Xaver and his employer, Dr. Gleitze, and, through reflective flashbacks, informs the reader about those unsatisfactory aspects of Xaver's employment that have induced his present physical problem of acute and painful constipation. During his thirteen years of work as Gleitze's driver he has had to conform to his employer's — quite incorrect — image of him as the ideal chauffeur: a careful driver with the skill of a champion marksman (which Xaver never was), a composed nondrinker,

[14]Cf. here Donna Hoffmeister's excellent analysis of this work, "Fantasies of Individualism: Work Reality in *Seelenarbeit*," *Martin Walser: International Perspectives*, eds. Jürgen E. Schlunk and Armand E. Singer, American University Studies: Series 1, Germanic Languages and Literature 64 (New York: Lang, 1987) 59-69.

[15]Hoffmeister, *Vertrauter Alltag, gemischte Gefühle*, p. 169.

[16]This aspect is examined in part by Siegfried Mews in the following essay.

[17]Hoffmeister, *Vertrauter Alltag, gemischte Gefühle*, p. 169.

whose only indulgence is ice cream (but who, in reality, prefers to indulge in a bottle or two of wine in his off-duty hours). He has constantly to endure the separation between front and rear in an automobile, rendered particularly intense by Gleitze's being constantly wrapped in his obsession with the world of opera on the back seat; the indignity of removal to cheap hotels with uncomfortable beds at night; the exclusion from the sybaritic pleasures of his thoughtless employer, who then, to make matters worse, rams home the false persona he has inflicted on his driver by insisting on Xaver's being treated to the sickly-sweet "treat" that he so hates, under the impression that he (Gleitze) is being generous. Their peripatetic *pas de deux* embodies with an intensity not found in Walser's other works the personal degradation inherent in the (at least European) class structure.

Xaver has in some way compensated for the fear of losing his somewhat privileged position with fantasies of aggression. This antagonism towards Gleitze is, in turn, further stimulated by the casual purchase of his "colleague" John Frey's memoirs of his life as a chauffeur to a German Nazi manufacturer, in which he recognizes his own experiences — above all, his real dependency on the whim of a man who, although to Xaver and all others seemingly decent in his treatment of his driver, has ultimate power over him: even Xaver's nominally free weekends are spent running errands for Gleitze and/or his wife, or for their friends. This power relationship, as with John Frey, in turn produces hatred for Gleitze, hatred which is, however, immediately suppressed, manifesting itself in Xaver's physical discomfort. His detailed physical examination in a Tübingen clinic turns out to be the climactic moment of the novel, exposing his apparent illness as ultimately psychosomatic and, at the same time, confronting him with the truth about his relationship to his employer. On learning that Gleitze has arranged for a close friend to examine him, Xaver at first feels that this is yet another example of the man's inherent kindness, but the series of painful tests convinces him that he has, in fact, been exposed to "those machines, because he [the boss] needs a man whose reliability has been scrutinized by every technological process." Moreover, Gleitze "was entitled to be informed about every square centimeter of his insides" (IM 156; SA 170). Just how true this is is revealed somewhat later. After his week in the clinic Xaver returns to his job and, on the surface, nothing seems to have changed apart from the fact that Xaver's aggressive feelings towards his employer are more intense: when the latter gets out of the car to urinate on a night journey home Xaver fantasizes about stabbing him with one of the six knives he by now has stashed away in the glove compartment. The next day — there is no suggestion of a causal link, except perhaps that the knife in Xaver's hand aroused Gleitze's suspicions — he is summoned into the office to see the secretary, who informs him that he has been relieved of his chauffeur's duties and is to return to the warehouse. She hints, with some empathy, at advancing age and mentions an apparent suggestion by Gleitze that Xaver was having increasing difficulty in getting through the day without a beer (he has had but one in public!), but the crucial thing is the totally impersonal way in which he is demoted by the man to whom he has been physically close for some thirteen years and who is widely held to be a considerate person. The nature of his demotion brings out with an intensity found nowhere else in Walser the full nature of Xaver's dependency on Gleitze.

On the same day the Zürns learn that their daughter Julia has failed the examinations necessary for her to proceed towards the high-school diploma (*Abitur*), the prerequisite for social advancement in Germany. This convinces Xaver of the inevitability and correctness of Gleitze's judgment of him, a failure from a family of failures (IM 247; SA 264) — a judgment confirmed by further personal calamities. In the acceptance of the inherent justice behind his degradation, with only sexual intercourse with his wife Agnes offering any sort of solace, is captured the extremely low self-esteem so quintessentially typical of the lower orders in European class society. Whereas in the other post-1973 prose works examined here the social origins of this malaise are frequently only alluded to somewhat cryptically, *The Inner Man* confronts us in graphic form with the social origins and psychological consequences of the "petty-bourgeois deformation" that marks all of Walser's later anti-heroes and, in turn, enhances the understanding — particularly that of the non-European reader — of the other works.

Works Cited

Bienek, Horst. *Werkstattgespräche mit Schriftstellern*. Munich: Hanser, 1962.

Bullivant, Keith. *Realism Today: Aspects of the Contemporary German Novel*. Leamington Spa, Hamburg, New York: Berg, 1987.

—— (ed.). *Englische Lektionen*. Munich: iudicium, 1990.

Hoffmeister, Donna L. "Fantasies of Individualism: Work Reality in *Seelenarbeit*." *Martin Walser: International Perspectives*. Eds. Jürgen E. Schlunk, and Armand E. Singer. American University Studies: Series 1, Germanic Languages and Literature 64. New York: Lang, 1987. 59-70.

——. *Vertrauter Alltag, gemischte Gefühle. Gespräche mit Schriftstellern über Arbeit in der Literatur*. Bonn: Bouvier, 1989.

Pilipp, Frank. *The Novels of Martin Walser: A Critical Introduction*. Studies in German Literature, Linguistics, and Culture. Columbia SC: Camden House, 1991.

Thomas, R. Hinton, and Wilfried van der Will. *Der deutsche Roman und die Wohlstandsgesellschaft*. Stuttgart: Kohlhammer, 1969.

Waine, Anthony. *Martin Walser*. Munich: Text + Kritik, 1980.

Walser, Martin. "Brauchen Romanhelden Berufe?" *Frankfurter Allgemeine Zeitung* (Literary Supplement) 11 Jan. 1992: 1-2.

——. "Freiübungen." *Erfahrungen und Leseerfahrungen*. Frankfurt/M.: Suhrkamp, 1965. 94-110.

——. "Goethe hat ein Programm, Jean Paul eine Existenz." *Literaturmagazin* 2 (1974): 108-09.

——. "Die Literatur der gewöhnlichen Verletzungen." *Die Würde am Werktag: Literatur der Arbeiter und Angestellten*. Ed. Martin Walser. Frankfurt/M.: Fischer, 1980. 7-11.

3

A Merry Departure from the Past? Master-Servant Relations in Bertolt Brecht, Martin Walser, and Volker Braun*

Siegfried Mews

HERR PUNTILA UND SEIN Knecht Matti (1948; *Puntila and Matti, His Hired Man*, 1972; henceforth *Puntila/Matti*) originated during Brecht's exile in Finland, and the play counts among his most frequently performed.[1] In the opinion of one literary historian, the play contains a dramatic dialectic which, despite the rural backdrop, has nothing to fear from comparison with *Mutter Courage und ihre Kinder* (1941; *Mother Courage and Her Children*, 1972) or *Leben des Galilei* (1943; *Life of Galileo*, 1972).[2] This literary value judgment from the early 1970s derives in part from the attempt to reassess *Puntila/Matti* with respect to the other, "classical" dramas of Brecht's exile period and confer upon it canonical status. Primarily, however, this judgment is based upon an assumption of both the applicability of the Brechtian model to capitalist society and the practicability of its proposed solution for surmounting the power relations which are paradigmatically expressed in the title of the play. The following observations proceed from a hypothesis which poststructuralist and postmodern theorems hardly touch upon. As Jan Knopf formulates, "Historischer Wandel — Veränderung und Veränderbarkeit —

*Translated by Martina Greene.

[1]For an account of the genesis of *Puntila/Matti* and Brecht's collaboration with Hella Wuolijoki, see Hans Peter Neureuter, *Brechts "Herr Puntila und sein Knecht Matti"* (Frankfurt/M.: Suhrkamp, 1987).

[2]See Jost Hermand, "*Herr Puntila und sein Knecht Matti*: Brechts Volksstück," *Brecht heute* 1 (1971): 117-36.

ist nicht nur Thema, sondern auch Ziel von Brechts Werk außerhalb der Kunst: der Mensch als 'Produkt' der Geschichte, aber auch als derjenige, der die Geschichte macht, Veränderung gewährleistet und Veränderbarkeit ermöglicht" [historical change and changeability are not only the theme, but also the goal of Brecht's work outside of art: the individual as the "product" of history, but also as the producer of history, the one who accepts responsibility for change and makes change possible].[3]

Indeed, in view of the radically new situation in Europe, which has arisen since the fall of the Berlin Wall, the opening of the internal German border, German reunification, and the presumable victory of capitalism in East Germany and Eastern Europe, the expectation of the elimination of the power relations thematized in Brecht's play rests on shaky foundations. However, the interpretation of the Brechtian work as "weitgehend ... unabgeschlossen, veränderlich und veränderbar" [largely ... unresolved, changing and changeable][4] does not find corroboration in recent political developments alone, for the continuing rewriting of *Puntila/Matti* by authors emulating Brecht — their reaction to the "jeweiligen Aktualitäten der entsprechenden Zeit" [respective actualities of the given time],[5] so to speak — implies criticism of Brecht's premises and intentions. Even greater censure of the social design implied by Brecht in *Puntila/Matti* can be found in the play's contradictory reception history.

Despite, or perhaps because of its "so widerspruchsvoll, so facettenreich, so satirisch und zugleich so 'genüßlich'" [so contradictory, so multifaceted,

[3]Jan Knopf, *Brecht-Handbuch: Theater. Eine Ästhetik der Widersprüche* (Stuttgart: Metzler, 1980) 1. All translations from the German are, unless otherwise indicated, those of the translator. In his review of Elizabeth Wright's study, *Postmodern Brecht: A Re-Presentation* (London: Routledge, 1989), Reinhold Grimm essentially proceeds from the same premises as Knopf and raises the following objection against Wright's "postmodern approach": "Was der marxistische Stückeschreiber bezweckte, ist nun laut Wright halt nicht länger, das Publikum zum 'eingreifenden Denken' zu erziehen und es dazu anzuhalten, die 'Verhältnisse umzuwälzen' und die 'Welt zu verändern,' sondern 'to force the audience into a continuous process of re-writing [the world]'" (Wright 75; quoted by Grimm) [What the Marxist playwright intended is according to Wright no longer to train the audience in "radical thinking" and urge it "to overthrow the prevailing order" and "change the world," but rather, "to force ..."]. See Grimm, "Brecht — auf den Postmodernismus gekommen," rev. of *Postmodern Brecht: A Re-Presentation*, by Elizabeth Wright, *Monatshefte* 82 (Spring 1990): 79.

[4]Knopf, p. 1.

[5]Knopf, p. 2.

so satirical and at the same time so "enjoyable"] construction,[6] *Puntila/Matti* was at first in no way understood or accepted as a model analysis of the master-servant relationship, a filiation which, though enjoying a long literary tradition, is primarily determined by the economic issue of property. Except for the reception of *Puntila/Matti* by a few literary historians who took Brecht's Marxism seriously, the stage history of the play, which was first performed in the Zurich Playhouse on 6 June 1948, was burdened by incomprehension of Brecht's intentions, or at least by a misunderstanding of them. This lack of understanding includes the blatant misreport by the Berlin Theater Service on 9 July 1948 that the playwright had made an attempt "die sozialen Gegensätze zwischen Herr und Knecht und ihre Tragik zu überbrükken und versöhnen" [to bridge and reconcile the social contrasts between master and servant and their tragedy].[7] Even spokespersons for the intended beneficiaries of Brecht's play about the exploitation of people by people seem not particularly to have taken to *Puntila/Matti*, for the Communist publication *Vorwärts* (Basel/Geneva, 6 December 1948) viewed the play as "für ein sozialkritisches Werk zu oberflächlich" [too superficial for a work of social criticism].[8]

While following the play's premiere the Western performance practice was characterized by a tendency to deemphasize its ideology, the premiere performance of the work by the Berlin Ensemble in 1949 gave rise to accusations of deficient topicality. With the agrarian reforms in the then Soviet occupation zone, later the German Democratic Republic (GDR), the problem of estates and the associated dependence-relationships had become irrelevant; critics argued that *Puntila/Matti*, which takes place in rural Finland, had become anachronistic. Brecht distanced himself from such criticism in part by remarking that one must learn not only from the struggle but also from the history of struggles. Continuing this line of thought, the playwright cited Karl Marx, who in *Zur Kritik der Hegelschen Rechtsphilosophie* (Critique of the Hegelian Philosophy of Law) described the genre of comedy as the "letzte Phase einer weltgeschichtlichen Gestalt — [d]amit die Menschheit

[6]Hermand, p. 127.

[7]Quoted by Siegfried Mews, *Bertolt Brecht: Herr Puntila und sein Knecht Matti*, 3rd [enl.] ed. (1975; Frankfurt/M.: Diesterweg, 1989) 74.

[8]Bertolt Brecht, *Werke: Große kommentierte Berliner und Frankfurter Ausgabe*, eds. Werner Hecht, Jan Knopf, Werner Mittenzwei, Klaus-Detlef Müller (Berlin: Aufbau; Frankfurt/M.: Suhrkamp, 1988) 6:469. All subsequent references to this edition of Brecht's works will be given in the text parenthetically (BuFA).

heiter von ihrer Vergangenheit scheide" [last phase of a construct of world history — designed to allow humankind to merrily depart from its past].[9]

This deemed merry departure from the past by means of a comedy or popular or folk play (*Volksstück*), reference to which can be found in the prologue of the Berlin production of 1952, is executed through the presentation of what was once an "arge Landplage" (BuFA 6:374) ["a plague"].[10] "... ein gewisses vorzeitliches Tier / Estatium possessor, auf deutsch Gutsbesitzer genannt" (BuFA 6:374) ["A certain prehistoric animal / Estatium possessor, in English, squire" (Manheim 6:107)] serves as the focal point for the exposition of a class society divided into masters and servants. Since the surmounting of the circumstances presented in the play was an issue in only part of Germany, however, the scope of Brecht's incantationlike moral — "Den guten Herrn, den finden sie [die Knechte] geschwind / Wenn sie erst ihre eignen Herren sind" (BuFA 6:370) ["They'll quickly find good masters when / The masters are the working men" (Manheim 6:191)] — appeared to be limited to the western part of Germany.

Standing in the way of any practical usefulness of Brecht's moral, however, was not only the tendency toward stressing the entertainment value and diversion aspects of the play but also critical doubt whether Brecht's "geschliffene Dialektik" [polished dialectic], "all die genußbringende Artistik" [all the pleasant artistry] was suited to expose the comparatively subtle forms of exploitation of the present day (1969).[11] This doubt seems justified inasmuch as a text as indebted to Brecht as Martin Walser's *Seelenarbeit* (1979; *The Inner Man*, 1984) may give more exact information about the forms of dependence in the pre-reunified Federal Republic of Germany (FRG) than its Brechtian model. In his novel — the genre difference between drama and novel and the resultant differing conditions for reception are not considered here — Walser offers a modern variant of the prototypical master-servant relationships crafted by writers such as Cervantes and Diderot, a

[9]Ruth Berlau, Bertolt Brecht, et al., *Theaterarbeit: Sechs Aufführungen des Berliner Ensembles* (Dresden: VVV Dresdner Verlag, 1952) 46.

[10]Bertolt Brecht, *Plays, Poetry and Prose*, trans. Ralph Manheim, eds. Ralph Manheim and John Willett (New York: Vintage, 1972) 6: 107. Subsequent translations of Brecht taken from this edition will be cited parenthetically in the text as (Manheim).

[11]Volker Canaris, "Zwei Brecht-Altmeister," *Theater heute* 10.7 (1969): 10-11.

variant which takes the form of the boss-chauffeur relationship.[12] While such a relationship contains a level of personal contact between master and servant which for industrial society is rather atypical, the chauffeur's position is particularly well suited to demonstrating dependence and being externally directed from a worm's-eye-view.[13]

In contrast to *Puntila/Matti*, where in the comparison and exposition of master and servant two perspectives come into consideration, Walser's novel has one central character, the petty-bourgeois driver Xaver Zürn. The last three months which Xaver spends chauffeuring his boss, Dr. Gleitze, are pondered exclusively from Xaver's point of view and developed into a personal "Bewußtseinsprotokoll" [protocol of consciousness].[14] Although the servant Matti was at first negatively assessed by critics — he was seen as "rather a prig"[15] and as an "anämische[r] Ideologieträger" [anemic ideological puppet][16] — and although less attention was devoted to him than to the well-rounded character of the vital, expansive Mr. Puntila, he gradually came to be revaluated. As a class-conscious proletarian, but hardly an active revolutionary, Matti represents a necessary counterpole to his master, Puntila; their relationship is based upon a dialectic interdependence, in which both rely upon each other. As a representative of an exploited class, Matti is predestined to be Puntila's opponent. Because of the economically determined power relations, however, there can be no real confrontation between master and servant. Thus, Matti delivers his tales, in which he criticizes existing conditions, in a sly and artful manner, acting as producer and secret director of the many plays within the play. Meanwhile, the dialogue which Puntila seeks, particularly when he is drunk, reveals the continuing ine-

[12]Chauffeur characters appear several times in Walser's work. See Mews (23, note) and Walter Seifert, "Martin Walser: *Seelenarbeit*. Bewußtseinsanalyse und Gesellschaftskritik," *Deutsche Romane von Grimmelshausen bis Walser*, ed. Jakob Lehmann (Königstein/Ts.: Scriptor, 1982) 550. Regarding the literary development of the master-servant relationship in general, see Hans Mayer, "Herrschaft und Knechtschaft: Hegels Deutung, ihre literarischen Ursprünge und Folgen," *Jahrbuch der deutschen Schillergesellschaft* 15 (1971): 251-79.

[13]Seifert, p. 550.

[14]Seifert, p. 552.

[15]Martin Esslin, *Brecht: A Choice of Evils*, 4th rev. ed. (1959; London: Methuen, 1983) 275.

[16]Volker Klotz, *Bertolt Brecht: Versuch über das Werk* (Bad Homburg: Gentner, 1957) 51.

quality: in a society ruled by class interests, dialogue cannot serve interpersonal communication.

The self-confident Matti accepts his social identity: as a skilled worker with technical abilities, he ultimately turns his back on Puntila's agrarian world, in which a change in the prevailing conditions cannot be expected. Before his departure in the final scene, Matti proclaims the warning cited above, which, though not meant to be a direct challenge to the audience like the closing lines of *Der Gute Mensch von Sezuan* (1943; *The Good Person of Szechwan*, 1972), nevertheless serves as an epilogue, summarizing the meaning of the staged events. The chauffeur in *The Inner Man*, on the other hand, hardly functions as an outspoken social critic, and this despite the dominance of his perspective in the novel. As a sedentary family man and father with deep local roots and a strong sense of tradition, Xaver lacks the independence of Matti, who has neither property nor attachment to any region. Xaver wins his social identity through his promotion from common laborer to the driver of factory manager Dr. Gleitze, and it is in this position that he hopes to find the meaning of his existence. Thus, he stylizes his working relationship into one of trust and loyalty.[17] Despite the physical proximity to his boss during long business trips, however, the contact and accompanying sense of intimacy for which Xaver longs do not materialize. In contrast to the "Hymniker des Genießens [und] genialischem Dionysiker" [hedonist and brilliant Dionysian] Puntila,[18] who in his drunken state sees his chauffeur Matti as a human being and includes him in his "ideal" of universal brotherhood and a free, unbridled existence — of course, with the master-servant relationship remaining intact — Dr. Gleitze devotes his attention primarily to the aesthetic pleasure afforded him by listening to Mozart operas. The headphones which Dr. Gleitze uses represent an extreme form of isolation from and aloofness toward Xaver, whom he acknowledges only in his capacity as driver.

Thus, Xaver, unlike Matti, is condemned to speechlessness, to nothing more than imagined participation in the conversations which Dr. Gleitze sometimes has with other passengers. In exchange for his loyalty and dedication to duty during his thirteen years of employment, he has been rewarded with digestive problems and chronic stomach pain, troubles which are obviously of a psychosomatic nature, even though Xaver at first shies away from attributing them to his work and dependence relationships. One

[17]Heike Doane, "Martin Walsers *Seelenarbeit*: Versuche der Selbstverwirklichung," *Neophilologus* 67 (1983): 263.

[18]Hans Egon Holthusen, "Versuch über Brecht," *Kritisches Verstehen* (Munich: Piper, 1961) 104.

reflection of the deformed state of Xaver's consciousness is his rigid self-denial, which manifests itself in, among other things, the suppression of his urinary urges during long drives. Xaver's boss, on the other hand, a man not plagued by physical ailments and able to enjoy a healthy nap, has the opportunity to stop the car at any time in order to "rasch mal verschwinden" (SA 254) ["go behind a tree" (IM 237)]. Here, too, there is a contrast to *Puntila/Matti:* in the shortest scene of the play, the ironically titled "Nocturno," the social boundaries between Puntila and Matti are suspended, if only for a moment, when the two men satisfy a common biological human need and relieve themselves together (BuFA 6:358; Manheim 6:179). This kind of common interest is nowhere to be found in *The Inner Man:* when the Gleitzes come for a visit, Xaver's initial hospitality turns to rage, all because he believes that the boss had his daughters "wie ein Tierarzt ... taxiert" (SA 143) ["had sized [them] up ... like a veterinarian" (IM 129)]. With this reaction, Xaver Zürn truly lives up to his name; he becomes angry or begins to *zürnen*.

Xaver's dependence, which is based upon massive self-denial — adherence to the fiction of being a nonsmoker and nondrinker, a fiction to which he owed his promotion — is extreme both in comparison to *Puntila/Matti* as well as within the context of the novel itself. Other characters in *The Inner Man* find themselves in similarly dependent situations, but they exhibit far greater self-confidence. For example, the Gleitzes' housekeeper, Aloisia, is indifferent to her employers' opinion of her — "Also, wenn ihr etwas egal ist, dann, wie Gleitzes über sie reden" (SA 218) ["She must say, if there was something she couldn't care less about, it was what the Gleitzes said about her" (IM 202)] — and she does not shy away from terminating her dependence relationship. Meanwhile, other fictional drivers place no special value upon a particularly loyal relationship with their bosses. Xaver, however, believes, as he so often states, that the Gleitzes value him as "nicht der Hellste ..., aber der Treuste" (SA 218 et passim) ["not the brightest, but the most loyal" (IM 202 et passim)], that he has been "vereidigt" (SA 19) ["sworn in" (IM 12)], thereby establishing mutual trust as the essence of his working relationship: "Er wollte keinen sinnlosen Beruf haben" (SA 272) ["He didn't want a job that made no sense" (IM 254)]. In accordance with this ethic, Xaver thinks that he must conceal from the Gleitzes that he has read the book by the chauffeur Frey, a man who "seine Arbeitgeber von Fahrt zu Fahrt mehr hassen lernte" (SA 122) ["with every trip learned to hate his boss{es} more and more" (IM 110)].

Xaver's efforts to assure himself of the meaning of his profession take on frankly grotesque form when he undertakes an excursion with Aloisia, including unpremeditated sexual intercourse, just to find out from her "wie die Gleitzes über ihn sprachen" (SA 221) ["how the Gleitzes spoke about him" (IM 205)]. The "vollkommene Ergebnislosigkeit" (SA 221) ["total failure" (IM 205)] of this endeavor casts an ironic light upon Xaver's vain effort to get closer to his boss. Matti can once again serve as a contrasting figure, because he rejects the intoxicated Puntila's attempts at contact as an unsuitable means of overcoming class barriers:

PUNTILA: Matti, bist du mein Freund?
MATTI: Nein. (BuFA 6:288-89).
[PUNTILA: Are you my friend, Matti?
MATTI: No. (Manheim 6:110)]

Only in the middle part of the novel is a change in the relationship between Xaver and his boss implied. When Xaver, at the suggestion of Dr. Gleitze, visits a clinic in Tübingen in order to have doctors look into his stomach and intestinal complaints, he is at first quite impressed by the apparent concern of his boss. During the examinations, however, he feels "tiermäßig ohnmächtig" (SA 161) ["like a helpless animal" (IM 147)], degraded to a "Vierbeiner" (SA 167) ["four-legged beast" (IM 153)], and it is then that he begins to gain greater awareness of himself. This process of becoming aware of oneself, the search for "the inner man" as the exploration of one's sense of self, leads Xaver more clearly than before to the understanding that it is ultimately his boss who is the cause of his suffering. But even at the university clinic in Tübingen Xaver is forced to acknowledge: "Er kam nicht los von denen [den Gleitzes]" (SA 171) ["He could not escape them {the Gleitzes}" (IM 157)], and he concedes complete authority over himself to his boss:

> Der Chef hat ihn nach Tübingen geschickt zu den Maschinen, weil er einen Mann braucht, dessen Zuverlässigkeit von allen Untersuchungstechniken überprüft ist. Und wenn er der Mann sein wollte und selber Anlaß zu Zweifeln gab, dann mußte er mit diesen Überprüfungen einverstanden sein. Der Chef hatte das Recht, über jeden Quadratzentimeter seiner Innereien Bescheid zu wissen, klar. (SA 170)

> [The boss sent him to Tübingen, to those machines, because he needs a man whose reliability has been scrutinized by every technological process. And if Xaver wanted to be that man, if he had himself given rise to doubts, it was up to him not to object to that scrutiny. The boss was entitled to be informed about every square centimeter of his insides, that was quite obvious. (IM 156)]

Here Xaver freely takes on a degree of subordination which other bosses achieve only through force. In the classic employee novel of the Weimar Republic, Hans Fallada's *Kleiner Mann — Was nun?* (1932; *Little Man — What Now?*, 1933), a saleswoman in a department store appeals in vain to the right to separate the working world from the private sphere: "'Was ich außer dem Haus tue, ist doch meine Sache!' ruft das Fräulein.... 'Da irren Sie sich,' sagt ernst Herr Spannfuß. 'Das ist ein Irrtum von Ihnen, Fräulein. Das Warenhaus Mandel ernährt und kleidet Sie, das Warenhaus Mandel ermöglicht die Basis ihrer Existenz. Es muß erwartet werden, daß Sie bei all Ihrem Tun und Lassen zuerst an das Warenhaus Mandel denken'"[19] ["'What I do outside the house is my business,' cried the girl. 'There you are wrong,' said Herr Spannfuss gravely. 'That is quite a mistake, Fräulein. The Mandel Store clothes and feeds you, the Mandel Store provides the basis of your existence. It is only to be expected that in all the transactions of your life the Mandel Store should be considered first'"].[20] In comparison with the right of self-affirmation implied in Fallada's novel, Xaver's position represents a considerable step backwards.

Despite his obsequious subordination, Xaver is not completely the "Hund" (SA 113) ["dog" (IM 101)] he believes himself to be, nor the "Sklave" (SA 140, cf. 21) ["slave" (IM 127, cf. 114)] others regard him to be. His ties to his native region and its landscape work against the growing crippling of his spirit brought on by his excessive accommodation. This sense of belonging, along with the trusting relationship he shares with his wife, serve as counterweights to his social and personal dependence upon his boss. At one point, in unconscious reaction to his repression, which he vents through bursts of aggression, Xaver is seized by the violent urge to buy a knife; he ultimately enters into murderous fantasies against Dr. Gleitze. After his demotion to forklift driver, Xaver symbolically takes leave of Dr. Gleitze by sinking the knife in a brook. Of course, the power relations are not affected by this farewell, and, likewise, nothing changes with respect to Xaver's psychologically rooted dependence, since the victor and the loser are clearly established: "Was ist denn ein Sieger? Der Unterschied zwischen dem Sieger und dem Besiegten besteht nur darin, daß der Sieger an den Besiegten nur denkt, wenn er will, während der Besiegte an den Sieger denken muß, ob er will oder nicht" (SA 283-84) ["After all, what is a victor? The difference between victor and vanquished is merely that the victor thinks of the vanquished only when he wants to, whereas the vanquished has to think of

[19]Hans Fallada, *Kleiner Mann — was nun?* (1932; Hamburg: Rowohlt, 1990) 264.

[20]Hans Fallada, *Little Man — What Now?*, trans. Eric Sutton (New York: Simon and Schuster, 1933) 315.

the victor whether he wants to or not" (IM 265)]. The roles of master and servant in this context are plainly written: "Der Chef kam ihm wie ein Sieger vor. Er war der Besiegte" (SA 116) ["The boss seemed to him like a victor. He was the vanquished" (IM 103)]. Xaver's defeat is all the more grave, in that the family history of the Zürns, as well as the history of social strife in general, especially the Peasant War of 1525, seem to have predetermined his fate. Xaver's way of looking at the world centers on performance and advancement; thus, when his daughter Julia fails in school, he assumes a fatalistic position: "der Versuch der Wigratsweiler Zürns, in der Welt um eine schlichte Stufe höherzusteigen, werde abgeschmettert, das müsse er hinnehmen" (SA 176) ["The attempt of the Wigratsweiler Zürns to move up a modest step in the world was being dashed to the ground, he had to accept that" (IM 161)]. All attempts by Xaver to give the familiar course of family and political history a new, more optimistic turn, to set a new reading of history against the official version, are founded upon his sense of powerlessness, which causes him to perceive "den Gang der Geschichte [die Niederlage der Bauern 1525] wie eine persönliche Niederlage" (SA 80) ["the course of history [the defeat of the peasants in 1525] as a personal defeat" (IM 70)]. The future-oriented Matti, who does not suffer from the historical burden of the defeats of his class, terminates his working relationship without the slightest reflection and augurs a time without masters or servants; conversely, for Xaver the problem of overcoming class differences gives rise to pessimistic reflections: "Warum gibt es noch Herren? Weil jeder hofft, er werde auch einer, sagte Xaver" (SA 200) ["Why are there still masters? Because everyone hopes to become one himself, said Xaver" (IM 184)].

The functioning model of social justice is completely absent from Xaver's thinking. For him, the production of an appearance of equal social opportunity in the FRG serves only to give the Soviet system the advantage of greater honesty in the brutal practice of repression: "Da es Gott offenbar nicht gibt, bleiben nur die Russen. Warum marschieren denn die Russen nicht endlich ein und machen Schluß mit diesem Pack und setzen ein offenes Unrecht ein, das ist doch besser als dieser Schein" (SA 263) ["Since God obviously doesn't exist, all that remains is the Russians. Why don't the Russians come marching in to do away with this whole gang and establish open injustice. Surely that's better than this hypocrisy" (IM 246)]. Xaver's assessment of the "Russians" is a sign of his ambivalent relationship to Dr. Gleitze, in which his air of subjugation and his courting of favor outstrip his feeble revolt. In one of Xaver's inconsequential "Dialogentwürfe" [dialog designs][21] about his brother Johann, who fell at the end of World War II during the defense of Königsberg, Dr. Gleitze's hometown, he muses: "Die

[21]Seifert, p. 553.

Familie Zürn hatte wirklich getan, was sie konnte, um die Heimat der Gleitzes nicht in die Hände der Russen fallen zu lassen" (SA 62) ["The Zürn family really had done all it could to prevent the Gleitzes' native place from falling into the hands of the Russians" (IM 54)].

Xaver's oscillation between voluntary conformity and occasional opposition manifests itself in his gestures when he accompanies his words about the hope of equal social opportunity with a "lavierende Handbewegung" (SA 200) ["finagling gesture" (IM 184)], which appears to legitimate this hope as commendable. His "wütende Grimasse" (SA 200) ["face ... distorted with rage" (IM 184)], however, gives this hope the lie, revealing it to be a position which conforms to and stabilizes the system. Thus, interpreters who, supported by one of Walser's statements, wish to see "die sozialistische Gesellschaft als weißen Schatten" [the socialist system as a white shadow] in his portrayal of a class society are only conditionally to be agreed with.[22] Certainly, the portrayal of Xaver's privation makes readers aware of this privation, thus bringing to bear the kind of consciousness-raising function to which Walser was referring.

Standing out in marked contrast to the Zürns, the losers of history, are its interim victors as they appear in Volker Braun's *Hinze-Kunze-Roman* (1985; Hinze-Kunze-Novel), a satirically exaggerated work which came under intense discussion in the former GDR. Of course, even the GDR in its real socialist end-phase could not adequately resolve the master-servant relationship, as the novel suggests. To be sure, the new social conditions in the GDR are reflected in the novel, so that a reversal of the social structure up to then has taken place: the functionary Kunze, who comes from a working class and farming background, is the new master; Hinze, the son of a clerk, rises much like Xaver from skilled worker (head lathe operator) to chauffeur, thereby escaping the drudgery of manual labor, which even in a socialist system does not have great appeal. The nonantagonistic society, to use GDR terminology, produces new modes of behavior for master and servant, boss and driver, modes which are supposedly founded upon the common interests of both parties. Furthermore, by choosing the names Hinz(e) and Kunz(e),[23] roughly equivalent to the English Tom, Dick, and Harry, Braun emphasizes the close connection between the two. Thus, as

[22]Frank Pilipp, *The Novels of Martin Walser: A Critical Introduction*, Studies in German Literature, Linguistics, and Culture 64 (Columbia, SC: Camden House, 1991) 90.

[23]Regarding the Hinze-Kunze motif in Braun's work, see Christine Cosentino and Wolfgang Ertl, "Das Hinze-Kunze-Motiv im Werk Volker Brauns," *Germanic Review* 64-65 (1989-1990): 168-76.

opposed to Walser and leaning upon Diderot's *Jacques le Fataliste* (1776) and Brecht's *Puntila/Matti*, dialogue comes back into its own again as a form of communication between Hinze and Kunze. It is a dialogue between near equals. On the one hand, they are united by the difficult-to-define "societal interest"; on the other hand, they remain separated by their functions, their degrees of responsibility, and their privileges. Still, Kunze takes the theoretical equality seriously, as his offer to Hinze to share in responsibility illustrates:

> KUNZE: Hilf mir regieren, Mensch!
> HINZE: Laß man. Ich steh so im Streß.[24]
> [KUNZE: Help me govern, man!
> HINZE: Forget it. I'm under a lot of stress.]

Hinze's negative response, his refusal, is less brusque than Matti's rejection of Puntila's attempts at contact, because Hinze accepts the role assigned to him by the authorial narrator and plays the part almost to the point of self-renouncement, without ever taking the possibility of changing roles with Kunze into serious consideration. Hinze suffers, just as Xaver, from digestive problems; moreover, Hinze is in a difficult position vis-à-vis the sexually potent Kunze, who outdoes Puntila in his libidinal desires and who seeks more tangible pleasures than the musical ones of Dr. Gleitze. Hinze "verkneift sich seine sexuellen Bedürfnisse [und] macht keine Anstalten, seine Würde zu verteidigen" [denies his sexual urges and makes no efforts to defend his dignity],[25] ultimately letting Kunze have his wife and child. Matti's superiority is in the end based upon his attractiveness to women; in the play within the play, the trial marriage which he arranges with Puntila's daughter Eva in order to test her suitability for a proletarian marriage, there is a reversal of the until then sanctioned sexual exploitation of the wives and daughters of servants by the masters. The expectations of the traditionally patterned characters, as well as those of the audience, are thus disappointed: "Not the prince, but the princess is found wanting, which goes to show that no legend is to be taken for granted. Comedy is thus used for an immediate political purpose, that of disturbing the interpretative procedures of the

[24]Volker Braun, *Hinze-Kunze Roman* (Frankfurt/M.: Suhrkamp, 1985) 26. All subsequent references to this novel are to this edition and will be indicated parenthetically in the text as (HKR).

[25]Ursula Heulenkamp, Hans Kaufmann, Siegfried Rönisch, and Bernd Schick, "*Hinze-Kunze-Roman* von Volker Braun," *Weimarer Beiträge* 32 (1986): 833.

characters and through them, the audience."[26] Hinze's resistance against this kind of sexual exploitation, on the other hand, is limited to resigned, recondite verbal opposition in the style of Brecht's *Flüchtlingsgespräche* (Conversations of Refugees), to the furtively clenched fist (HKR 51 et passim) borrowed from a character in Uwe Pfeifer's oil painting *Feierabend* (1977; Quitting Time), and, like that of Xaver, to an act of destruction against an object manifesting the master-servant relationship, the boss's limousine.

In light of Hinze's servile behavior, which stands in sharp contrast to that of Matti, it is fair to ask "warum Hinze so ganz auf sich selbst verzichtet, selbst auf seine Sinnlichkeit.... Denn Kunzes Selbstherrlichkeit setzt Hinzes Unmündigkeit voraus und nicht umgekehrt" [why Hinze so completely denies himself, even his sexuality, for Kunze's self-aggrandizement depends on Hinze's inferior status and not the other way around].[27] Rolf Schneider assumes that Volker Braun "vielleicht ... auch bloß die Handlungsunfähigkeit des ehemaligen Kleinbürgers denunzieren und eine vollzogene Emanzipation an seinem proletarischen Siegertypus Kunze dartun [wollte]" [may simply have wanted to denounce the inability of the one-time member of the petty bourgeoisie to act, and to give complete emancipation to his proletarian victor Kunze].[28] On the one hand, the question posed at the beginning and the end of the novel, a question which recurs frequently with only minor variations, speaks against such an assumption: "Wie hielten sie es miteinander aus?" (HKR 7, 196 et passim) [How did they stand one another?]. The narrator's pretended lack of understanding, his incomprehension of Hinze's actions, reflects doubt as to both the justification of the portrayed relationship between master and servant and the desirability of its continuation. Whether under such conditions one critic's assumption about Braun's Brechtian writing premises still holds true — "[die] Gewißheit von der Überzeugungsfähigkeit des Lesers, ... [die] Gewißheit von der Durchschaubarkeit gesellschaftlicher Zusammenhänge und schließlich ... [die] Gewißheit von der Veränderbarkeit der Welt" [the certainty that the reader is convincible, the certainty of the transparency of social conditions, and finally, the certainty of the changeability of the world][29] — may reasonably

[26]Elizabeth Wright, *Postmodern Brecht: A Re-Presentation* (London: Routledge, 1989) 53.

[27]Heulenkamp, p. 833.

[28]Rolf Schneider, "Herr Kunze und sein Knecht Hinze," rev. of *Hinze-Kunze-Roman*, by Volker Braun, *Der Spiegel* 18 Nov. 1985: 267.

[29]Hermann Kähler, "Unordentliche Bemerkungen zu einem nicht abseitigen Thema," rev. of *Hinze-Kunze-Roman*, by Volker Braun, *Sinn und Form* 38 (1986): 438.

be doubted. After all, the obscene parable of the penises, which is relayed and greatly elaborated upon by the narrator, suggests the impossibility of leveling individual differences and creating complete equality. This parable, however, points the way to a potential suspension of social differences in the patriarchal GDR, inasmuch as the parable appropriately values the role of women, whose behavior is characterized by solidarity rather than by hierarchical thinking.

Kunze, like the euphorically intoxicated Puntila, is capable of envisioning a brotherly and sisterly human community; but while the men passively await the future of communism, Hinze's wife Lisa, who after advanced study in the Soviet Union can lay claim to a leadership position, embodies the behavioral ideal of the new socialist human being. She does not develop into the type of official represented by Kunze; rather, she tends to ignore her authority, an attitude which Kunze notes "beglückt" (HKR 164) [happily]: ".... sie war nicht von dieser Welt, ein zukünftiger Mensch" (HKR 164) [she was not of this world, a person of the future]. Within the existing socialist system (*real existierender Sozialismus*), such a person was "unerhört" (HKR 164) [unheard of], and Lisa's "Gleichgültigkeit gegen ihre Stellung" (HKR 163) [apathy with respect to her position], her unassuming association with her "Leibeigenen" (HKR 163) [serf] Hinze, is at first "unverständlich" (HKR 163) [incomprehensible] to Kunze, for this kind of intimacy creates an uncontrollable "utopisch[es] Durcheinander" (HKR 163) [utopian disarray].

That Volker Braun resolves the master-servant relationship by escaping into Utopia is an indication of his skepticism regarding the Marxist principles of the old master Brecht. In his volume of poetry entitled *Training des aufrechten Gangs* (1979; Practicing Walking Upright) Braun employs the form of Brecht's sociocritical sonnets to distance himself from the one-time teacher, now literary classic, and his "suggestion" to speak the truth: "So was ist noch auf dem Papier zu haben. / Wir haben ihn [den Vorschlag] nicht angenommen, nur / Gewisse Termini und die Frisur" [Such a thing remains available on paper / We did not accept it [the suggestion], only / Certain terms and the coiffure].[30] Similarly, some lines of the poem "Rechtfertigung des Philosophen" [Justification of the Philosopher] in the same volume read: "Aber Marx wußte was er sagte, was weiß ich?? / .... / ... Die große Gewißheit der Klassiker und die langen / Gesichter der Nachwelt" [But Marx knew what he was talking about, what do I know?? /.... / ... the great certainty of classical authors and the long / Faces of posterity].[31] The uncer-

[30]Volker Braun, "Zu Brecht, Die Wahrheit einigt," *Training des aufrechten Gangs* (1979; Halle-Leipzig: Mitteldeutscher Verlag, 1981) 23.

[31]*Training des aufrechten Gangs*, p. 36.

tainty of future generations and the inadequate preparedness of the little people to work together on the Marxist and Brechtian design for the future is articulated by Hinze in the novel: "Sie [die Leute] denken an sich und nicht daran, daß eine Idee zum Sieg zu führen ist! Es scheint jetzt geradezu ein Fehler der Idee, daß sie Tugenden erfordere wie frühere Ideen auch" (HKR 195) [The people think only of themselves and not about the fact that an idea must be led to victory. Frankly, now it seems that the idea, like earlier ideas, makes the error of requiring virtue]. Hinze's doubt about the validity and usefulness of great ideas, a doubt expressed from the proletarian perspective, had been anticipated by Brecht in his *Flüchtlingsgespräche*, written about the same time as *Puntila/Matti*. In the chapter entitled "Trauriges Schicksal großer Ideen / Die Zivilbevölkerung ein Problem" [Sad Fate of Great Ideas / The Civilian Population a Problem], the emigrant Ziffel says: "Alle großen Ideen scheitern an den Leuten" [All great ideas are frustrated by the people].[32] Granted, the distanced and skeptical attitude of the little people concerning the machinations of their superiors had a certain justification in Brecht's "dark times" of exile, but the survival of this attitude in the then existing socialist system raises a question as to the grounds for the need to call upon the self-sacrificing virtues of the little people, draws attention to the contradictions in the former GDR, and awakens doubts about the validity of the Brechtian social project. After all, as Galileo said to Andrea when the latter bitterly accused the former of lacking the courage of his convictions in the face of torture: "Unglücklich das Land, das Helden nötig hat" (BuFA 5:93, 173, 274) ["Unhappy the land where heroes are needed" (Manheim 5:85)].

In Christa Wolf's controversial text *Was bleibt?* (1990; What Remains?), which she first wrote in 1979 and reworked in November 1989, it is said about Brecht's *Leben des Galilei:* ".... dies war ein Stück aus der Zeit, in der die reinliche Dialektik noch Geltung hatte, ebenso wie die Wörter 'positiv' und 'negativ,' und in der es einen Sinn hatte, die 'Wahrheit' auszusprechen, und böse war, sie zu verschweigen..." [this was a play from the time in which tidy dialectic still had validity, just like the words "positive" and "negative," a time in which it made sense to speak the "truth" and was bad to conceal it...].[33] The "tidy dialectic" had been applicable to the fight against fascism which characterized Brecht's exile period, the period in which the first and second versions of *Galilei* as well as *Puntila/Matti* were written. However, as Christa Wolf noted in 1979/1989, not without regret,

[32]Bertolt Brecht, *Gesammelte Werke in 20 Bänden: Werkausgabe edition suhrkamp* (Frankfurt/M.: Suhrkamp, 1967) 14: 1425.

[33]Christa Wolf, *Was bleibt?* (Darmstadt: Luchterhand, 1990) 30.

the GDR in its final phase could no longer rely upon antifascism for its legitimacy nor appeal to it as its moral principle, leaving Brecht's dialectic without meaning. In the end, the fall of the GDR leads one to the conclusion that the merry departure from the past for which Brecht was aiming was of only a temporary nature. In the changed and changeable postsocialist society there is a need for new literary impulses, a need to go beyond Brecht in the literary representation of the master-servant relationship — including new suggestions for its dissolution.

Works Cited

Barthes, Roland. "Brecht and Discourse. A Contribution to the Study of Discursivity." 1975. Reprint of the translation from the French in *Critical Essays on Bertolt Brecht*. Ed. Siegfried Mews. Boston: G.K. Hall, 1989. 245-53.

Berlau, Ruth, Bertolt Brecht, et al. *Theaterarbeit. 6 Aufführungen des Berliner Ensembles*. Dresden: VVV Dresdner Verlag, [1952].

Braun, Volker. *Hinze-Kunze-Roman*. Frankfurt/M.: Suhrkamp, 1985.

——. *Training des aufrechten Gangs*. 1979. 2nd ed. Halle, Leipzig: Mitteldeutscher Verlag, 1981.

Brecht, Bertolt. *Gesammelte Werke in 20 Bänden. Werkausgabe edition suhrkamp*. Vol. 14: Prosa 4. Frankfurt/M.: Suhrkamp, 1967.

——. *Plays, Poetry and Prose*. Vols. 5, 6. Trans. Ralph Manheim. Eds. John Willett, and Ralph Manheim. New York: Vintage, 1972.

——. *Werke. Große kommentierte Berliner und Frankfurter Ausgabe*. Eds. Werner Hecht, Jan Knopf, Werner Mittenzwei, and Klaus-Detlef Müller. Vols. 5, 6: *Stücke*. Berlin: Aufbau; Frankfurt/M.: Suhrkamp, 1988-1989.

Canaris, Volker. "Zwei Brecht-Altmeister." *Theater heute* 10.7 (1969): 10-11.

Cosentino, Christine, and Wolfgang Ertl. "Das Hinze-Kunze-Motiv im Werk Volker Brauns." *Germanic Review* 64-65 (1989-1990): 168-76.

Doane, Heike. "Martin Walsers *Seelenarbeit*. Versuche der Selbstverwirklichung." *Neophilologus* 67 (1983): 262-72.

Esslin, Martin. *Brecht: A Choice of Evils*. 1959. 4th rev. ed. London: Methuen, 1983.

Fallada, Hans. *Kleiner Mann — Was nun?* 1932. Hamburg: Rowohlt, 1990.

——. *Little Man — What Now?* Trans. Eric Sutton. New York: Simon and Schuster, 1933.

Grimm, Reinhold. "Brecht — auf den Postmodernismus gekommen." Rev. of *Postmodern Brecht: A Re-Presentation*, by Elizabeth Wright. *Monatshefte* 82 (Spring 1990): 73-80.

Hermand, Jost. "*Herr Puntila und sein Knecht Matti*: Brechts Volksstück." *Brecht heute* 1 (1971): 117-36. Reprinted in *Die deutsche Komödie. Vom Mittelalter bis zur Gegenwart*. Ed. Walter Hinck. Düsseldorf: Bagel, 1977. 287-304.

Heulenkamp, Ursula, Hans Kaufmann, Siegfried Rönisch, and Bernd Schick. "*Hinze-Kunze-Roman* von Volker Braun." *Weimarer Beiträge* 32 (1986): 830-45.

Hoffmeister, Donna L. "Fantasies of Individualism: Work Reality in *Seelenarbeit*." *Martin Walser. International Perspectives*. Eds. Jürgen E. Schlunk, and Armand E. Singer. American University Studies: Series 1, Germanic Languages and Literature 64. New York: Lang, 1987. 59-70.

Holthusen, Hans Egon. "Versuch über Brecht." *Kritisches Verstehen*. Munich: Piper, 1961. 7-137.

Jarmatz, Klaus. "Realismus mit Ecken und Kanten." Rev. of *Hinze-Kunze-Roman*, by Volker Braun. *Neue Deutsche Literatur* (February 1986): 132-39.

Kähler, Hermann. "Unordentliche Bemerkungen zu einem nicht abseitigen Thema." Rev. of *Hinze-Kunze-Roman,* by Volker Braun. *Sinn und Form* 38 (1986): 438.

Klotz, Volker. *Bertolt Brecht. Versuch über das Werk*. Bad Homburg: Gentner, 1957.

Knopf, Jan. *Brecht-Handbuch: Theater. Eine Ästhetik der Widersprüche*. Stuttgart: Metzler, 1980.

Mayer, Hans. "Herrschaft und Knechtschaft: Hegels Deutung, ihre literarischen Ursprünge und Folgen." *Jahrbuch der deutschen Schillergesellschaft* 15 (1971): 251-79.

Mews, Siegfried. *Bertolt Brecht: Herr Puntila und sein Knecht Matti*. 1975. 3rd enl. edition. Frankfurt/M.: Diesterweg, 1989.

Neureuter, Hans Peter. *Brechts "Herr Puntila und sein Knecht Matti"*. Suhrkamp Taschenbuch Materialien. Frankfurt/M.: Suhrkamp, 1987.

Pilipp, Frank. *The Novels of Martin Walser: A Critical Introduction*. Studies in German Literature, Linguistics, and Culture 64. Columbia, SC: Camden House, 1991.

Schneider, Rolf. "Herr Kunze und sein Knecht Hinze." Rev. of *Hinze-Kunze-Roman*, by Volker Braun. *Der Spiegel* 18 Nov. 1985: 266-68.

Seifert, Walter. "Martin Walser: *Seelenarbeit*. Bewußtseinsanalyse und Gesellschaftskritik." *Deutsche Romane von Grimmelshausen bis Walser*. Ed. Jakob Lehmann. Königstein/Ts.: Scriptor, 1982. 545-61.

Solbach, Andreas. "Herr und Knecht bei Kafka, Walser und Hegel." *Zeitschrift für deutsche Philologie* 106 (1987): 218-36.

Waine, Anthony. "Productive Paradoxes and Parallels in Martin Walser's *Seelenarbeit*." *German Life & Letters* N.S. 34 (1980-1981): 297-305.

Wallace, Ian. *Volker Braun: Forschungsbericht*. Amsterdam: Rodopi, 1986.

Wolf, Christa. *Was bleibt?* Darmstadt: Luchterhand, 1990.

Wright, Elizabeth. *Postmodern Brecht. A Re-Presentation*. London: Routledge, 1989.

4

Reading on the Edge: Martin Walser's California Novel *Breakers*

Bernd Fischer

AT A TIME WHEN it seems more appropriate to talk about Martin Walser's affair with the unified Germany, this essay instead discusses once more his rapport with the U.S. Suspicions that these two affairs of the heart might somehow be related are reinforced by a recent essay in the *New York Times Magazine* on the current fate of East German authors. According to the author, Katie Hafner, the writers from the former GDR have lost their readers and face "harsh re-evaluation or, worse, the ash heap of history." In this context Hafner quotes Walser's comments on Christa Wolf's current reclusion in Santa Monica: "I think we'll see astonishing sentences from her.... A little California always does good.... Especially for the East German writers. They should all get stipends to go to California." What they need, according to Walser, is real distance "from this terribly confining place. Germany."[1]

Walser speaks from experience.[2] What is more, he has sent one of his protagonists, the school teacher Helmut Halm, as a visiting lecturer to Washington University in Oakland, California.[3] With this plot line, *Breakers*

[1]Katie Hafner, "A Nation of Readers Dumps its Writers," *The New York Times Magazine* 10 Jan. 1993: 23.

[2]Cf. his numerous statements about his frequent stays on the North American continent in *Auskunft: 22 Gespräche aus 28 Jahren*, ed. Klaus Siblewski (Frankfurt/M.: Suhrkamp, 1991). See also Heinz D. Osterle's interview with Walser, "Wo viel Schatten ist, ist auch viel Licht. Eindrücke eines verhinderten Einwanderers," *Bilder von Amerika: Gespräche mit deutschen Schriftstellern*, ed. Heinz D. Osterle (Fulda: Englisch-Amerikanische Studien, 1987) 219-27.

[3]Walser himself held visiting appointments and lectured at universities in

not only contributes to the genre of the campus novel, which is suspiciously underrepresented in German literature, but it also positions itself in the tradition of the German-American novel, whose remarkable popularity reaches back to the beginning of the nineteenth century.[4]

Most readers remember Halm as the self-conscious and self-doubting vacationer in *Runaway Horse* (1978), who managed to fend off a dangerous attack on the ways of his bleak German middle-class lifestyle. In the novella the assault was launched by Halm's ex-friend Klaus Buch, who seemed to possess all those vital things that Halm both lacked and fought against: worldliness, intellectual awareness, respect, success, admiration, women, love, friendship, a contemporary mind, a trained body, and, most important, the ability to relate to others in unrestricted and mutually beneficial ways — the list seemed endless. Having somehow survived this frontal attack, Halm, at the beginning of *Breakers*, seems more withdrawn than ever into his last bastion, the nuclear family. Already in the first few pages, the reader becomes aware that Halm's persecution has continued in between the novels in all the familiar ways: his reflection in the mirror, his colleagues with their sneaky success stories, his demanding and undisciplined pupils, the undeserved right to live in the house of his wife's family, his unhappy daughters with their sad marriages and affairs (with older men), his still unpublished Nietzsche manuscript — the list of Halm's persecutors is at least as long as that of his deficiencies and fears. Ultimately it is, of course, the same list. Halm survives by turning himself into an untouchable and impenetrable fortress dependent on only one person to supply him with the essentials for survival: his wife, Sabina.

In *Breakers* this fortress of German manhood has to withstand the ultimate onslaught: California. Survival demands that Halm accept the offer of his old friend Rainer Mersjohann to escape his hometown, Sillenbuch, for a semester and take on a visiting appointment in Oakland. It seems more than questionable, however, whether the battleship Halm can withstand the breakers off the coast of California: the most western edge of the most western civilization. "There was no going any farther west. This was it" (B 87).

Washington, D.C.; West Virginia; Texas; and California.

[4]Siegfried Mews explored the novel within the framework of the campus-genre; "Martin Walsers *Brandung*: Ein deutscher Campusroman?," *German Quarterly* 60 (1987): 220-36. Mark E. Cory has looked at *Breakers* in the topical context of escaping to America and interprets the fictional coed as a new metaphor for America as the land of promise; "Romancing America: Reflections of Pocahontas in Contemporary German Fiction," *German Quarterly* 62 (1989): 320-28.

In the Greek tradition, *Sillen* are parodistic squibs on thinkers and writers. A *Sillenbuch*, therefore, offers us a book of intellectual mockery, a parody — what else could a teacher novel or campus novel look like these days? It is important, however, to take Halm's origin seriously, for it establishes the tone of Walser's narrator, who is one of the most daring he has employed so far. In this novel the explorations of and elaborations on the fifty-five-year-old Halm's most private hopes, needs, and fears and his repeatedly unsuccessful attempts to find some sort of adequate and winning identity-constructs end over and over again in moments of heightened embarrassment, humiliating awkwardness, and desperate silliness.[5] The narrator seems to envision a reader who has the stomach and humor to face these unbearable, unspeakable moments and even find delight in them. This is brought about because Halm speaks and lives the literary language of hiding while uncovering and revealing while denying. Here we have *in nuce* an important aspect of Walser's poetic theory to which we will return.

Halm's flight across the Atlantic and his arrival in California offer all the pathos of a true and yet very stereotypical experience of freedom, an enthusiastic sensation of having escaped once again. Like generations of German immigrants before him, Halm feels that America could set him free and is at once aware of the seemingly endless possibilities that his new environment can offer him. At the same time, however, he also knows that Rainer Mersjohann, the pal from his student days in Tübingen, is not his friend any more and that living in the U.S. must have done something terrible to him. These are, one might say, the two opposing stereotypes of America that have been prevalent in the German mind for at least a century. For Halm, the emotional and physical experiences of freedom and optimism prevail. He sees light, sun, air, sea, bays, hills, picture-book houses, tree-lined streets, a comfortable pace, and upbeat people of impressive shapes and colors with perpetually optimistic smiles: from his German perspective, he has arrived in the otherness of middle-class elysium. This is a land where he can even take up driving again. While his motto used to be: "Feel nothing, live for the day, as shallowly as possible," he now wavers:

> But how could he do that here? This land was an invitation to live big, act big, talk big. The heat, the gas stations, the blacks, the women, the treetops, the luscious gardens, the parched hills, the dogs walking dreamily across the street, and how that's respected, and the

[5]In an interview with Ulf Erdmann Ziegler of 31 August 1985 Walser states that Halm's pathos in *Breakers* can indeed be seen as ridiculous. However, he, as author, has no means to expel ridiculousness from this world, but rather is left with attempting to restore some dignity to it; cf. *Auskunft*, p. 160.

> light, that light — as Sabina says — which sets everything apart.... (B 142)

Sabina too grows more and more fond of California, until she has to return to Stuttgart to take care of her father. After a few weeks even their daughter Lena emerges from the lonely seclusion into which she had withdrawn after a failed marriage and an accident that left her scarred for life. That is what California can do. Everything seems possible. While Halm attends receptions and parties during the course of the academic term, he, for the first time, is able to experience the possibilities of personal style: what architectural details in a family home can disclose, what decorating and landscaping can imply, what clothes and bodies can reveal. In short, he finds himself in a society in which self-expression is everything, in which everybody seems to be taken for what he or she expresses. There are no boring people on campus — with the exception of the Silesian mini-Solzhenitsyn Dempewolf, perhaps, and Zipser, a visitor from the GDR. This does, of course, imply that in California the German question is little more than boring.

California's challenge for Halm is direct and instant. During his only swim in the Pacific he is almost swallowed up by the breakers. This is what he sees in the uncounted mirrors in his California house or in Carol's eyes when he sits in front of her desk to be examined and to confess: his body is inadequate, his conservative suits are laughable in the California light, his guarded language and his protective mannerisms fail. Everything about him falls short and needs improvement, and yet Halm's presence is being taken seriously by everyone. Here he actually has a presence, he is respected. Colleagues and their spouses, staff and students alike, all want to connect with him and they seem to care. Nothing is expected of him, and yet everything he does is noticed and counts. This could be a utopian community or it might very well be the Californian version of a Kafkaesque bind.

California's attack on Halm is simply too manifold in all its different facets to be listed here exhaustively, the most direct and important aspect being love. Halm is hit by an erotic fascination with the undergraduate student Fran Webb, and he sets out in search of his own erotic persona. He is told repeatedly that he resembles Marlon Brando, or he sees himself as the comical Shakespeare character Malvolio.[6] He also feels that he resembles the campus rapist or the type of sexual molester described in the university's harassment policies. The possibilities truly seem endless in California. Nearly every male colleague shows off a wife fifteen to thirty years his junior, although none of them feels very secure in his relationship. But that is not

[6]See Hellmuth Karasek, "Malvolio in Kalifornien," *Der Spiegel* 26 Aug. 1985: 158-59.

what sex and love seem to be about here. At fifty-five, Halm experiences a very specific male identity crisis. Throughout all his California dreaming though, he knows that, no matter what happens, he will not be able to function without the security of his marriage. Back in Sillenbuch, Halm finally assures us that it was all just a play, an act he put on in order to hide that at fifty-five it is all over: "You were pretending.... You wanted to be as heartbroken as a younger man. Scream like a thirty-year-old.... You have to pretend to have a horrendous disease, put on an act to avoid admitting to yourself that all is over. Everything. Just an act, that's all" (B 294). Subsequently Halm receives the news that it is Fran who has literally been swallowed up by the breakers; once again he has managed to survive. Soon afterwards it is his old dog Otto who gets killed — representative of all the old dogs in the habit of chasing the young bitches on Washington's campus — while the aging Halm will truly grow old. Although Halm does not escape completely without injury — he slipped while dancing with Fran — his damage is negligible in comparison with Fran's accident or Rainer's suicide.

Halm knows that Rainer died from being denied the love to which he felt entitled by his marriage contract. Halm might not possess Rainer's stubborn sense of justice, but he would never take that kind of a risk in any relationship. In his case it is the institution of marriage that keeps him going. As a sexual being, Halm is all but autistic. There is a constant bristling and sometimes highly charged erotic atmosphere within him which, at times, reaches a point of near-explosion. However, nothing or almost nothing of this is transmitted to the outside world. Sex is (with the exception of one pitiful marital scene) actually absent from the novel. Whatever Halm's erotic core might try to signal, love outside the family seems hardly accessible to him. His erotic fantasies are dominated by infantile oral images and self-censored observations of T-shirts and running pants. The absence of sex or coming to terms with an age without sex is the main topic of Halm's struggle. At the same time, there is an abundance of names, scenes, images, quotes, and symbols in the novel that signify Eros and Death — all the way down to puns like "Benedick" (B 167) and "Littlewood" (B 211). And where there are no more deeds, there is the realm of the dirty old man, the seasoned language of literary desire.

> Th' expense of spirit in a waste of shame
> Is lust in action; and till action, lust
> Is perjur'd, murderous, bloody, full of blame,
> Savage, extreme, rude, cruel, not to trust.... (B 80)

These are lines of a Shakespeare sonnet that Halm and Fran read and interpret together. It is Halm's literary interpretations that need to be investigated in more detail. Granted that the novel can be (and has been) approached from other angles, there is reason to believe that some of Halm's concerns — such as age, death, competition, jealousy, family, emotional economy, individualism, media, self-expression, talking instead of doing, dreaming instead of talking, and, once again, talking instead of thinking — are within reach from the vantage point of Walser's poetic theory.

While it is not unusual for a campus novel, it is nevertheless eye-catching that Walser intersperses *Breakers* with numerous citations of the particular literary theory that he himself favors. As mentioned above, the central idea is that literary writing can, according to Walser, be defined as revealing while concealing and, conversely, disguising what it illuminates. According to this seeming paradox, literature is camouflage and spotlight at the same time, and it can only be the one because it is also the other. Halm asks himself:

> Didn't Freud have a somewhat punitive notion of self-suppression? Isn't every language a foreign language, Halm would have liked to say — to exclaim even? Foreign to what we are. What we are must not be revealed. In any language. So, today's contention: every language is designed to conceal more than it reveals.... Too bad that the girl didn't participate. (B 59)

In addition, both writing and reading are seen as reactions to the experience of a void, a fault, a privation, or a want.[7] And again, most important seems to be the avoidance of what Halm calls the diagnostic "linguistic supermarket of psychology." For writing and reading constitute possibilities of responding, of coming up with soothing replies to personal experiences. Literature, therefore, is on the side of life; it is a kind of survival technique, while psychology, on the other hand, is a diagnosis, a "ready-made interpretation" (B 50). Indeed, Halm's first attempt to translate his feelings for Fran while translating Rilke's "Panther" from German into English is depicted as an illustration of Walser's own approach to reading. Writing and reading are closely related. The reader replies to written fiction with his own fiction. He constructs his own fictive world according to his own experiences, needs, and desires. The common psychological ground is, according to Walser, that reader and writer both wish for a happier end to every story, i.e., they wish for a happier history in general. Readers are writers who produce their

[7]Walser has explained his poetic credos in numerous interviews, essays, and lectures. For a summary see Frank Pilipp, *The Novels of Martin Walser: A Critical Introduction*, Studies in German Literature, Linguistics, and Culture 64 (Columbia, SC: Camden House, 1991) 19-46.

private books by filling what they read with their own most personal fate. Those who feel they are already at the top and have nothing to fear or to wish for can no longer read.[8] For Walser, reading, like writing, is always therapeutic.

However, just as there are professional writers there are also professional readers. Halm himself is that type of reader; one who makes a living by teaching how to write on what one has read. Therefore, the plot offers ample opportunity to confront Halm and his readers with the question of the nature of academic interpretation. Walser's standard answer to the demands of scholarly criticism has always been that there can never be only one method and only one result. Hence the idea of a correct reading of a text, as opposed to a false reading, is a self-serving invention of teachers. What counts for Walser in an interpretation is not *what* the reader responds, but rather *how* this response is unfolded. That has nothing to do with the interpreter's judgments on the text or what he might have found in it. All depends on how much of himself the author of such an interpretation brings to his reading and to his own text.[9] In Halm's case, the reader soon discovers that even when two people read and translate — together and in dialogue with each other — a loaded and enigmatic text, such as Rilke's "Panther" poem, their reading can be so private and so intense that the attempt to share this experience with one another is pathetically ridiculous and yet, it simultaneously presents, in Halm's eyes, the biggest chance for happiness, if not life. There may not be any communication, but at least there is the illusion of it, just as the fiction itself is an illusion of reality:

> This poem can only be translated by two people sitting, at the end of August between twelve and one, all alone at a little table outdoors, who have nothing in common in the whole wide world except for these three verses of a Rilke poem. Admit that this is a fantastic day, he said to himself. I admit it said the I to the I who had addressed it.... Not that he considered his English good enough to translate this poem. But this very presumptuousness was what inspired him. He

[8] I am paraphrasing Walser's mini-credo of reading as stated in his essay "Über den Leser," *Wer ist ein Schriftsteller? Aufsätze und Reden* (Frankfurt/M.: Suhrkamp, 1979) 94-97 and "Über den Umgang mit Literatur," *Martin Walser: International Perspectives*, eds. Jürgen E. Schlunk and Armand E. Singer (New York: Peter Lang, 1987) 195-214.

[9] I am paraphrasing Walser's response to a question on the quality of interpretations; "Über den Umgang mit Literatur," p. 208.

> wanted to do something that was beyond him, to transcend himself. (B 51-52)

The same afternoon Halm's "I" is challenged by a "He-Halm," who calls him a coward for having left the girl so suddenly. Halm finds out that he has already talked too much; already he has transcended himself. "Halm liked to use inflated language.... He knew he couldn't speak calmly. He had to get worked up, otherwise he remained silent. Whenever he began to speak he felt like a man from the Stone Age striking a rock to produce a spark" (B 83). Perhaps the biggest Californian assault on Halm is language. Rainer explains:

> Perhaps all this could be attributed to the English language, he said. To its California version. This was the land of words. A world of words. People here were crazy about words. Words took care of things here. So then there were no things left. Elissa had grown up in this tradition, in which words were less dependent on things than where he had grown up. (B 92)

At least for Rainer's stubborn Westphalian sense of reality and justice, there is still this epistemological question of how much renaming, camouflaging, and reinterpreting is permissible before any chance for truth and justice is lost. What Rainer says about his son Jamey — that he had left because he could not stand lies and demanded truth — also holds true for himself concerning his personal relationships as well as his writing. Neither truth nor justice are attainable; this is a lesson Rainer and the reader must learn.

In *Breakers* Walser presents three literary critics: Rainer Mersjohann, who, for months, is supposedly working on a paper on Schubert's understanding of texts; Halm, who is writing a paper on Heine; and Fran Webb, who — with Halm's help — is writing essays for her class on several literary topics. Surprisingly it is Rainer who, seemingly so well-versed in the academic rites and rules, suffers the most dramatic defeat. Confronted with the fundamental campus law of "publish or perish ..., he opts for perish" (B 272). Halm faints before he can utter the first word of his lecture. And Fran repeatedly has to settle for a C-minus for her interpretive efforts. All three rebel against the academic demands of communicable readings within the canon. While Rainer and Fran fail clearly and fatally, Halm's case is not quite so clear-cut. After all, he uses his "literary affection" for Fran primarily as an aid to cross the line of old age, expressed in symbolic terms when the two cross Okra Creek: "But she walked with him over that bridge. It swayed slightly as one walked across it, that humpback bridge over dry Okra Creek" (B 96). He virtually instrumentalizes almost everyone he meets in order to get what he wants, and Rainer, at least, feels persecuted by him.

"'Oh well, that's life,' said Halm. 'Persecutors tend to feel persecuted'" (B 123). To himself he thinks: "Lena didn't know that he had become involved in a struggle here.... The more one knew about someone without that person's knowledge, the better armed one was against him.... After all, that was part of his struggle, having to wage it clandestinely. From Nietzsche to Mersjohann" (B 136). Carol judges that, on account of his "calculated benevolence" (B 113), Halm "seem[s] a positive menace" (B 141). By no means as harmless to the outside world as his helpless private suffering might suggest, Halm's inner turmoil makes him a potentially dangerous man.

Everything Halm reads turns into raw material for his manic infatuation with Fran. When he reads Faulkner's *The Hamlet*, he identifies with the teacher Labove, who had tried to rape his beautiful student Eula, only to hear from her: "Stop pawing me, you old headless horseman Ichabod Crane" (B 235). Thanks to Faulkner's incomprehensibly precise language, the meaning of this name — untranslatable, yet so befitting Halm himself — will occupy him for weeks. Unlike Labove, however, Halm is "incapable of madness! This fear! Not fear of punishment! Sexual harassment ... ridiculous. He was only afraid of the words: 'Stop pawing me.' To hear those words from her would, he feared, be more than he could endure" (B 239). While the not yet thirty-year-old Labove "had been able to imagine wounding her seriously enough to draw blood," Halm claims that "at fifty-five strangling is as far as one can go" (B 237). Thus, instead of Fran, Halm butchers Faulkner, Shakespeare, Rilke, and Heine; newspaper accounts, television movies, and radio shows, as well as the newly published university rules on sexual harassment. There seems no limit to this reader's ability to occupy and affiliate, to convert and assimilate. Even when it comes to television commercials, he lets his guard down.[10] They translate easily and forcefully into the illusions he needs: "A girl running through a shady, idyllic landscape, in slow motion, her legs, her shorts, her T-shirt, her hair, herself" (B 37). If it is true that reading and interpretation depend on how much of their own lives readers bring to the text, then this milk commercial is Halm's ultimate text: "Or was it because of a certain universal quality in her face? Or was it her? She also drank only milk! She went jogging twice a day! Jogging was obviously her top priority! Idiot! As if a commercial spot must have any connection with reality! Yet why shouldn't it happen once in a while?" (B 37).

One of Fran's course assignments is to write an essay on a Shakespeare sonnet. She responds to the poem by retelling how she would not let her

[10]Halm's radical turn to TV-consumerism American style could make for a paper in itself.

boyfriend touch her while she was writing her composition. As truthful as the essay may be (in Walser's sense), it could hardly be more trivial.

> Halm was at a loss. She said anxiously: "But you mustn't believe that that's how it was. Never. It's all my invention." "Or an answer," said Halm.... He asked her please not to change anything, merely to go on trying to react to her experiences in words that revealed her to herself more clearly than had her actual experiences. (B 149-50)

Halm reads the final version of the essay and approves: "Marvelous, every word of it. Congratulations" (B 156). He means the girl, of course, and how the two are sitting together, and not the text:

> Only when she had walked away ... did he come to his senses again. He wanted to call after her, run after her, to tell her that his judgment was warped by his downright heroic struggle to be objective. He hadn't been able to read at all. He had skimmed the lines, aware of who was sitting across from him, with no idea as to what he was going to say. So then that enthusiasm had burst out of him. He should have at least told the girl that it seemed as though, here in California, he was capable of producing only one tone of voice — that of enthusiasm. Would she please go and see Carol, who could prove better than anyone else how absurdly small that modicum of reality was in every one of Halm's enthusiastic utterances. It was quite true that he was enthusiastic about her essay, but it was precisely in this enthusiasm that he was aware of his diminished responsibility. (B 156-57)

At this point the question arises for Halm whether there is, after all, a reality that could matter and could demand subjectively valid reactions to a text. Is it possible for a reader to bring a mood to a text that is inadequate, and if so, could the text then stand up to this brutalization? Finally, is uncontrolled enthusiasm not the most likely culprit? Fran's professor surely thinks so, as the grades he gives her indicate. Indeed, Halm's and Walser's interpretive theory seems to have been carried to a most critical edge in this episode. If it is true that those who believe that they have conquered the world and have it all can no longer read, then it might also well be true that those who need too much, whose enthusiasm is too excitable, desires too great, and emotions too autistic, are equally inadequate readers.

Let us expand on at least one aspect of what it implies to teach canonical texts. Reading the canon relies upon a set of learned cultural tropes, a system of cultural semiotics, to use Pierre Bourdieu's frame of reference.[11] Learning to read is part of being educated in the vocabulary of a particular society with a particular tradition. Even those who feel the need to rebel against such readings can only do so in an effective way if they are familiar with the rules. Reading a literary text is more than reading oneself, although it also is that. The problem presented by Walser/Halm is not one of an absolute bipolar opposition: of a societally accepted and, therefore, correct reading as opposed to a personally meaningful but unacceptable reading. Rather, it is a problem of degree, which is also the true difficulty in grading a student's literary interpretation.[12] In other words, Fran's/Halm's C-minus is warranted. Fran might be right when she complains that her professor "only wants stupid clowns who write the way he does" (B 174).[13] At the same time, however, she needs to be made aware that in his uninhibited identification, Halm rapes the text just as he would like to rape her. In that sense, one goal in teaching students how to read might be, among other things, to find ways to sublimate the impulse for unconditional identification — a form of relating to other humans' stories, which children, "dumb beaut[ies]" (B 37), and old rapists have difficulty escaping.

Another of Fran's essays deals with *Much Ado About Nothing*. Halm suggests that she write about Benedick and Beatrice, the secondary couple which he sees as the principal couple in the play.

> Has the girl suggested this play because Benedick and Beatrice unceasingly attack one another polemically, merely because they can't confess so-called love for one another? ... Regardless of what she has in mind, he can only advise her to write about Benedick and Beatrice: the tone of hostility as a declaration of love. Language as the exact opposite in emotion. The explicitness of the unsaid in the said. Revealing merely by hiding. Perhaps then she would at least have an inkling of all that he was not saying. If he was not allowed to say anything, he could use this bickering couple to signal that he was saying nothing and all that he was not saying. Why has she chosen this play? (B 176)

[11]Pierre Bourdieu, *La distinction: critique sociale du jugement* (Paris: Les editions de minuit, 1979).

[12]Cf. Walser's remarks on grading in literature classes in "Über den Umgang mit Literatur," *Martin Walser: International Perspectives*, p. 205.

[13]Steve Dowden in his article on Walser's literary essays also addresses the question of "correct" readings.

It is time to ask how Halm's/Walser's theory of reading and interpreting, which assumes a reader who reacts to a text with her/his own fiction, is connected to the idea of language as a form of communication that reveals by hiding. The common denominator seems to be the assumption that literature today is a kind of self-therapy without the need for an objective diagnosis. Although this can hardly be denied, it typically provokes questions about other possible qualities of literary communication: Is there, for instance, anything in the reading and writing of texts that might have informational value or provide views of the world that are not already present in the conscious or subconscious mind of the reader? Can texts lead the reader to envision worlds that are not already a part of her/his perspectives, desires, or interests; worlds that are bigger, even more encompassing than what the reader might have experienced up to this point? Can a text provide another aspect, an exotic angle on a common story or even an interest in the other for its own sake and right? Or is otherness always only an extension of self, a different way of looking at oneself?

Halm reaches a limit in his self-therapeutic reading when he writes a paper on Heine titled "One of the Tribe of Asra" (B 208). Implicitly, Halm's own essay lends more validity to the above questions. He answers his reading of Shakespeare's work on Halm/Fran with Heine's work on Halm/Fran:

> They loved one another, though neither
> Would speak to the other thereof;
> They looked at each other like strangers
> The while they were dying of love. (B 193)

"Let her comment on that!" (B 193), Halm writes with the blood of his and her heart. He reads "with a pencil" (B 184) and writes "Fran and Helmut" into whatever he reads. Much later, back in Sillenbuch, a dream recaptures the moment of his breakdown in California: "The disgrace would immediately be revealed on the stage in theatrical exaggeration. When embarrassment became unbearable, Otto bit his hand. The pen, filled with red ink, sprayed red ink over the sheet of paper and fell to the floor" (B 303). This is what happened at the moment when Halm's private story of "Fran and Halm" was about to become public as "One of the Tribe of Asra."[14] After a close encounter with the remains of the German student movement (or Klaus Buch, for that matter) on the California beach, after too much sun during his morning run, after Schubert's *Dichterliebe* being performed right before his presentation, Halm was excited and enthused to the point of

[14]Mews has investigated Walser's use of Heine; "Ein entpolitisierter Heine? Zur Rezeption Heines in Martin Walsers *Brandung*," *Heine-Jahrbuch* 27 (1988): 162-69.

emotional explosion. While the campus paper does state a medically correct diagnosis — "HEART ATTACK STRIKES SPEAKER DURING LECTURE" (B 222) — Rainer brings it to the point: "Don't forget the *Dichterliebe*" (B 220).

Halm's theory of reading and writing has suffered a serious defeat as far as publicity and publishing are concerned. Still, "'at least you produced a manuscript,' said Rainer. 'A whimsical whimsy, whatever, you can be satisfied, the minor experience has passed through the filter of verbal expression, you're a fine fellow again" (B 221). This is, of course, true, as far as scholarly papers are judged for their therapeutic value. Halm will ultimately be a fine fellow again, who can live with himself. However, academia in Stuttgart, Berkeley, or Houston has, with equally good reasons, limited room for this approach. There are too many conditions of the heart. Rainer, as we know, never finished his paper on Schubert's understanding of texts. As for the novel's fascination with Schubert, this would implicitly be the most difficult topic of all.

Fran, too, fails with her last essay, another C-minus. Halm is outraged:

> That asshole! What's his name? W. Martin Littlewood. Where does he live? Where's his office? That's the limit! It's deliberate! And if it isn't deliberate, then it denotes an incompatibility that shouldn't be expressed by marking! "He'll be hearing from me," said Halm. All these question marks! ... "'Fran, don't worry. You are the victim of deliberate malice on the part of a teacher. He is in love with you. He is having his revenge. I'm quite sure of it. You can believe me. There are teachers who are as weak as that. There are teachers who are weaker than any student can imagine. How old is he?" (B 211)

Halm later knows that he is speaking of himself that he is "to blame, to blame, to blame. His colleague had obviously been totally baffled, could only resort to question marks." Just like the teachers at his school back in Stuttgart, the California colleague shows no tolerance for Halm's reading. After all, the professor here, too, as Fran points out again, has to be "a generator of clowns" (B 212). There is no escape for Halm. The dreaded "suppressive" mode of reading reaches to the very edge of the most Western civilization:

> He has the feeling of having fled his pursuers as far as the extreme edge of this continent and of now standing at the brink of a sheer cliff. So it has all been for nothing. But how could everything not have been for nothing? Idiot. The language doesn't contain words harsh enough to teach you a lesson; you need a treatment going beyond that. If only he had nerves strong enough to bear such a silence! (B 211-12)

But while Halm only looks down the abyss, Fran falls over the edge and is swallowed up by the surf. Her boyfriend survives and tells reporters: "We were so shocked, we went kind of silent as we hurtled and bounced down the cliff face" (B 296).

This brings us back to what Halm has been trying to escape. One potential oppressor of the raping reader is, as mentioned before, Freud, whom Halm calls the "worried theoretician of self-suppression of the Viennese/Victorian school" (B 227). "If you wished to understand dreams, you must not translate them. There was no second language for a dream" (B 264). The class, however, takes Fran's

> lovely dream ... apart ... as if it were a slaughtered wild animal that had to be gutted, boned, and carved up to prepare it for pot, pan, and stomach. And they were pretty skillful in carving up and identifying. They were all psychologists. Fortunately they couldn't agree.... "It's some kind of compulsion, evidently. Instead of experiencing, people want to know." He didn't tell her that, while the class was dismembering her dream, he had been waiting nervously and greedily for someone to discover him, Halm, in some part of the dream. Surely Jeff should have mentioned Halm in connection with Marlon Brando? It would have embarrassed Halm very much, yet he had been hoping for it. (B 266-67)

One of the binary oppositions that underlie Walser's/Halm's reader-response theory is that of experience and knowledge. Halm repeatedly makes a valid point that experiencing a text has to precede any claim to knowledge of it. Yet, here he concedes that knowledge is also a compulsion. What is more, wanting to know and wanting the other to know are, in a way, much more social and, therefore, risky compulsions than any private reading experience that remains silent can ever be. Halm also realizes that there is no escape in the incomprehensibly diffuse otherness of a foreign language. At times, even he cannot "let it rest at mere understanding: He had to translate the contents word for word. What sometimes so appealed to him over there — to leave everything pleasantly vague — was now unthinkable. He wanted to be absolutely sure of every detail" (B 296).

Although Halm must go back to teaching high-school English and composition in his home town on the "continent of death agonies" (B 233), he knows that he will manage. Once again he will be able to play the role of one of those whom he himself had tried to escape: "All those who through some blockage are in danger of succumbing to a negation-routine or a utopia-idea" (B 228). There is one profession, however, that seems to have succumbed beyond repair. During a Monteverdi performance of *Lettera amorosa* Halm follows

> the text of the *Love Letter* in the program and envied the past its freedoms.... He would have loved to use such inflated language. Who, after all, has scared us away from the words that say more than can be meant? The art arbiter! Halm had a vision of either Kiderlen or a metropolitan gentleman who wears fur coats in the heat of summer and, to justify this, gobbles down unending quantities of ice cream. Someone who condemns life but enjoys it. (B 249)

It is, of course, a tragedy that German schools, universities, and feuilletons are still stuffed with Kiderlens and ice cream-eating gentlemen in fur coats. The question remains, then, whether we should indeed go so far as to embrace what the teacher and critic Helmut Halm was for those few months in California.

Works Cited

Bourdieu, Pierre. *La distinction: critique sociale du jugement*. Paris: Les éditions de minuit, 1979.

Cory, Mark E. "Romancing America: Reflections of Pocahontas in Contemporary German Fiction." *German Quarterly* 62 (1989): 320-28.

Hafner, Katie. "A Nation of Readers Dumps its Writers." *The New York Times Magazine* 10 Jan. 1993: 23-26, 46-48.

Karasek, Hellmuth. "Malvolio in Kalifornien." Rev. of *Brandung*. *Der Spiegel* 26 Aug. 1985: 158-59.

Mews, Siegfried. "Martin Walsers *Brandung*: Ein deutscher Campusroman?" *German Quarterly* 60 (1987): 220-36.

——. "Ein entpolitisierter Heine? Zur Rezeption Heines in Martin Walsers *Brandung*." *Heine-Jahrbuch* 27 (1988): 162-69.

Heinz D. Osterle, "Wo viel Schatten ist, ist auch viel Licht. Eindrücke eines verhinderten Einwanderers." Interview with Martin Walser. *Bilder von Amerika: Gespräche mit deutschen Schriftstellern*. Ed. Heinz D. Osterle. Fulda: Englisch-Amerikanische Studien, 1987. 219-27.

Pilipp, Frank. *The Novels of Martin Walser: A Critical Introduction*. Studies in German Literature, Linguistics, and Culture 64. Columbia, SC: Camden House, 1991.

Walser, Martin. *Auskunft: 22 Gespräche aus 28 Jahren*. Ed. Klaus Siblewski. Frankfurt/M.: Suhrkamp, 1991.

——. "Über den Leser — soviel man in einem Festzelt darüber sagen soll." *Wer ist ein Schriftsteller: Aufsätze und Reden*. Frankfurt/M.: Suhrkamp, 1979. 94-101.

Walser, Martin. "Über den Umgang mit Literatur." *Martin Walser: International Perspectives*. Eds. Jürgen E. Schlunk, and Armand E. Singer. American University Studies: Series 1, Germanic Languages and Literature 64. New York: Peter Lang, 1987. 195-214.

5

Martin Walser's *Breakers* and Walter Kempowski's *Dog Days:* Reflections of Two Unpolitical Men?*

Frank Pilipp

GIVEN INCONTROVERTIBLE DIVERGENCES WITH regard to their "literary" status in the Federal Republic, a juxtaposition of novels by Martin Walser and Walter Kempowski may, at first glance, not necessarily appear all that compelling. That Kempowski is predominantly received as a popular writer is underscored by the rather scarce attention scholarly criticism has paid to his novels. By contrast, Walser's works have consistently generated an abundance of critical reactions. Beyond these essentially qualitative differences, however, Walser's *Breakers* (1985) and Kempowski's *Hundstage* (1988; *Dog Days*, 1990) share a number of characteristics that virtually demand a contrastive discussion. Apart from the relative proximity of their respective publications and the comparable age of their authors and their protagonists,[1] there exist numerous fundamental similarities, both on a formal and thematic level, which seem to be accented by more or less explicit textual references in *Dog Days* to Walser's novel. A comparison of the two texts under literary

*This article also appears in German in vol. 3 of the *MIFLC Review* (1993) under the title "Martin Walsers *Brandung* und Walter Kempowskis *Hundstage*: Betrachtungen zweier Unpolitischer?"

[1]While these parallels alone would not constitute a sufficiently compelling reason for comparison, they are no doubt conspicuous: Walser was born in 1927, Kempowski in 1929; their heroes: Walser's Helmut Halm is fifty-five years of age, Kempowski's Alexander Sovtschick sixty. These facts are insofar relevant as they establish a thematic premise. References to *Dog Days*, the first English translation of Kempowski's novel published by Camden House, will be given parenthetically as (DD).

and literary-historical categories is furthermore supported by certain parallels concerning their authors' literary careers as well as their concept of writing, which may generally be understood as the fusion of autobiography and history.[2]

While both Walser and Kempowski belong to the first generation of postwar German authors, neither became established as an independent writer until the mid-seventies — Kempowski achieved wider public recognition only after his second novel, *Tadellöser & Wolff*, had appeared in 1971, fourteen years after Walser's initial, if limited, success with his collection *Ein Flugzeug über dem Haus und andere Geschichten* (1955; An Airplane over the House and Other Stories). Although both authors regard writing as a process of self-definition, neither Walser nor Kempowski is usually listed as a representative of the literary movement of the so-called New Subjectivity that crystallized in the early seventies. In spite of the subjective premises of their writings, the meticulously detailed and empathetic depiction of their protagonists' inner lives does not result in an escape into the ivory tower of emotional self-reflection but rather serves to illuminate external, that is, sociohistorical conditions, even though primary emphasis lies on the character's/narrator's personal claims to truth.[3] *Breakers* and *Dog Days*, however, seem to indicate a subtle shift in the respective author's approach to his subject matter, a shift that allows the component of individual self-reflection and the quest for self-definition to emerge as the central theme of the novel. Accordingly, the novels under discussion increasingly tend to illustrate existential concerns.

When Walser, who, like his protagonist Helmut Halm, taught for a semester in California, acknowledges the autobiographical component of his novel as an attempt "to get to know oneself,"[4] the same can be said for

[2]Walser considers his writing "a chronicle of everyday life" (*Wer ist ein Schriftsteller* [Frankfurt/M.: Suhrkamp, 1979] 25), Kempowski calls it "simply recording what happened there" (*Freisinger Tagblatt* 7 Jan. 1980, quoted by Patricia H. Stanley, "Walter Kempowski," *Dictionary of Literary Biography 75: Contemporary German Fiction Writers Second Series*, eds. Wolfgang Elfe and James Hardin [Detroit: Gale Research Company, 1988] 141).

[3]In Walser's novels of the sixties, the Kristlein trilogy, the protagonist is also the narrator, whose actions and perceptions are intended to mirror the social atmosphere of the time. In Kempowski's previous novels it is always a meticulous and most precise first-person narrator (often named Kempowski), who aims to create a chronicle of the changing times.

[4]Walser in an interview with Anton Kaes, "Porträt Martin Walser: Ein Gespräch," *German Quarterly* 57 (1984): 448.

Kempowski, whose protagonist, the writer Alexander Sovtschick, the author's fictitious alter ego, confirms the "all-too-autobiographical nature" of his novels (DD 284) and admits his goal to be "get[ting] to know himself better by writing" (DD 286).[5] The autobiographical component in Kempowski's case is further suggested by his volume of intimate confessions published two years after *Dog Days*, whose title, *Sirius: Eine Art Tagebuch* (1990; Sirius: A Diary of Sorts), supports the impression of a nonfictional sequel to the novel.[6] Without postulating congruity of author and protagonist, the scattered account of the protagonists' past lives (Halm's childhood and adolescence marked by dire financial straits, Sovtschick's stint as a POW in Russia) clearly evidence major biographical parallels to the lives of their authors.

Despite the fact that the narrative perspective in both novels maintains the point of view of the main character, the use of the third person and the simple past point to a mediating narrative voice. As in his other novels since 1976, Walser rigorously narrows the narrative perspective of *Breakers* to relay exclusively Halm's perceptions. Oftentimes this results in narrated monologue, a highly subjective narrative mode that effects a high degree of dramatic and mimetic representation of external as well as internal events, including the penetration of a character's subliminal zones. This, then, entails a process of identification between reader and character, and the reader is invited to meet the character with empathy and benevolence.[7] Subjective perception is thus mediated through the guise of the grammar of impartiality. Except for a few passages, this narrative mode does not seem to transcend notably the mental framework of the main character. *Dog Days* presents the same narrative setup; the novel is narrated from Sovtschick's perspective, and the implied narrator's knowledge appears to be identical with the charac-

[5]Kempowski has Sovtschick create yet another "sort of self-portrait" (DD 11) that carries this 'portrait of the author as an aging man' to a metafictional level. Sovtschick designates "Gottfried Fingerling, the aging writer" (DD 20) to be "his poetic alter ego" (DD 156), who is at work on a novel whose title, "*High Tide*," may be a potential reference to Walser. The same passage reads: "He thought of surf pounding the shore..." (DD 156) ["Er dachte an Brandung, die ans Ufer schlägt..." (*Hundstage* 195-96).

[6]Cf. Kempowski's preamble to the novel, where he links the "dog days" to "Sirius, the Dog Star."

[7]See Dorrit Cohn's chapter on "Narrated Monologue," *Transparent Minds: Modes for Presenting Consciousness in Fiction* (Princeton: Princeton UP, 1978) 99-140, esp. 112-17 and 126.

ter's self-knowledge.[8] By virtue of their linguistic brilliance, minute perceptiveness, and subtle sensitivity in registering the inner workings of their characters, Walser and Kempowski are able to create a convincingly authentic and well-rounded portrait of their protagonists. It should be noted, though, that Walser succeeds in designing a far more profound and sophisticated psychological makeup for his character than is the case with Sovtschick.[9] In both cases the coexistence of the character's perspective and implied narrator's voice creates a tension for the reader between identification and distancing effect,[10] a tension that gives rise to a subtle yet witty form of irony, making for a humorously entertaining and, at the same time, intellectually stimulating reading experience. It should be pointed out, however, that the ironic tonality of Kempowski's novel manifests itself more explicitly, tending to satire that pokes fun via the protagonist's foibles at Germany's literary marketing strategies. Walser's irony, on the other hand, exists on a deeper, more sophisticated plane and often with a blend of melancholy pathos. While Walser clearly sympathizes with Halm's faux pas, he simultaneously draws the reader's attention to specific (external) conditions adverse to the character's quest for self-realization.

The introjection of the narrative perspective lays the formal foundation for the authors' individual case studies of an identity crisis and their increasing preoccupation with psychological and emotional concerns. This also marks a thematic shift of accent from a more sociological view in their early novels to a distinctly psychological approach in the works discussed here. The subjective perspective renounces the depiction of external reality as a trustworthy totality. The outside world in these texts is presented as an individual inner problematic. In this vein, Walser's acutely self-conscious Halm tries to cope by developing and upholding survival strategies to ward

[8]In both novels the presence of an implied narrator is signalled by an (occasional) tense change from simple past to present tense. This time shift disrupts the flow of narrated monologue and draws attention to the subjective nature of the narrated events.

[9]For example, Halm's tendency to intellectualize his fears, hopes, and anxieties and mediate them through his literary readings; see esp. the discussion of this aspect by Kurt Fickert, "A Literary Collage: Martin Walser's *Brandung*," *The International Fiction Review* 15.2 (1988): 96-102, and Siegfried Mews, "Martin Walsers *Brandung*: Ein deutscher Campusroman?," *German Quarterly* 60 (1987): 220-36.

[10]For a sound analysis of this aspect see Jean-Maurice Martin, *Untersuchungen zum Problem der erlebten Rede. Der ursächliche Kontext der erlebten Rede, dargestellt an Romanen Robert Walsers*, Europäische Hochschulschriften: Series 1, Deutsche Sprache und Literatur 1009 (Bern: Peter Lang, 1987) 125-26.

off society's impinging dictates and to secure himself a minimal range of personal autonomy. Like Halm, Sovtschick is portrayed as a constantly reflecting intellectual, well-versed and conversant in literary matters. In contrast to Halm, Sovtschick is rather cheerful, but he also displays a propensity for emotional-intellectual self-reflection and a certain existential anxiety sparked by the inescapability of aging, which are so characteristic for Walser's antiheroes.[11] Thanks to his eminently developed sense of self, however, Sovtschick is able to confront the outside world with a healthy measure of self-assurance, self-complacence, and at times with undisguised arrogance.[12]

On a generally thematic level, both novels deal with the self-doubts of aging intellectuals and their attempts at compensating for or coping with a lack essentially sexual in nature; their growing certainty after almost thirty years of matrimony of having missed their (erotic) opportunities in life: a midlife crisis of sorts. In addition, further thematic premises and parallels are evidenced in the respective contrast of old age and death, on the one hand, and youth and sexuality, on the other,[13] a contrast of which Halm is acutely and dismally aware under the inspiring aura of his new environment. Upon his arrival in California, the blooming radiance of the land with its glorious weather, its glistening bay, its nocturnal cicada choruses, and suntanned, youthful people convinces Halm that life is worth living. Despite his hopes in *Runaway Horse* that the torture of sexuality would soon be over (RH 45), he involuntarily but consciously falls prey to the new splendor of life surrounding him and finds himself face to face with a sexual temptation of

[11]For example, the "screams for help" (DD 8) Sovtschick utters in his sleep are reminiscent of Halm's "screams" (RH 87) after sexual intercourse with his wife in *Runaway Horse* (1978). Whereas no reasons for Sovtschick's screams are given, in Halm's case it is a feeling of despair and devastation for having submitted once again to society's performance pressure by engaging in sexual activity.

[12]The two characters furthermore differ in their physical appearance. Whereas Halm finds his — apparently overweight — figure ridiculous and grotesque to look at, Sovtschick feels "youthful and fresh, full of energy and elasticity" (DD 332) and all too readily surrenders to spells of self-admiration, seeing himself as the "world-famous author" (DD 314), the irresistible pickup artist (e.g., DD 295, 301), and the progressive *Lebenskünstler* (DD 301), who has mastered the art of living by virtue of his superior intellectual capabilities. Sovtschick's physical appearance resembles more that of Klaus Buch, Halm's hated counterpart in *Runaway Horse* (cf. also their daily workout routine). Buch's cult of fitness and youth serves, of course, nothing but to compensate for his professional failures.

[13]While Walser uses Schubert's "Death and the Maiden" as a leitmotiv, the title occurs at least once in *Dog Days* (DD 10).

major proportions, especially when he develops a burning infatuation with a student thirty-three years his junior.[14] Sovtschick on his part, with his avowed preference for "young women" (DD 323), consciously seeks such encounters.[15] He — who, in another conspicuous parallel to *Breakers*, has also "taught in California" before (DD 74) — thrives on the excitement he gets from the charms and attractions of the females around him under the blistering heat wave. While Halm, in the course of events, becomes thought-controlled by and obsessed with his student, Sovtschick's life, too, revolves around his juvenile guests, although he pretends to engage in the contacts with them as a mere diversion, in order "to bridge the bleak intervals in time" (DD 65) left by his rather sporadic work on his new novel.

Like Gustav Aschenbach in Thomas Mann's *Death in Venice* (1911), both characters try to camouflage their aging complex[16] by mimicking an all-too-youthful appearance, an endeavor which, of course, only serves to further underscore the pathetic makeup of their respective situations. Both of them, however, are recurrently called back to reality by *memento mori* alerts that

[14]In this context see also my chapter on *Breakers* in *The Novels of Martin Walser: A Critical Introduction*, Studies in German Literature, Linguistics, and Culture 64 (Columbia, SC: Camden House, 1991) 71-78.

[15]The German text has the more telling "Kindfrauen" (*Hundstage* 396). Likely references to *Breakers* become manifest, for instance, when Sovtschick frequently remembers the young girl Freddy, a Californian beach beauty, who went "hurtling down the cliff" in Santa Barbara, a tragedy he links to his own "hurtling down the cliff of old age" (DD 305). This, of course, corresponds exactly to the accident of Fran Webb, who "hurtled and bounced down the cliff" (B 296), and to Halm's sensation of looking down the cliff of old age (see also Bernd Fischer's essay, p. 60). Similarly, Sovtschick's repeated recollection of an — intentionally vague — episode in a hotel in Italy ("... and it was noisy all night long" [DD 323]) duplicates Halm's unpleasant memory of a previous Italian vacation, where he was shown the limits of his sexual prowess by a veritable sex machine in the adjacent hotel room (B 155). Furthermore, Halm's doubts "if a spiritual plane exists" (B 200) correspond to Sovtschick's gripe, "don't the things of the spirit count for anything?" (DD 323); likewise, both characters entertain sexually loaded fantasies of strangling girls (B 226; DD 288). Another striking parallel arises when Halm recognizes himself in his blind infatuation as Malvolio, the enamored old dunce in Shakespeare's comedy *Twelfth Night*, while Sovtschick identifies himself as Nick Bottom, the duped jackass in *Midsummer Night's Dream* (DD 292).

[16]At times Sovtschick feels "old and withered" (DD 50); Halm obviously suffers from his age (e.g., B 29, 50, 54, 97).

run through both novels in a leitmotivlike fashion.[17] To counter these frustrations, the characters either compulsively exude make-believe optimism[18] or envision salvation from their depressing and unfulfilled lives in bouts of flagrant escapism.[19] While both are constantly plagued by the impression of being filmed or watched (B 224; DD 49), it is perhaps precisely their self-conscious nature that hints at — and at the same time renounces — a societal theme: both characters display a behavior that has obviously been conditioned by bourgeois standards of status and success propagated through the public media of an affluent society. In this vein, the contradictory goal of their role play is to live up to social dictates while trying to fend off the manipulative influence of the outside world. While Sovtschick, thanks to his grand-bourgeois self-esteem, wages this perpetual battle with relative ease, the petty-bourgeois Halm has to endure a seemingly never-ending series of setbacks.

In both texts the setting is removed from immediate social conflicts, and like *Breakers*, where the transience of Halm's stay evokes the impression of an exotic vacation experience,[20] *Dog Days*, too, creates the impression of rather atypical summer interludes. As the plot, perhaps because of the protagonists' well-established social status, focuses exclusively on their private problems, sociopolitical issues are categorically excluded. The characters' trials and tribulations experienced early in life may be seen as the catalyst for their nonchalance about social problems. While Halm remains comparatively indifferent to such issues, Sovtschick is at least peripherally aware of such "catastrophic topics" as "the arms race, AIDS, smog, and the burning of the South American rain forest" (DD 20-21), though his intention

[17]In *Dog Days* this is implicitly manifest in the title — cf. "Dog Days, these are days in which life seems to stand still.... After that, the days rush on toward the autumn; melancholy sets in with thoughts of departure and death" (DD 283) — and furthermore in Sovtschick's frequent interpolation "Out! Out! It's all over!" (DD 25 et passim), as well as explicitly in *Breakers* through Halm's downright fatalism (e.g., B 97, 134, 225, 260).

[18]When Halm wants to be convinced "that life ... was beautiful" (B 258), he forebodes Sovtschick's proclamation that "life was really beautiful, after all" (DD 332).

[19]Sovtschick feels certain that "the television set would help him salvage the evening" (DD 323), and Halm "capitulate[s]" helplessly "at the sight of the TV set" (B 228), knowing: "Life is better on TV than at your front door" (B 256).

[20]See Mark E. Cory, "Romanticizing America: Reflections of Pocahontas in Contemporary German Fiction," *German Quarterly* 62 (1989): 325.

to work them into his novel remains unrealized.[21] Otherwise he feels rather annoyed with "political slogans" (DD 178) and would much rather replace them with poetry. Halm, on his part, admits his strong preference for "direct experiences" over "political or ideological themes" (B 139-40) and tends to accept unquestioningly the given conditions as irreversible (B 228), thus affirming Franz Horn's motto in *Letter to Lord Liszt* (1982) of the liberating effects of conformism, "Those who conform think of themselves as free" (LL 66).

Kempowski's satirical portrayal of a writer who deliberates the "utilization" of social and political issues simply for commercial reasons evidences unambiguous criticism of a bourgeois political apathy and complacency. On the other hand, Halm's defensive petty-bourgeois withdrawal from society — in the past Halm had been known to be "all for the class struggle" (RH 31) ["ein Klassenkämpfer" (FP 50)] — may be seen as an apology for this bourgeois impassivity. Both characters are conformists — one might call Sovtschick a sycophant — in a society that propagates disparate cultural values (classical music and literature, on the one hand, physical and sexual fitness, on the other) to create the illusion of freedom and equality while effacing actual social hierarchies. The illusion of freedom virtually eliminates the individual's willingness and ability to reflect on the anonymous societal apparatus since the inequalities, oppression, and exploitation that exist in reality (although not specifically addressed within the social context of either novel) are veiled, that is, made bearable.

Both protagonists fail to realize that their mentalities are in fact second-hand ideals borrowed from the public-opinion sector and originate in a capitalist ideology rooted in social prestige and material affluence. When Halm suddenly advocates the compulsive enjoyment of life and subscribes to a daily fitness program, reducing his consumption of alcohol and cigars to a minimum (a sensible resolution, at least from a health-conscious point of view), it is clear that he has simply succumbed to the influence of Fran Webb, the epitome of the student-conformist. For Sovtschick, too, ideal values only seem to exist on a materialistic basis. He revels in his presumption that his writing "would give Western culture a significant nudge

[21]The following observations illustrate Sovtschick's alleged social commitment: "A man who has 'arrived' is confronted with problems arising from differences in what is called 'social status.' ... Overall it would be a pleasant, 'upbeat' thing, and a bit risque, with its political message wrapped in eroticism.... The advantage ... was that he could *act like* he was politically involved..." (DD 331; emphasis added). On the other hand, it is disturbing to Sovtschick when critics accuse him — alluding to Handke's self-proclaimed subjectivism — of being "someone living in an ivory tower" (DD 218; cf. 65).

forward"; most important, however, it "would also help drive the column of mercury in his bank account upward" (DD 331). His continual reflections on women are tinged with flagrant chauvinism, and his material wealth at times proves advantageous for his seductive strategies. Halm, on his part, tries to discredit sexual activity as an extension of the societal dictate for greater physical and sexual fitness. On the one hand, his rekindled though unfulfilled sexual needs deeply disturb his already shaky inner balance, and he is desperately inclined to end the repression and confinement of his natural drives and seek unrestricted fulfillment in sexual "recklessness" (B 177). Lacking Sovtschick's nerve and forwardness, however, Halm, the eternal failure, does the opposite and negates the validity of all sexual activity. He persistently seeks theoretical proof that sex is nothing but a highly repugnant, mechanical "pseudoservice" (B 155) that one performs for the sake of physical pleasure. His strategy is clearly to fabricate a rational construct that will justify the denial of his sexual desires, thus defusing the Californian temptation and reaffirming his position as an intellectual.

The ending suggests identical solutions for both characters. After a calamitous incident[22] both, perhaps in an opportunistic turn, seek recourse to their wives, whose empathy delivers them from their individual isolation and in whose commitment and dedication they discover a new, fortifying intimacy, a reservoir for genuine communication. Thus, conjugal community constitutes a social microcosm that allows for a limited context within which such ideal values as friendship, solidarity, and unity can still be actualized. This "New Intimacy" signifies a new sense of self, which seems to be limited to this most private familial circle. Halm's conclusion in the dramatic version of *Runaway Horse* (1985) that being married allows one to ignore the rest of the world[23] and his desire to regain the "old harmony, solidarity" (B 115) with Sabina are echoed in Sovtschick's aspiration: "Sit on the sofa for the rest of his life with Marianne and just stare straight ahead. Create some privacy that really was private!" (DD 337). Surely this somewhat cheerless image depicts a rather ambiguous idyll. The irony is undeniable, for this companionship in social isolation is effected by a capitulating retreat from a greater community in which the tormented self finds neither support nor validation.

[22]In Sovtschick's case, the vandalization of his mansion by a group of youths; in Halm's case, an accident he had caused dancing with his student while heavily intoxicated — an accident that leaves him with bruises but may be the reason why Fran later was unable to rescue herself in a landslide and drowned in her car.

[23]Martin Walser and Ulrich Khuon, *Ein fliehendes Pferd. Theaterstück* (Frankfurt/M.: Suhrkamp, 1985) 77.

Like Sovtschick, who often lives his desires vicariously through writing, Halm envisages relief by verbalizing his problems, that is, by fictionalizing them and imparting them to a potential listener. However, this "narrative in which he c[an] hide away" (B 117) does not begin until the last sentence of *Breakers*, when Halm launches into a confession to his wife, a confession that will be a retelling of the preceding events. Halm's narration is, thus, akin to Walser's concept of writing as a "fictional response"[24] in order to compensate for the "inadequacies of his self-identity."[25] Walser's premise seems straightforward. He considers writing as a "means to promote a sense of self" ["Mittel zur Identitätsbildung"] for the socially underprivileged.[26] Apart from this somewhat doubtful assumption which assigns to the lower classes an existential impulse to write, Walser's premise would not necessarily hold up either in light of the elevated social status of the *Gymnasium* teacher Halm, even if Walser insists that the proletarian past of his protagonist identify him — like all of his other protagonists — as a societal underdog.[27]

Kempowski, too, seems to place primary emphasis on the character's quest for self-definition, without, however, relating it to a specific theoretical premise. First and foremost it is the act of narrating to which both protagonists dedicate themselves. With his final confession and his productive conjuration of "everything worth telling" (RH 15) ["Das Erzählbare überhaupt" (FP 28)], Halm recaptures his long-lost "adventure" (RH 15) and rises from a figural medium to an authorial narrator, while Sovtschick concludes:

> He held the world captive ... and the world probably longed to be set free. Sovtschick had locked it out of his magic kingdom.... He sat here in his enchanted castle ... the creator of all, and held sway over life and death, at least in his books. If he did not depict these crazy weeks of summer, if he did not sketch the girls, then they did not exist and had never lived. (DD 295)

[24]"Porträt Martin Walser: Ein Gespräch," p. 434.

[25]Walser, *Wer ist ein Schriftsteller*, p. 37.

[26]*Wer ist ein Schriftsteller*, p. 40.

[27]I discuss this issue in depth in my article "Von den Nöten des Kleinbürgers: Individueller und gesellschaftlicher Determinismus in Martin Walsers Prosa," forthcoming in *Leseerfahrungen mit Martin Walser: Neue Beiträge zu seinen Texten*, eds. Gertrud Bauer Pickar and Heike A. Doane (Munich: Fink, 1994).

Romanticizing the storyteller as a godlike creator celebrates the act of narrating as an escape from realty[28] and elevates poetry to a wondrous act of (self-)liberation and self-actualization. The protagonists' private retreat thus turns into an escape into fantasy/poetry where everyday restrictions are no longer valid, allowing them infinite freedom for self-expression.

In their highly personal and subjective mode of presentation, *Breakers* and *Dog Days* integrate autobiographical elements and evidence a radical candor that even extends to the most private sector. Nevertheless, the two novels can only be conditionally categorized as examples of the subjectivist literature that has firmly established itself since the early 1970s. Especially represented by the second postwar generation of writers, this literature also claims such authors as Max Frisch, Thomas Bernhard, and Elias Canetti on the grounds of their later quasi-autobiographical fictions. Generally characterized by its disregard for political themes while celebrating the rediscovery of the self,[29] it illustrates the dissonances of an individual (usually the first-person narrator) with external reality. Clearly the utmost importance is attached to the subjective disposition of the individual — external reality is largely disregarded or (as in Sovtschick's case) casually dismissed or glossed over. Nevertheless, Kempowski depicts his character's societal impassivity and unconcern due to material surfeit not without poignant criticism. Walser presents Halm's tacit acceptance of the reigning conformity and political stagnation as an apology for the indifference of his formerly activist protagonist, but he also illustrates the private deformations caused by such introversion.

In Walser's novel the reasons that compel the protagonist to seek refuge in inwardness are disillusionment, pessimism, and unfulfilled expectations. Since external reality can no longer be perceived and depicted as a whole, the individual centers on the self, which still implies a societal perspective *ex negativo*: self-reflection as a means to stabilize self-identity. Individual deformations — one might argue — are imputed to society's manipulative influence, but this influence is no longer concretely comprehensible since the societal apparatus is perceived exclusively as a threat that necessitates the

[28]Cf. Sovtschick's unassailable "sanctuary" (DD 334) ["Fluchtburg" (*Hundstage* 410)] that frequently grants him his last retreat from the outside world. Halm's flight attempts are more concrete (not only in regard to *Runaway Horse*) as a territorial escape from the "restrictions that regulate his life at home and limit his freedom" (Heinrich Vormweg, "Bittersüß die Schmerzen des Alterns," rev. of *Brandung*, *Süddeutsche Zeitung* 31 Aug. 1985: 104).

[29]See Helmut Koopmann, "Tendenzen des deutschen Romans der siebziger Jahre," *Handbuch des deutschen Romans*, ed. H. Koopmann (Düsseldorf: Bagel, 1983) 576.

retreat into subjectivity. In his collection of aphorisms, *Meßmers Gedanken* (1985; Messmer's Thoughts) published concurrently with *Breakers*, Walser seemed to announce his (temporary) "farewell to history" in the guise of the faceless title character. When Meßmer proclaims that the deformations of his identity are attributable to the effects of capitalism, he also admits that except for this global verdict his tirades contain "nothing political" (MG 94).

As these observations show, *Breakers* and *Dog Days* implicitly acknowledge sociopolitical or sociocritical issues by drawing attention to societal disinterest as a product of a zeitgeist marked by reactionary apathy. The critical potential usually inherent in Walser's prose manifests itself more explicitly in his texts after *Breakers* — for instance, in his novella *No Man's Land*, which deals with the then divided Germany; in his latest novel, *Ohne einander* (1993; Separate Lives); and, albeit with great moderation and an unmistakable sense of nostalgia, in *Die Verteidigung der Kindheit* (1991; In Defense of Childhood).[30]

In light of Halm's "unpolitical reflections" it is astonishing that Walser has mocked Thomas Mann for the selfsame nonpolitical attitude, which he found displayed in *Tonio Kröger* (1903). According to Walser, Thomas Mann's title character is a hero "utterly without problems and sorrows due to his aristocratic identity, a hero whose unshakable self-confidence allows him to be aloof from any social discrepancies.[31] Walser's novella *Runaway Horse*, the predecessor of *Breakers*, has rightly been interpreted as a subtle parody of *Tonio Kröger*.[32] In presenting a petty-bourgeois individual, highly unstable and vulnerable under the existing social pressures, *Runaway Horse* counters Mann's/Kröger's social detachment with a distinctly critical stance. At the same, time the reader is repeatedly reminded that Halm covets this sublime, grand-bourgeois sense of self-worth for which he so envies his colleagues in Germany. On the other hand, his inherited lack of self-confidence prevents him from transgressing mentally the social confines imposed on him by birth, a step which Sovtschick has long undertaken. While nearly

[30]Cf. the essays by Heike Doane and Gertrud Pickar in this book.

[31]Martin Walser, "Die Ironiker," *Selbstbewußtsein und Ironie. Frankfurter Vorlesungen* (Frankfurt/M.: Suhrkamp, 1981) 93. This essay was written before 1976, thus preceding publication of *Runaway Horse* (1978).

[32]See Manfred Dierks, "'Nur durch Zustimmung kommst du weg': Martin Walsers Ironie-Konzept und *Ein fliehendes Pferd*," *Literatur für Leser* 7 (1984) 44-53. In *Breakers*, too, there exist striking thematic parallels to another novella by Thomas Mann, *Death in Venice* (1911): for example, Halm's and Aschenbach's journies abroad, their subsequent erotic obsessions, and their pathetic attempts at rejuvenation.

ten years later the very same volatile and socially "underaffirmed identity"[33] makes Halm a comical-grotesque figure who does not miss an opportunity to expose his foibles, a sociocritical momentum can be claimed at least conditionally with regard to *Breakers*.

One might argue that Kempowski has weaved the parallels to *Breakers* (which often appear like allusions) deliberately into his novel, only to distance himself from Walser in the psychological makeup of his protagonist.[34] Sovtschick's character, which has evolved — not only materially, but also mentally — from a proletarian to a true grand bourgeois, surely contradicts Walser's claim that his protagonists' weaknesses are inherited and thus irreversible. In fact, Sovtschick's personality comes closer to that "overaffirmed" (grand-)bourgeois identity indifferent to all social discord for which Walser sardonically chided Thomas Mann. Flaunting the insignia of the ruling class, Sovtschick, unlike Tonio Kröger, finds himself by no means in an impasse between the existence of an artist and that of a bourgeois but rather seems to identify himself wholeheartedly with the *(Bildungs-)Bürgertum*. While Kempowski's novels are generally designated as chronicles of the German bourgeoisie as they depict everyday bourgeois reality from the subjective viewpoint of his characters, Kempowski has not exactly made a name for himself as a harsh social critic. Quite to the contrary, critics ordinarily point out Kempowski's rather moderate, nonpartisan position, as well as his conspicuous reluctance to discuss sociopolitical issues.[35] This position is manifest in *Dog Days* as an ironic commentary on bourgeois *savoir vivre* which assimilates the status quo.[36]

In contrast to Kempowski, Walser's innumerable essays and speeches attest to his ever-active participation in the political affairs of the Federal Republic of Germany, although in recent years Walser appears to have moved from distinctly leftist persuasions to a slightly more moderate stance. Perhaps this alleged conservatism can be perceived in Walser's prose of the 1980s as a peculiar mixture of pragmatic affirmation, muted opposition, and

[33]Walser, "Selbstbewußtsein und Ironie," *Selbstbewußtsein und Ironie*, p. 178.

[34]In this context, see also Martina Wagner-Egelhaaf's conclusion on intertextual readings, p. 106.

[35]Manfred Dierks, *Walter Kempowski*, Autorenbücher 39 (Munich: Beck, 1984) 16.

[36]As Dierks comments, Kempowski exposes the bourgeois attitudes while looking for its positive components (*Walter Kempowski* 128).

weary resignation, with the former remaining dominant at the end of his fictions.[37] His characters, the Halms, Zürns, and Horns, eventually have to put up with their lives and "find everything as fine as it was" (B 291). Walser's hesitant affirmation and Kempowski's ironic presentation of bourgeois living may accurately reflect the authors' "eigene Lebensstimmung" [existential ambience].[38] Both react to an existential impulse to write and the process of narrating becomes, as Sovtschick states, the "center of the universe" (DD 295). This does not mean, however, that writing assumes a self-serving function and that these authors are simply interested in self-affirmation within the subjectivist arena. Both the formal and thematic characteristics of their narratives suggest a self-consciously parodistic distance from the once-New Subjectivity: the subtle implication of an objectifying narrative voice sheds irony on the subjective point of view that is mediated. Both authors seem to act on an autobiographical-existential impulse to treat the theme of aging in their fictions. However, the theme of the protagonists' disinterest in political themes, albeit secondary to the illustration of their mid-life crisis, should be viewed as a critical commentary on the motives that induce them to renounce a critical reflection on extant conditions. Hence, neither needs to feel implicated by Günter Grass' sarcastic rebuke of 1985 when he denounced that literature which, to him, seemed to contain nothing but the authors' overt admission of their societal insouciance.[39]

[37]This excludes the novella *No Man's Land*, which reflects Walser's personal commitment to a national concern. For a detailed discussion, see the essay by Alexander Mathäs.

[38]Walser in an interview with Paul Reitze, "Mit kleinen Magneten auf Jagd nach Figuren," *Die Welt* 4 Oct. 1988: 21.

[39]Grass reproaches contemporary authors with narcissism and political nonchalance: "Ichbefindlichkeit ist im Schwange; wer sollte da noch den Blick frei haben auf Armut und Elend, Unrecht und Tyrannei, auf Polen und Nicaragua oder auf uns, die wir doppelt gemoppelt deutsch sind," "Vorrede," *Der Traum der Vernunft — Vom Elend der Aufklärung*, vol. 2 (Darmstadt, Neuwied: Luchterhand, 1986) 8.

Works Cited

Cohn, Dorrit. *Transparent Minds: Modes for Presenting Consciousness in Fiction*. Princeton: Princeton UP, 1978.

Cory, Mark E. "Romanticizing America: Reflections of Pocahontas in Contemporary German Fiction." *German Quarterly* 62 (1989): 320-28.

Dierks, Manfred. "'Nur durch Zustimmung kommst du weg': Martin Walsers Ironie-Konzept und *Ein fliehendes Pferd*." *Literatur für Leser* 7 (1984): 44-53.

——. *Walter Kempowski*. Autorenbücher 39. Munich: Beck, 1984.

Fickert, Kurt. "A Literary Collage: Martin Walser's *Brandung*." *The International Fiction Review* 15.2 (1988): 96-102.

Grass, Günter. "Vorrede." *Der Traum der Vernunft — Vom Elend der Aufklärung*. Vol. 2. Darmstadt, Neuwied: Luchterhand, 1986. 7-8.

Kaes, Anton, "Porträt Martin Walser: Ein Gespräch." *German Quarterly* 57 (1984): 432-49.

Kempowski, Walter. *Dog Days*. Trans. Norma S. Davis, Garold N. Davis, Alan F. Keele. Columbia, SC: Camden House, 1990.

——. *Hundstage*. Munich: Knaus, 1988.

Koopmann, Helmut. "Tendenzen des deutschen Romans der siebziger Jahre." *Handbuch des deutschen Romans*. Ed. H. Koopmann. Düsseldorf: Bagel, 1983. 574-86; 655-56.

Martin, Jean-Maurice. *Untersuchungen zum Problem der erlebten Rede. Der ursächliche Kontext der erlebten Rede, dargestellt an Romanen Robert Walsers*. Europäische Hochschulschriften: Series 1, Deutsche Sprache und Literatur 1009. Bern: Peter Lang, 1987.

Mews, Siegfried. "Martin Walsers *Brandung*: Ein deutscher Campusroman?" *German Quarterly* 60 (1987): 220-36.

Pilipp, Frank. *The Novels of Martin Walser: A Critical Introduction*. Studies in German Literature, Linguistics, and Culture 64. Columbia, SC: Camden House, 1991.

Stanley, Patricia H. "Walter Kempowski." *Dictionary of Literary Biography 75: Contemporary German Fiction Writers Second Series*. Eds. Wolfgang Elfe, and James Hardin. Detroit: Gale Research Company, 1988. 139-45.

Vormweg, Heinrich. "Bittersüß die Schmerzen des Alterns." Rev. of *Brandung*. *Süddeutsche Zeitung* 31 Aug. 1985: 104.

Walser, Martin. *Selbstbewußtsein und Ironie. Frankfurter Vorlesungen*. Frankfurt/M.: Suhrkamp, 1981.

——. *Wer ist ein Schriftsteller? Aufsätze und Reden*. Frankfurt/M.: Suhrkamp, 1979.

——, and Ulrich Khuon. *Ein fliehendes Pferd. Theaterstück*. Frankfurt/M.: Suhrkamp, 1985.

6

Letter to Lord Liszt as an Epistolary Novel

Richard H. Lawson

NOT EVEN SAMUEL RICHARDSON identified his novels generically in his short titles with quite the aplomb of Martin Walser in the latter's *Brief an Lord Liszt* (1982). The English version of the title, *Letter to Lord Liszt* (1985), yields an impressive alliterative series to boot — but what is of interest here is not the sound of the title but rather the novel as an epistolary novel. It should be noted, however, that a completely accurate title might well be "The Second Letter to Lord Liszt." Franz Horn has already sent Horst Liszt a short letter or note, which has gone unanswered. Horn thereupon decides to write the letter referred to in the title.

The unanswered note had dwelt on their recent quarrel and on Horn's lack of interest in establishing whose fault it was. Indeed, in the note Horn conceded that, in contrast to their many previous quarrels, the responsibility for the most recent row may well have been his, Horn's. It is clear that such a pro forma concession is not likely to have resulted in the unburdening, the merciless self-revelation that threads through the titular letter.

Critical examination of *Letter to Lord Liszt* as an epistolary novel is surely justified, perhaps required, by the very title. Not surprisingly, the letter in question has a supremely important thematic function. Its prolonged and somewhat agonizing composition enables Horn to get hold of himself in the imminence of corporate split and its potential confirmation — by relegating him to the scrap heap — of his sense of worthlessness. *That* will test this newfound determination to stay alive nevertheless. *That* will require him to come to some distancing self-awareness, and supposedly — the ending of the novel like the whole is redolent of Walserian irony — to avoid a recurrence of "that nonsense with the pills" (LL 2 et passim): his earlier failed suicide attempt at the end of *Jenseits der Liebe* (1976; *Beyond All Love*, 1982). As Bernd Fischer summarizes, Horn is given the opportunity in his prodigious letter to come to grips with a new stage in his suffering, revealing himself in what has been called the most exhaustive of all forms of self-revelation: the epistolary novel.[1]

The novel consists mostly, then, though not exclusively, of one long letter from Franz Horn to Horst Liszt, a letter of a hundred pages more or less, including nineteen postscripts. As in Kafka's long unsent letter to his father, of which Horn's is a descendant in tone and spirit, writing emerges as the last best therapy for the letter writer.[2] Even in the eighteenth-century heyday of the epistolary novel that would have been quite long; in the twentieth century it is all but unimaginable: a protean letter composed by Horn in the course of a hectic night of solitude, a letter most likely not meant to be sent, and indeed not sent. Support for the idea that Horn's letter was from the first not meant to be sent is contained in the novel's first sentence, which informs the reader that the time is Friday before the Whitsun weekend holiday — referred to shortly after as a "long" weekend. In other words, Horst Liszt — the title "Lord" reflecting both envy and ironic disdain, occurred to Horn only upon taking up his pen — cannot possibly receive it before the next Tuesday's mail delivery, when it would be separated from immediacy by eighty-some hours of weekend and Whitmonday. If Horn really wants to get in touch with Liszt — communicate, engage in actual dialogue — all he has to do on Friday evening is pick up the phone and dial the number. That course of action is three times rejected — the central rejection, no doubt significantly, coming right after Horn takes an unsatisfying phone call from his wife Hilde, from whom he had been separated and with whom his marital relationship is now strained: what was keeping him from the agreed-upon family gathering at his mother's on the latter's name day?

Still, after that disconcerting call — additionally disconcerting in the light of new corporate alignments that would confirm Horn's role as a has-been — Horn does tentatively pick up the phone to call Liszt. But to follow through, he feels, would amount to accepting the blame for the monumental quarrel he had had with Liszt on Ascension Day, a few days earlier. The time is perfect to write Liszt a second letter, containing a calm recitation of the facts of the quarrel in proper sequence. The unanswered first letter is included among the legitimations for the second, legitimations that now

[1]"Walser und die Möglichkeiten moderner Erzählliteratur: Beobachtungen zum *Brief an Lord Liszt*," *Martin Walser: International Perspectives*, eds. Jürgen E. Schlunk and Armand E. Singer, American University Studies: Series 1, Germanic Languages and Literature 64 (New York: Peter Lang, 1987) 105.

[2]Frank Pilipp, *The Novels of Martin Walser: A Critical Introduction*, Studies in German Literature, Linguistics, and Culture 64 (Columbia, SC: Camden House, 1991) 62.

include the tactical disadvantage of the phone, the negative aura of his wife's phone call, plenty of time (he told his wife he would not be joining the family celebration until the next morning), his psychological lability owing to the recent unhappy corporate tidings, resulting in Horn's suffering a perturbing attack of weakness on his way to his parked car. And finally the presence of a bottle of local rosé, one of several such bottles that he keeps on hand for Liszt's visits, although Horn himself does not "particularly care for this wine" (LL 23). Everything conduces to writing the letter.

One further compelling reason to get in touch with Liszt should not be overlooked: the self-immolation in the ruins of his burned-out factory of the chief business rival of their boss, Arthur Thiele, and the certain effect of that personal and corporate demise on Thiele's now monopoly enterprise. As Horn's star has already fallen, so is Liszt's certain to fall, and everything is set to confirm a new corporate whiz kid as Thiele's new satrap and the relegation of *both* Horn and Liszt to supernumerary status. It may well require a letter, just such a one as Horn will write, to get the sense of their new, *equal* relationship to Liszt. It seems odd, however, that precisely in a letter designed to elaborate on their new equality Horn should for the first time endow Liszt with such an aristocratic title. In fact, it is the essence of Walser's irony, which depends for its effect on the forever vulnerable self-confidence of the petty bourgeois, even — actually, especially — the petty bourgeois like Horn, whom the capitalistic expansionist wave has elevated well above his marginal socioeconomic origins. Furthermore, Horn, at a deeper level, did not intend to send the letter elucidating his and Liszt's new parity. Rather, the real task of the letter, its therapeutic goal, or part of its therapeutic goal, is to get the sense of that new parity across to Horn, the writer of the letter. In that cause, even the local rosé, which Horn doesn't like, apparently becomes drinkable — at least, three bottles of it are consumed.

Already the survivor of one suicide attempt, Horn stands in dire need of readjustment. On the one hand, the reader of the novel is given to understand, not least by the phrase "nonsense with the pills," that that parlous phase of Horn's life is over. On the other, he has not recovered entirely, and, owing to a recurrent paresis of the vocal cords, will never regain his full voice. The "nonsense with the pills" is ironic too, and one had better assume that, in accordance with the tendency of most failed suicides to try again, Horn remains at mortal risk and knows it. Besides preferring the pen to the telephone, a man deprived of his full voice may bear another connotation, and one inevitably thinks of the historic papal castrati, of eunuchs. It is hard to imagine that Horn is oblivious to that relationship just because he does not specify it. No doubt Horn's future looks problematic, and not less so because Lord Liszt is very soon to join him in the ranks of the corporate castrati.

Walser's narrative frame around Horn's remarkable letter consists of several pages before and after, embracing third-person narration by an apparently reliable narrator in the traditionally omniscient mold, who is especially privileged with respect to Horn and Horn's mind, narrating from inside Horn's head as well as outside Horn's body. The result is a narrowed perspective that focuses on Horn's point of view, not, however, without preserving enough inner distance or angle to convey a somewhat ironic impression of Horn. The thrust of that irony, as frequently in Walser's fiction and as developed in Walser's theoretical essays dating back to 1973, depends on petty-bourgeois class consciousness, devoid of confidence, oriented to subordination and self-denial.[3] In the first few frame pages Walser reveals Franz Horn's petty-bourgeois origin and, as far as that goes, his illegitimate origin as well. The more obvious avenue of this revelation lies in Horn's family background, the less obvious in his notable penchant for saving oddments of junk, his hoarding fixation — a trait also of his stepfather.

Nor is the third-person narration strictly confined to the opening and closing frames. There are shorter passages intercalated among the postscripts, so that the reader is, as it were, kept on the ironic track in his view of Franz Horn's view of events and attitudes, that is, the first-person narration of the polemical and, after all, not so calm letter and its appendices. While the letter is not meant to be sent, and while its writing is, above all, therapeutic, the question remains whether it is truthful as well.[4] Probably it is not consciously deceptive, yet it leaves the question whether one can write objective (or even subjective) truth of oneself.[5] Walser's third-person introduction tends to draw the reader's sympathies to Horn, to effect an identification, at the same time its irony ought to make the reader critical. In the resulting narrative tension it is probably the reader's sympathy that prevails. By the very nature of the presentation we are enlisted in Horn's corner. The third-

[3]Dieter Liewerscheidt, "Die Anstrengung, ja zu sagen: Martin Walsers Ironie-Konzept und die Romane von *Jenseits der Liebe* bis *Brief an Lord Liszt*," *Literatur für Leser* 9 (1986): 74-88.

[4]"Die Polemik des nächtlichen Schreibens gegen die Gewalt des Tages erweist sich als Therapie: aber auch als Wahrheit?" (Fischer 109).

[5]See Heike Doane, "Die Anwesenheit der Macht: Horns Strategie im *Brief an Lord Liszt*," *Martin Walser: International Perspectives*, p. 86: "Obwohl Horns Brief an Liszt impulsiv und ohne Vorüberlegung niedergeschrieben wird, ist er nicht planlos."

person introduction does not present Horn as devious or as any more devious than the nature of his job requires. Maybe *less* devious than required, he is not the monster of duplicity that his boss is. Arthur Thiele is a successful corporate player, whereas Horn has failed.

The nature of the presentation, that of the epistolary novel, represents a genre with no small history and perhaps, as demonstrated by Walser and by such luminaries as Nabokov, Barthes, and Atwood, a promising present and future as well. In a late twentieth century much given to confession-making it may well seem the apposite genre, although there is also apparent reason why it may equally well be anomalous. Walser, by the way, was not completely an epistolary tyro when he wrote *Letter to Lord Liszt*. If his earlier production of letters in fiction was far short of a *Briefroman* as such, still there occur scattered letters in previous novels. For example, in *Die Gallistl'sche Krankheit* (1972; Gallistl's Disease) we are presented, ironically enough, with the formal appurtenances of a letter — a letterhead, a date, the signature of Dr. Helm Lohrer (GK 43-45) — but the content is a market analysis of Josef Gallistl's poems. In *Der Sturz* (1973; The Fall) there is a letter of instruction from Gertrud Müller to Frau Kristlein, and in the more recent *Jagd* (1988; On the Prowl) Anna reads a letter addressed to daughter Julia. The most conspicuous episode, however, which seems to prefigure Horn's letter, occurs in *Runaway Horse* (1978) when Halm drafts a letter to his antagonist Klaus Buch (FP 36-37; RH 20-21) — a letter in which he intentionally reveals himself to a degree that makes sending impossible. Like Horn, Halm is of petty-bourgeois origin and suffers from low self-esteem vis-à-vis his antagonist and from profound doubt about the values and norms that contemporary society — the socioeconomic structure — foists onto the individual. Like Horn, Halm finds relief in unburdening himself in a letter that remains unsent.

While one is not likely to suggest that the epistolary novel totally dropped from view in the nineteenth century — when it did fall upon hard times — its earlier peak, as all readers of British literature know, occurred with Samuel Richardson in the eighteenth century, the same Richardson whose "bourgeois novels" are commonly cited as an influence on Gellert, Lessing, and Goethe. Epistolary literature hardly began with Richardson, however: Ovid, attentive to his own fame, claimed that his *Epistulae Heroidum* represented a new genre. In any case, as Janet Gurkin Altman points out, there was no lack of descendants in the classical and the medieval periods, nor, above all, in late-seventeenth- and early-eighteenth-century France, and less notably in Spain and Italy.[6] In the French case, Marivaux, Montesquieu,

[6]Janet Gurkin Altman, *Epistolarity: Approaches to a Form* (Columbus: Ohio State UP, 1982) 3, 14.

and Crébillon *fils* are names to be reckoned with. In Germany, later in the eighteenth century, after Richardson, Goethe contributed his *The Sorrows of Young Werther* (1774; final version 1787). It is instructive to see to what degree some of the classic features of the Richardsonian novel are replicated in Walser's *Letter to Lord Liszt*. Fundamental is that the letters are primary in the novel, expanding naturally to determine the length of the work. For Richardson the novel was conceived as a series of letters, and he seems to have proceeded spontaneously rather than schematically. Although we may at first be tempted to greet *Letter to Lord Liszt* as something like a *tour de force* — the startling number of postscripts helps incline the reader in that direction — the following details align Walser's novel with those of Richardson rather convincingly.

Instead of letters, plural, Walser presents the text of a letter, singular, with nineteen formalized afterthoughts, some short, some long, some simple, some complex, as a series of letters might be. Because Franz Horn imputes Horst Liszt's replies to his proposals, the whole takes on the aspect of a spirited correspondence whetted by antagonism. Horn's much-adumbrated letter is indeed primary to the novel, as its title suggests in the first place. The initial letter from Horn to Liszt, whose text is not presented but merely alluded to at intervals, and which *was* sent, is secondary in narrative importance if first in sequence. The unsent but textual and central letter, expanding naturally by way of postscripts as Liszt's responses are hypothesized and in turn responded to, effectively determines the length of the novel. The third-person narration, constituting an expository frame amounting to slightly more than a fifth of the total novel, not minimal but terse, contributes to the length of the novel but scarcely determines it.

Although we run the risk of imprecision and distortion in attempting to compare mid-eighteenth-century English society to that of Germany in the twentieth century, we can at least posit the overarching descriptor, "bourgeois." In the case of Richardson, "bourgeois" was an original perspective; it is at the least a self-conscious perspective on the part of Walser, consistently concerned with the petty bourgeois who has "made it" into the higher bourgeois reaches of the Federal Republic but who has not freed himself from his habit of subordination. After all, Walser's irony — so different from that of Thomas Mann, which is rooted in the self-confidence of the *haute bourgeoisie* — depends on the very lack of self-confidence on the part of his protagonist: the petty-bourgeois arriviste.

It is remarkable to what a degree Walser and Richardson coincide, given the distance, temporal as well as spatial, between them. Granted, *Letter to Lord Liszt* contains no multipartite letter. A diarylike effect is probably an inevitable but not an unimportant result of a group of letters taken together, as in Richardson, as well as of a cumulatively supplemented single letter, as in Walser. That effect is notably therapeutic. In the case of Horn's letters it may be difficult to say whether the more accurate formulation is that they are therapeutic because diarylike and revelatory, or diarylike and revelatory because therapeutic. In any case, the therapeutic function is closely tied to the diarylike form.[7]

Finally, proceeding from the obvious therapeutic function, the fact — or, at least, the critical consensus — is that the Horn letter was never intended to be sent. So also in Richardson's epoch-making *Pamela* (1741), many of whose letters seem to be written "with something like a conviction that they will never reach their destination."[8] In both Richardson and Walser there seems to exist a characteristic double level of illusion: first, the reader's disbelief having been suspended, that the novel describes a reality rather than a fiction; and second, that the letters, though not sent and thus incapable of generating other than a hypothecated reply, are nonetheless letters and not simply a transparent narrative device and an extra burden on the reader's patience. On the whole, the accumulation of illusion would seem to constitute no small burden on the reader's perseverance.

With the last observation in mind — and admittedly difficult to prove — we may speculate on why the epistolary novel flourished in the eighteenth century, declined in the nineteenth, and with Walser and others shows signs of vigorous life again in the twentieth. The eighteenth-century reader is said to have been blessed with patience even as he or she was an adherent of individual emancipation — as reflected in letter writing. In Hans Rudolf Picard's opinion, choosing to write a letter as a means of personal expression reveals one's personal inclination toward emancipation.[9] To follow Picard's reasoning, the nineteenth-century reader was much more impatient than his eighteenth-century predecessor. The nineteenth-century reader, less devoted to individualism, wanted the solace of that directing voice from on high. The epistolary novel is limited to what the letter writer can observe and rationally comprehend. That precludes comporting with the personal-tragic spirit that purportedly typifies the nineteenth century, which accordingly was less hospitable to the epistolary novel. In Picard's view, the ambit of the epis-

[7]Cf. also the essay by Martina Wagner-Egelhaaf, where the diarylike aspects of Horn's letter are discussed further (esp. p. 92).

[8]Godfrey Frank Singer, *The Epistolary Novel* (Philadelphia: University of Pennsylvania Press, 1933) 65.

[9]Hans Rudolf Picard, *Die Illusion der Wirklichkeit im Briefroman des achtzehnten Jahrhunderts* (Heidelberg: Carl Winter, 1971) 123.

tolary novel increasingly narrowed as public confidence in *ratio* declined.[10] One is forced to wonder where that would leave the twentieth century, especially in its later years less than conspicuously devoted to *ratio*, vis-à-vis the epistolary novel, for instance, *Letter to Lord Liszt*. In any case, Picard's chief time perspective, duly reflected in the title of his book, is from the eighteenth century. And some might contend that *Letter to Lord Liszt*, classical epistolary that it has been shown to be, does not a century make. But that would be to overlook the fact that it has some vigorous and worthy company.

Walser's novel, after all, does not stand alone in this century, one has to realize, even as one is amazed that it could escape mention in such a work of contemporary criticism as that of Linda S. Kauffman bearing the comprehensive title *Special Delivery: Epistolary Modes in Modern Fiction*.[11] Goethe, in his "Reflections on Werther," Kauffman reminds us, "pinpoints the contestatory dialogic nature of epistolarity as well as its solipsism" (56). The matter could hardly be better put, granted that individualism and solipsism share a large common ground. Kauffman dwells on Viktor Shklovsky, Vladimir Nabokov, Roland Barthes, Jacques Derrida, Doris Lessing, Alice Walker, and Margaret Atwood as praiseworthy practitioners of "epistolary modes" in modern fiction. Where, one wonders, is the discussion of Martin Walser's *Letter to Lord Liszt*, which had been translated into English seven years prior to Kauffman's study?

A reader of the latter will have begun to understand her original and not unpersuasive point of view much earlier on, but she summarizes it concisely late in her work: "epistolarity — the genre traditionally associated with women's voices, feelings, and textual production...."[12] That equation or association, which Kauffman does not insist on too much, may, however, go some way to explain the absence of Walser's name from a pantheon to which he is otherwise surely equal. On the other hand, we are arguing from an absence, from a negative, and inadvertent omission is not out of the question, despite the accessibility of Walser's novel in English. In any case, the Horn letter is decidedly not a woman's voice; it is a man's voice, reflecting a man's point of view. Horst Liszt's hypothecated responses are equally those of a man. Although Liszt's wife is obviously involved in a lesbian relation-

[10]Picard, p. 121.

[11]Chicago: University of Chicago Press, 1992.

[12]Kauffman, pp. 190-91.

ship, that only throws Liszt's straightness into sharper relief as Horn's antagonist.

The variety of signatures that Horn appends to his letter and its nineteen postscripts may be read as a summary shorthand version of the texts and of Horn's progress toward self-liberation. The signature of the letter proper is the full and formal "Franz Horn." The first and second postscripts are signed "Franzl Horn," as Horn ironically appropriates the nickname that Liszt gives him, familiarly-condescendingly, when talking to their boss. Indeed, the second "Franzl Horn" is preceded by a complimentary close, "Yours sincerely." Horn signs the next three postscripts — as he would perhaps sign an interoffice memo — with the noncommittal initials "F.H.," followed in the next postscript by the more intimate "Franz." That is followed by the familiar and ironically self-deprecatory "Your humble servant, Franz" — this after having warned himself to keep his distance from those conspiring against him. Another "F.H." and then Horn distances himself by signing "Most insincerely, Horn." What has preceded this frank, scarcely complimentary close? A detailed revelation that those remembering Thiele before the advent of his hairpiece — thus including Liszt — are condemned to be out of the running for corporate preferment.

Postscripts ten through eighteen bear the minimum signature "F.H." — in the seventeenth the initials are preceded by "Yours sincerely." The signature to the nineteenth and final postscript, howecer, tells us that Horn's epistolary unburdening is truly completed. He signs "Your truly relaxed Horn." The final postscript itself consists of markedly brief — one to three lines — paragraphs, ironic and paradoxical summaries of Horn's triumphant insight, including the conviction that a good relationship between himself and Liszt is now impossible. Was it ever possible? — we are tempted to ask. Not likely. Horn's attainment of insightful letter-writing relaxation has been accompanied by the consumption of three bottles of the rosé he did not like and kept in readiness only for Liszt's visits. We may infer that a certain amount of unpalatability facilitates epistolary unburdening — and that the remaining rosé won't be needed for any more visits by Lord Liszt.

Works Cited

Altmann, Janet Gurkin. *Epistolarity: Approaches to a Form*. Columbus: Ohio State UP, 1982.

Doane, Heike. "Die Anwesenheit der Macht: Horns Strategie im *Brief an Lord Liszt*." *Martin Walser: International Perspectives*. Eds. Jürgen E. Schlunk, and Armand E. Singer. American University Studies: Series 1, Germanic Languages and Literature 64. New York: Peter Lang, 1987. 81-102.

Fischer, Bernd. "Walser und die Möglichkeiten moderner Erzählliteratur: Beobachtungen zum *Brief an Lord Liszt*." *Martin Walser: International Perspectives*. 103-10.

Kauffman, Linda S. *Special Delivery: Epistolary Modes in Modern Fiction*. Chicago: University of Chicago Press, 1992.

Liewerscheidt, Dieter. "Die Anstrengung, ja zu sagen: Martin Walsers Ironie-Konzept und die Romane von *Jenseits der Liebe* bis *Brief an Lord Liszt*." *Literatur für Leser* 9 (1986): 74-88.

Picard, Hans Rudolf. *Die Illusion der Wirklichkeit im Briefroman des achtzehnten Jahrhunderts*. Heidelberg: Carl Winter, 1971.

Pilipp, Frank. *The Novels of Martin Walser: A Critical Introduction*. Studies in German Literature, Linguistics, and Culture 64. Columbia, SC: Camden House, 1991.

Richardson, Samuel. *Pamela; or, Virtue Rewarded*. 1741 [1740]. Ed. T. C. Duncan Eaves, and Ben D. Kimpel. Boston: Houghton Mifflin, 1971.

Singer, Godfrey Frank. *The Epistolary Novel*. Philadelphia: University of Pennsylvania Press, 1933.

7

Walser's *Letter to Lord Liszt* and Hofmannsthal's "Letter of Lord Chandos": On Comparing Literary Texts*

Martina Wagner-Egelhaaf

"DEAR LORD LISZT: WHY do I call you that?" (LL 23). It is with these words that the executive employee Franz Horn in *Letter to Lord Liszt* (1982) begins his seemingly endless letter to his professional rival, Dr. Horst Liszt. Indeed, the reader will ask the same question and wonder why Horn chooses this lordly form of address. As Horn explains, "the title presented itself as I picked up my pen. I am probably trying to convey a certain distance between us and at the same time recommend that neither of us takes this distance too seriously. Or should we?" (LL 23). This passage contains three indications for the understanding of the text.

First of all, the salutation is already at hand when Franz Horn picks up his pen. The sudden and immediate availability of this opener at the beginning of the writing process stresses that the actual act of writing has taken over Horn's principal incentive to write — much in the same way as Kleist claims it to be in his essay "On the Gradual Fabrication of Thoughts While Speaking."[1] Second, Horn's suggestion not to take the distance between himself and his colleague Liszt too seriously sheds light on their close reciprocal relationship. Liszt only *appears* to be another person; in reality he is Horn's alter ego. Readers of Walser are familiar with the principle of

*Translated by Frank Pilipp and Holt Meyer. This article first appeared in German under the title "Franz antwortet: Martin Walsers 'Brief an Lord Liszt' (1982) und Hugo von Hofmannsthals 'Ein Brief' (1902) oder Über das Vergleichen literarischer Texte," *Germanisch-Romanische Monatsschrift* 39.1 (1989): 58-72.

[1]*An Abyss Deep Enough: Letters of Heinrich von Kleist with a Selection of Essays and Anecdotes*, ed., trans. Philip B. Miller (New York: Dutton, 1982) 218-22.

inner dialogues communicating the protagonists' simultaneous loss of and search for self in intense and continual battles between conflicting components of the self. Helmut Halm in *Breakers* (1985) is a prime example of such a dialogically constructed consciousness. However, it is primarily the parallels in their careers that intimate the congruence of Horn and Liszt. Years ago, Franz Horn had ousted the bookkeeper Ochs from his position as the right-hand man of the company's boss, Arthur Thiele, while he himself, as readers know from the novel *Beyond All Love* (1976), was later supplanted by Horst Liszt as Thiele's favorite. Now, Horn witnesses how Liszt has to yield his position to the young and ambitious Rudolf Ryynänen. *Nomen est omen*: the characters' names are a further indication of the intricately interwoven fate of Franz Horn and Horst Liszt; switching their first names gives rise to an assonant and somewhat clumsy Horst Horn and a masterly Franz Liszt.

Third, the fundamentally ironic tone of the work has the effect of achieving a constant distance between writer and addressee. While the distance expressed by the lordly form of address is not to be taken too seriously, its undoubted legitimation should not be overlooked. Here, Walser presents the fundamental concept of his poetics: irony, as expounded in detail in his Frankfurt lectures.[2] The character Franz Horn, who defines himself by means of self-reflection between reality and ideality, between Horst Horn and Franz Liszt, so to speak, corresponds to the "underaffirmed" or "negative identity" in Walser's conception of irony. While the unhindered formation of self-confidence of such "overaffirmed" ironic heroes as those depicted by Thomas Mann results in majestic haughtiness and self-complacency completely oblivious and irresponsive to the outside world, the "underaffirmed" heroes negate themselves by accepting and affirming their environment.[3] According to Walser, this type of irony gives rise to a genuinely ironical style,[4] a style found in Robert Walser's and Kafka's novels: a self-deprecating ironic perspective after which Martin Walser, too, models his protagonists, especially Franz Horn. It befits the criteria of Walser's definition of irony that Franz Horn's story takes place in the world of work; work and productivity are the criteria for self-confidence, since they

[2]*Selbstbewußtsein und Ironie: Frankfurter Vorlesungen* (Frankfurt/M.: Suhrkamp, 1981).

[3]*Selbstbewußtsein und Ironie*, pp. 82, 177-78.

[4]*Selbstbewußtsein und Ironie*, p. 117.

bring — or, in the case of the underaffirmed hero, deny — public recognition.[5] In *Beyond All Love* Walser illustrates Horn's self-destructive feelings of his own "worthlessness" (BAL 66), "wretchedness" (BAL 97), and his pessimistic self-perceptions as a "typical loser" (BAL 78) and "classic failure" (BAL 98) — a self-image that ultimately leads to an unsuccessful suicide attempt. In *Letter to Lord Liszt* Horn still finds himself in a fundamental crisis, lacking self-confidence, permanently convinced of his own "insignificance" (LL 17). The "sense of worthlessness" (LL 18) that dominates him after he proved incapable even of committing suicide induces him to write. It is precisely this process of writing that concerns us here.

As he observes the decline of his colleague, Horn's self-loathing and his hatred for Liszt are mixed with a degree of sympathy and affection for his rival. But since Liszt is in no way prepared to accept the new situation and even refuses to admit it to himself, still less to others, he turns all his aggression against Horn. As Liszt had once triumphed over him, Horn is the only person left over whom he can exercise any kind of superiority. Because of Liszt's ill will and continued arrogance, Horn's initial friendship and sympathy turn into hate much stronger than ever before. This is precisely the crisis which suddenly inspires Horn to write his letter as an attempt to ease their tense relationship and to counteract the tremendous emotional pressure that weighs upon him. In this letter, he accuses and approaches his addressee at the same time, while he simultaneously elevates and denigrates himself. Horn recalls the entire history of their constantly changing relationship and reconstructs events leading to quarrels or to the few harmonious moments together. With the pedantry of a bookkeeper, he notes and analyzes both his own and the other's statements and actions and re-creates situations down to the most minute details. While writing, he relives the broad range of moods and emotions which the relationship between Franz Horn and Horst Liszt has been capable of producing. This letter, which ultimately Horn will not send, is mainly a medium for confrontation with himself. As a process of self-reflection it dissects the self into individual actions, utterances, and motivations, and sends the writer on a journey of self-discovery:

> Here I go, trying once again to wrangle a right for myself. I would like so much to confess *why* I unleashed the torrent of hatred on Ascension Day. But I don't know why. I can only confess that you are innocent. Of that. You have probably never done me any harm. And suddenly I lash out at you and accuse you of inflicting the worst damage you could on me without running the slightest risk. Why?

[5] *Selbstbewußtsein und Ironie*, pp. 169, 179-81.

> Tell me, please: why do I make such monstrous claims? And all that during an outing in May that seemed destined to yield a succession of lovely idylls. If you continue to keep silent and abandon me to the riddle of this unfortunate affair, I shall regard it as an act of meanness justifying everything I did to you! (LL 29)

This passage elucidates the movement of the letter writer's self-consciousness, which is typical of the text as a whole. It emphasizes that writing constitutes a form of merciless surveillance over oneself, that this activity of the writer serves as his judge and jury. Every attempt at evasion is duly noted: "Here I go, trying once again to wrangle a right for myself." Thus, Horn's letter to Dr. Liszt is intended not as much for the addressee as for himself: it is a kind of diary which serves the purpose of achieving distance from himself.

This is precisely what Elias Canetti means in his essay "Dialog mit dem grausamen Partner" (Dialogue with the Cruel Partner) when he calls the diary a conversation with oneself.[6] In fact, Canetti's description of the diary characterizes very aptly the intention and the effect of Franz Horn's letter. Canetti writes, for instance, that the diary can help one to calm down, and that it is possible to keep a diary only when one is dissatisfied with oneself and the world.[7] Both of these criteria obviously apply to Horn's dilemma. At the end of the novel we see Horn both totally exhausted from the tremendous effort of writing, and, at the same time, relatively satisfied and relaxed as he leaves for a family gathering. This is no doubt due to the effect of writing. The communicative partner in his diary is his own fictitious self:

> It doesn't pretend to be interested, it is not polite. It doesn't interrupt, and allows one to finish one's thought. It is not only curious, but also patient.... But you shouldn't fool yourself into thinking that this listener makes it easy for you. Since he has the advantage of understanding you, you can't pull the wool over his eyes. He's not only patient, but also vindictive. Since he has x-ray vision, he doesn't let you pull any tricks. He makes note of every single detail, and as soon as you begin falsifying anything, he returns immediately and vehemently to this very detail.... His instinct for stirrings of power

[6]In Canetti's *Macht und Überleben. Drei Essays* (Berlin: Literarisches Colloquium Berlin, 1972) 43.

[7]Canetti, pp. 38 and 44.

> and vanity is uncanny. Of course it comes in very handy that he knows you extremely well.[8]

One should keep in mind Canetti's idea that the other self, the one that is being addressed, undergoes a role change,[9] a change that is also characteristic of Horn's letter. While Liszt unscrupulously takes advantage of his triumphant defeat of Horn, he also needs Horn's sympathy and friendship. The passage quoted above (LL 29) suggests that Horn also changes roles. And it becomes clear that writing has serious advantages vis-à-vis "reality," that it becomes a substitute for this reality, and, in a sense, even its source: "All the conversations one can never finish in reality, since they would end in violence, all the absolute, merciless, devastating words one would often have to use with others are registered here."[10] Horn does not engage in an open quarrel with his colleague, either; instead, he notes: "Writing is now my substitute for everything" (LL 130).

Horn's "cruel partner" is Liszt, whose cruelty toward his colleague not only exists in real life but becomes even more apparent in his role as an imaginary correspondent — it is in this role that he embodies Horn's own cruelty to Ochs, to Liszt, and especially against himself. So the adversaries switch roles, and despite Horn's disciplined efforts to maintain his self-control, it becomes clear how taxing a task it is for him to maintain a sense of justice. Beneath this fragile surface of impartiality, Horn's enormous potential for aggression is ready to break free. The above quote contains several such phrases that intimate an imminent outbreak of aggression: "I can only confess that you are innocent. Of that" — that means there are other things still to be discussed. "Tell me, please: why do I make such monstrous claims? ... If you continue to keep silent ... I shall regard it as an act of meanness justifying everything I did to you!" In the course of a few lines, the self-accuser turns into an accuser of the other, and the mild-mannered posture turns into rage. The most significant characteristic of Horn's letter, however, is that in the course of its writing it generates an autonomous dynamic energy that virtually demands its continuation and prevents Horn from achieving closure with a single effort. After he supposedly finishes with the words "Good Night. / Yours / Franz Horn (LL 29), the text continues: "There was something he had to add to his letter to Lord Liszt" (LL 30). Only after Horn has added a total of eighteen postscripts can he sign off

[8]Canetti, p. 45; quotations given in English are those of the translators.

[9]Canetti, p. 47.

[10]Canetti, p.48.

"Your truly relaxed Horn" (LL 142). The entire novel thus becomes a letter in which Horn, as in his "Revenge Calendars" (LL 78), registers, classifies, interprets, and comments upon important and unimportant matters alike, in order to arrive at a coherent and complete picture of both his partner and himself. However, as the repeated reopening of the letter proves, a coherent picture is either completely unattainable or attainable only to a minimal degree. Every single statement gives rise to an abundance of associative impulses which in turn initiate new ideas and trains of thoughts, thus revealing ever more new facets of a complex personality. One may assume that this movement is not even completed with the nineteenth postscript, and that Franz Horn simply stops writing due to exhaustion. It is crucial, however, that he has achieved at least a temporary equilibrium that will allow him to survive the next few hours and days.

In his fit of writing, Horn is also driven by his enjoyment of language and linguistic experimentation. Evidently he likes to speak in metaphors: "You only wanted to bite my fur. I was supposed to bite back in the same way" (LL 53). Horn is equally aware of the intimidating synthetic rhetoric of the business world: "'restructuring,' development of 'goal-oriented guidance resources,' a 'new controlling concept — vertical, horizontal, and functional'" (LL 89). The phrases of his "social physics" (LL 36) are elaborate yet precise and highly sophisticated, as, for example: "the failure of his rival is the success of the unsuccessful" (LL 139). It is this linguistic tautness that creates a textual dynamic as captivating for the reader as it is for Horn, who pens his colossal letter in one fast-paced, breathless, and uninterrupted session. The text gains a Franz Lisztian virtuosity whose self-propelling dynamic causes both reader and writer to swirl around on the merry-go-round of Horn's thoughts.

The question still remains why Horn addresses his colleague as "Lord." The text suggests an ironic position on Horn's part; he engages in self-analysis, where he constantly shifts between, as it were, concave and convex vision. By using this aristocratic form of address ironically he can experiment with different modes of referring to and addressing his counterpart, thus *play*fully probing into the multifaceted dimensions of amity and animosity.

The book's title is reminiscent of another literary letter which is also addressed to a "Lord": Hugo von Hofmannsthal's famous "Letter of Lord Chandos," published in 1902, a "letter Philipp, Lord Chandos, younger son of the Earl of Bath, wrote to Francis Bacon, later Baron Verulam, Viscount St. Albans."[11] Here we are dealing with a letter from one Lord to another.

[11]Hugo von Hofmannsthal, "The Letter of Lord Chandos," *Selected Prose*, trans. Mary Hottinger, and Tania and James Stern (Kingsport, TN: Pantheon Books, 1952) 129; henceforth cited parenthetically as (Ch).

No doubt Walser, as a scholar of German literature, is most familiar with this seminal document of the so-called language crisis, whose pivotal role in the history of literature of the twentieth century reflects the conditions of art in the modern period. Chandos writes to Bacon to apologize "for his complete abandonment of literary activity" (Ch 129).

Lord Chandos, who used to write works that were "reeling under the splendour of their words" (Ch 129-30), who used to delight in the reconstruction of Latin periods and whose earlier "sensual and spiritual desire" (Ch 131) was to speak in tongues, has now abandoned all literary plans. No longer will he write his all-encompassing *Apophthegmata*, a work that was to contain noteworthy sayings of various luminaries, aphorisms and thoughts of writers new and old, as well as descriptions of significant events and incidents (Ch 131-32). Chandos has lost the sense of unity and wholeness which gave him security and pleasure in his work; he has fallen into a state of "despondency and feebleness" (Ch 133) and is now going through mental agony. "My case, in short, is this: I have lost completely the ability to think or to speak of anything coherently" (Ch 133). He has lost faith even in everyday words and can no longer say "spirit," "soul," or "body," because "abstract words," to quote the famous passage, crumble in his mouth "like mouldy fungi" (Ch 134). Chandos now realizes that words are abstract and intangible, are completely detached from the world of objects they signify, and cannot come anywhere near capturing the complexities of the phenomenal world. On closer inspection, this phenomenal world divides and multiplies: "For me everything disintegrated into parts, those parts again into parts; no longer would anything let itself be encompassed by one idea" (Ch 134). Words and phrases are only positions in a game:

> These ideas, I understood them well: I saw their wonderful inter*play* rise before me like magnificent fountains upon which *played* golden balls. I could hover around them and watch how they *played*, one with the other; but they were concerned only with each other, and the most profound, most personal quality of my thinking remained excluded from this *magic circle*. (Ch 135; emphases added)

Instead of a "literary" life, Chandos now leads a life "lacking in spirit and thought"; at the same time, however, this life is not without moments of happiness. In describing these moments, Chandos is at pains to stress the inadequacy of words: "It is not easy for me to indicate wherein these good moments subsist; once again words desert me. For it is, indeed, something entirely unnamed, even barely nameable..." (Ch 135), "a character so exalted and moving that words seem too poor to describe it," so "why seek again for words which I have foresworn!" (Ch 136). What Chandos now tries to concretize through that language which he has forsworn are moments of the divine feeling of "the fullest, most exalted Present" (Ch 136-37). This present — or presence — is communicated by certain concrete objects which become "vessels of revelation": a pitcher, a harrow abandoned in a field, a dog in the sun, the notion of poisoned rats, and so on. Experiencing these moments as the "presence of the Infinite," Chandos feels as if he is "flowing over" into those objects (Ch 137). Despite his attempt to depict this feeling as supralingual, his description is grounded in language and cannot escape it. Paradoxically, total presence can only be re-created through discourse. Thus, in these moments of divine presence, it seems to Chandos as though his "body consists of nought but *ciphers*" (Ch 138; emphasis added).[12] Although in this heightened state of perception he seems "to think with the heart" (Ch 138), this is, as he admits, still a form of thinking, irrespective of the fact that he has forsworn both the mind and language, which are obviously interdependent. The mystical experiences Chandos describes are moments of absolute, ideal speech: "What was it that made me want to break into words which, I know, were I to find them, would force to their knees those cherubim in whom I do not believe?" (Ch 137). The proclaimed renunciation of language cannot transcend linguistic categories. Chandos cannot elude language itself; his *altered conception of language* is merely a "language of objects," "a *language* in which inanimate things speak to me" (Ch 141; emphasis added), which admits its own inadequacy and in which objects become "vessels" (Ch 135). This language is not that accomplished language which Chandos believed to be writing in his youth. It is a symbolic language which does not signify anything but uses images to reveal the impossibility of naming things.

Philipp Chandos's mental state recalls that of Franz Horn. Having arrived at the nadir of his self-esteem and being constantly aware of his own insignificance — the premise for ironic writing — he also suffers from the loss or lack of language. Clumsy and awkward in conversations, Horn is easily at a loss for words, and "he often had no idea what people meant, even when they spoke in whole sentences" (BAL 67). Of course, he draws different conclusions from the fundamental awareness of the gap between the realm of phenomena and their representation in language: while Chandos has decided not to write any more (although he does so nevertheless in his letter), Franz Horn attempts to achieve clarity and security in thought precisely through writing. These attempts are exemplified by his "Revenge Calendars" (LL 78), in which Horn "entered on two lists everything he had heard from the

[12]See Waltraut Wiethölter, "Der 'Fall' des Lord Chandos," *Hofmannsthal oder die Geometrie des Subjekts: Psychostrukturelle und ikonographische Studien zum Prosawerk* (Tübingen: Niemeyer, 1990) 68.

Thieles about the Liszts and from the Liszts about the Thieles" (BAL 80). Incidentally, these notebooks, which also serve the function of self-definition, look like an ironic reminder of Lord Chandos's planned *Apophthegmata*. "My notebooks are full of Liszt phrases" (LL 77), Horn writes; that which Chandos fails to put into writing is carried out by Horn with wrathful obstinacy. Walser, of course, with his penchant for ironic allusions, did not miss the opportunity of setting the date for Horn's letter to Lord Liszt on Whitsun weekend, the holiday commemorating the gift of tongues.

The change toward a "perception of objects" described in the Chandos letter is analogous to the "ever-increasing density of objectification" (LL 147) in Franz Horn's shed. Walser exemplifies the dimension of the objective world with a "round shiny object" (LL 6) which Horn notices on various occasions, including the day before the long Whitsun weekend in the parking lot:

> He walked over and picked it up but waited until he was in the car before examining it more closely. A ball caster. Probably from an office chair. After having ignored the ball caster for several days he felt justified in keeping it. His desk chair at home had casters like that. One never knows.... To Franz Horn's mind, even on a day of great disasters one should pick up oddments and save them. (LL 6)

One should note Horn's passion for collecting things: "Franz Horn was meticulous.... By this time he had even become passionately meticulous. Keeping things tidy gave him satisfaction. He never tired of filing, putting away, storing things" (LL 10). Much to the chagrin of his wife, Franz Horn is incapable of throwing anything away. He has hoarded

> pipes he no longer smoked, old rosaries, boxes that some day might come in handy, a slightly damaged Thermos flask, obsolete loudspeakers and record players, shoes not yet quite beyond wearing, intact parts of picture frames, children's beds, as well as patio umbrellas, motorized bikes, lamps, lawnmowers, temporarily unemployed locks, orphaned keys, parts of shelves, lampshades, unmatched screws and nuts, randomly acquired nails and tacks to be straightened out at some point in a leisurely future, saddles from scrapped bicycles, intact parts of obsolete household appliances.... (LL 11)

As if that were not enough, Horn brings home all discarded household items he can find that might be in some way useful, and keeps his vast possessions in perfect order. For this purpose he has built a shed which he calls in his

Ravensburg dialect a *Schopf* ("tuffet" [LL 57 et passim]), a word he has difficulty explaining to the Hamburg native Liszt: "The unmistakable and heartwarming capacity of a tuffet doesn't interest you" (LL 57). Horn proclaims the "tuffet" to be his "creation" (LL 146), built with his own hands, where each item has its place. Furthermore, he can recall "precisely how, when and where he had picked up each item" (LL 146). In this sense, his creation is "unmistakable and heartwarming." The shed is, therefore, a structure designed to systematize Franz Horn's eccentricities, an instrument for coping with his own existence. It facilitates his coming to terms with himself by imposing on himself some kind of order:

> The shed had been crammed to the roof for a long, long time. For every new object for which he wanted to find a spot, he had to pick up a hundred others and rearrange them more closely, more ingeniously. That was the glorious part about it. The result was an ever-increasing density of objectification. (LL 147)

This passage describes the inner mechanics of association and interrelation that also characterize Franz Horn's carousel of self-reflection constitutive of his other major "work," his letter. Just as he picks up the objects in his shed again and again und arranges them anew, he thinks the same thoughts again and again in his letter, turns them this way and that, puts them in different contexts, and looks at them from different points of view. The "caster," however, has not yet found its place in the shed. For the time being Horn places it on his desk until his abrupt movements while writing cause it to roll off the desktop: "Horn crawled around and finally found the caster under the radiator, but, in getting impatiently to his feet, he banged his head against the windowsill. He wanted to resume writing as quickly as possible" (LL 56). Here the particular function of Horn's writing becomes painfully clear: in contrast to Lord Chandos's letter, Horn's/Walser's text does not regard writing as an abstract activity removed from reality but rather shows that the act of writing, in its most concrete and literal sense, brings something into motion, that language does indeed create reality. Only after completing his letter does he notice that in picking up the caster he hurt himself. Thus, his written altercation does not end without injuries. Not until his letter is finished can Horn find a place for the caster in his shed. His fanaticism for order corresponds to his motivation for writing; writing also enables him to classify and arrange temporarily (i.e., events and incidents) for future reference without achieving a sense of finality or closure. We are specifically made aware that, for lack of space, Horn only finds "a makeshift place for the ball caster between a coaster hub and a ball faucet" (LL 147).

The caster would not seem to be a very serious matter — its paltriness, paralleling Horn's own sense of insignificance, does not seem to justify such intricate interpretation — were it not for the fact that in Lord Chandos's letter it is precisely the trifling and unimportant things that are filled with the "presence of the Infinite" (Ch 137). Lord Chandos writes to Francis Bacon: "I cannot expect you to understand me without examples, and I must plead your indulgence for their absurdity" (Ch 135). Is the caster not comparable to the lamprey of Crassus, mentioned by Lord Chandos, whose death caused Crassus to weep bitterly?

> And about this figure, utterly ridiculous and contemptible in the midst of a world-governing senate discussing the most serious subjects, I feel compelled by a mysterious power to reflect in a manner which, the moment I attempt to express it in words, strikes me as supremely foolish. (Ch 140)

Lord Chandos experiences the divine immediacy of objects through a process of radical self-negation and adulation of the insignificant that leads him straight "into the deepest womb of peace" (Ch 140). This humble attitude, then, induces Chandos to renounce literary activity — which, evidently, always serves as a vehicle for personal self-assertion and self-glorification. Franz Horn's humility is of a different nature. It is an ironic humility which belittles the self and uses the external aspect of objects as a screen for self-projection. So Franz Horn eventually finds at least a transient balance that allows him to join his family gathering with a sense of contentment: "... wearing his clean socks and his sandals he walked toward his car and, almost light-headed with composure, drove out onto the street. He was on his way to a party. He had no problems. The void hummed intriguingly. And ahead of him the Allgäu wore the sun like a diadem" (LL 149).

The "fulfillment" (cf. Ch 135) in experiencing everyday phenomena claimed by Chandos is analogous to Horn's perception of an emptiness to be filled by the individual. Objects themselves can lay no claim to immediacy — on the contrary, they only assume a constitutive function as the external component in the process of self-reflection through writing. This process presupposes a fundamental semantic void — a void which is to be understood ironically but, precisely for this reason, will engender new and unique layers of meaning. The example of the caster shows how the effects of these kinds of meaning can be even painfully tangible. As Walser's novel illustrates, language is the only mode of mediation between inner and outer world. External reality can never be experienced authentically but only in its function as external referent in the process of self-reflection. It is the interplay of reflection, its movement between self and the world of objects, that constitutes the experiential knowledge of the writing or speaking subject.

The magical "object" (LL 6), then, is a ball caster of a chair which belongs to a desk (i.e., a tool for writing), which is placed on the desk while Horn is writing, and perhaps this *Kugelfuß* even connotes the *Kugelkopf*, the "golf ball" in the author's typewriter. While in Chandos's letter *Begriffe* engage in a "wonderful interplay" ("like magnificent fountains upon which played golden balls" [Ch 135]), Walser chooses this "round shiny object" (LL 6) to turn the "divine immediacy of objects" (which does not really exist in Philipp Chandos's letter either) into a play with irony. Through the pen of Franz Horn (or, to be more exact, through the ball of the author's typewriter), the "language of *things*" (Ch 141) conjured up by Chandos becomes the "*language* of things."

Hofmannsthal's "Letter of Lord Chandos" and Walser's *Letter to Lord Liszt* represent two different models of reaction to the same fundamental experience. Both Lord Chandos and Franz Horn realize that language is too ineffectual and inadequate to grasp real phenomena, and, what is more, that the concepts of language bear no connection to physical reality. While Chandos, due to this realization, declares his renunciation of language altogether, Horn bursts into a verbal exuberance that can hardly escape its autonomous, spiraling movement. When Horn states that the lordly form of address simply "presented itself" (LL 23) as he picked up his pen, this also conveys the intrinsic meaninglessness of language. Nevertheless, and precisely because of that lack of meaning, Horn takes pleasure in the use of language, experimenting freely with the boundless possibilities it allows him. His writing, eager and passionate, illustrates that even the intangibly abstract use of language can assume an epistemological function. It is significant that Chandos, at the end of his letter, also arrives at this *other* concept of language, that is, at a symbolic language which is aware of its own inadequacy. The only difference is that Chandos silently awaits this language, while Horn uses it in writing: his memory flashes of images, situations, conversations, and trains of thoughts make language — like his shed — a surrogate reality-construct, a construct that cannot itself appropriate but merely approximate reality. When Horn makes a statement only to retract it a few pages later, he tries to "zero in" on the truth; at the same time, his letter evidences that Walser's text does not allow for any kind of truth in an absolute sense. The "fullest, most exalted Present" (Ch 136-37) and the "presence of the Infinite" (Ch 137) in Chandos's letter are thus analogous to Franz Horn's "attack of truth" (LL 128), to a subjective form of truth that constitutes itself in the process of writing.

Horn himself overtly attests to his own skepticism: "Truth: what is it after all?" (LL 128). While Horn's letter is an homage to writing, his vehement absorption lets the world of objects come to life when the ball caster rolls off the desk. This loss of control causes the writer to collide with the "objects," while this collision provides the counter-stimulus for the ironic process of self-reflection. Language is necessary to classify objects, if only provisionally, and to establish a constitutive connection to the world of objects so that 'reality' can be experienced *and* mastered. Without language the world of objects does not exist; there is no nonlinguistic immediacy of experience. This is the message for Philipp Chandos delivered by *Franz* Horn in the guise of *Francis* Bacon, who had criticized Chandos's literary idleness (Ch 140), thereby causing Chandos to justify himself in his "Letter." Franz Horn, who shares not only Francis Bacon's first name (sometimes playfully altered to "Franzl" [LL 55 et passim]) but also the location of the plot in *Beyond All Love* (England), as well as his appreciation of the written word, not only writes a *Letter to Lord Liszt* but at the same time a "Letter to Lord Chandos."

The comparison of literary texts is no doubt one of the most frequently applied methods of interpretation. It therefore seems worthwhile to address some fundamental questions of this type of literary analysis through this particular example. The affinities of two single texts will establish the factors that not only allow for intertextual analysis but also, and most important, are constitutive of the autonomous meaning of one text. Reading *Letter to Lord Liszt*, as it were, through the mirror of Hofmannsthal's "Letter to Lord Chandos" establishes layers of meaning which would be difficult to perceive on the basis of an immanent treatment of Walser's novel. Thus, without the background of the "experience of objects" in the Chandos letter, the "ball caster" Horn picks up could hardly be understood as an autonomous referent that serves to accentuate the symbolic character of language. When the texts are juxtaposed, the caster emerges as a signifier for the possibility of experiencing a world mediated through language — in contrast to Philipp Chandos's letter which proposes the nonlinguistic immediacy of objects. The present contrastive analysis has applied the same creative play with language that distinguishes *Letter to Lord Liszt* as a celebration of the written word. Viewing this comparison as a game by no means implies arbitrariness or mere coincidence. Texts cannot be compared randomly, just as a game can only be played with sensible moves. However, just as the nonchalant and sometimes careless "juggling" with words and concepts (note the metaphoric use of "balls" at "play" in connection with meaningless words in "Letter of Lord Chandos" [Ch 135]) can give rise to new dimensions of meaning, a contrastive discussion can construct one text's meaning via potential points of reference of the content and context of the other text.[13] The act of comparison, a dynamic movement in itself, enhances the determination and demarcation of a text's meanings. In Lord Chandos's letter one reads that ideas are "concerned only with each other" (Ch 135) and that the most profound and personal aspects of being will always be missing. In this sense the compared texts — to stick to the metaphor — pass each other the ball.

This playful interrelation of the two texts is not only a matter of interpretation, but also delineates their formal structures and psychological strategies. This is reflected in the epistolary form of both works. Like Franz Horn, who creates his own self in his *alter ego* Horst Liszt, Philipp Chandos constructs an "external self" in the recipient of his letter, Francis Bacon. Though formally addressed to his friend Francis Bacon, Chandos's justification of his plans to stop writing is clearly a justification to himself. That Chandos and Bacon are *one* character becomes clear from the works Chandos has previously written or had planned to write. Among his literary plans, he mentions an account of the first years of the reign of Henry VIII: "True, I did plan to describe the first years of the reign of our glorious sovereign, the late Henry VIII" (Ch 130). In 1622, it was Francis Bacon who published a *History of the Reign of Henry VII*. Lord Chandos's intention to write on Henry VIII make the planned volume appear as a sequel and definitely a direct reaction to Bacon's book. Another of Chandos's projects should be mentioned: "I wanted to decipher the fables, the mythical tales bequeathed to us by the Ancients, in which painters and sculptors found an endless and thoughtless pleasure — decipher them as the hieroglyphs of a secret, inexhaustible wisdom whose breath I sometimes seemed to feel as though from behind a veil" (Ch 131). Quite obviously, this work is inspired by Bacon's *De sapientia veterum* (1609), a work which "deciphers" the "wisdom" of ancient myths in allegorical interpretations. In a way, Chandos's plans for his *Apophthegmata*, a collection of "the brilliant maxims and reflections from classical and Italian works" (Ch 132), among other things, are fragmentarily realized in his "Letter" in the form of Hippocrates' aphorism, "Qui gravi morbo correpti dolores non sentiunt, iis mens aegrotat (Those who do not perceive that they are wasted by serious illness are sick in mind)" (Ch 129). Chandos quotes Hippocrates, but he has taken the saying from Bacon, who used it in his own letter as a warning to Chandos.

[13]See, for example, Karlheinz Stierle, "Werk und Intertextualität," *Das Gespräch*, eds. Karlheinz Stierle and Rainer Warning, Poetik und Hermeneutik 11 (Munich: Fink, 1984) 141.

This shows to what degree the individual text is actually an intertextual fabric[14] and how that which its author writes is always a reflection of and reaction to other texts. Considering Hippocrates' saying, one might claim Bacon's text to be already an "intertext." Similarly, had Chandos realized his historical project, it would have had a number of different authors — we read, for example, that he had planned to make use of the "papers bequeathed to [him] by [his] grandfather" (Ch 130). Foucault's definition of an author can be applied here:

> Critics doubtless try to give this intelligible being [the "author"] a realistic status, by discerning, in the individual, a "deep" motive, a "creative" power, or a "design," the milieu in which writing originates. Nevertheless, these aspects of an individual which we designate as making him an author are only a projection, in more or less psychologizing terms, of the operations that we force texts to undergo, the connections that we make, the traits that we establish as pertinent, the continuities that we recognize, or the exclusions that we practice.[15]

While Foucault applies this account to the methods of critics, it is equally valid for the author of literary texts, who — as our discussion of the Chandos letter showed — is also an interpreter of other texts.

Just as the "Letter of Lord Chandos" is a reaction to Bacon's writings, Walser's *Letter to Lord Liszt* is a reply to Hofmannsthal's famous text: Francis Bacon had written to Philipp Chandos in order to encourage him to continue his literary activity; Chandos writes a reply to Bacon in which he justifies himself and explains why he will not write any more. In his letter Franz Horn, too, addresses someone who does not write, who feels no urge to write, and who refuses to look into the discord of his own self: "A week ago today he had written the letter [a letter which preceded Horn's long "letter to Lord Liszt"]. No reaction from Liszt. No reaction at all! Incredible!" (LL 16). Apparently the reason why Liszt cannot deal with the recent decline of his career is that he, unlike Horn, refuses to engage in self-reflection through writing. The relationship between Franz Horn and Horst Liszt illustrates to what degree this self-reflection is dependent on the presence of an "other." Both Horn and Walser facilitate an entrance to the other text

[14]See Roland Barthes, *The Pleasure of the Text*, trans. Richard Miller (London: Jonathan Cape, 1976) 64: "Text means *Tissue*...."

[15]Michel Foucault, "What Is an Author?," *The Foucault Reader*, ed. Paul Rabinow (Harmondsworth: Penguin, 1986) 110.

through the conception of the character of Dr. Liszt: Liszt *is* the "other" as well as Horn's alter ego, and Horn simply must seek confrontation. In rebuking Liszt for not writing, "Lord" Liszt implicitly quotes the text of Lord Chandos, who refuses to write any longer.

While not all texts are composed in letter format or in an explicitly dialogical form, they all constitute responses to other texts, and in developing their own positions they necessarily also formulate counter-positions. For this reason, each interpretation virtually invites comparisons to other texts, at the same time, however, calling into question the text's originality. Thus, a contrastive textual analysis consciously and explicitly reflects that operation which implicitly informs every literary production — in fact, any verbal or written expression. In the same vein, every reading is guided by previous reading experiences; hence, a comparison to an "other" exemplifies an imperative and essential approach to the reading of a text.

Works Cited

Barthes, Roland. *The Pleasure of the Text*. Trans. Richard Miller. London: Jonathan Cape, 1976.

Canetti, Elias. "Dialog mit dem grausamen Partner." *Macht und Überleben: Drei Essays*. Berlin: Literarisches Colloquium Berlin, 1972. 38-56.

Foucault, Michel. "What Is an Author?" *The Foucault Reader*. Ed. Paul Rabinow. Harmondsworth: Penguin, 1986. 101-20.

Hofmannsthal, Hugo von. "The Letter of Lord Chandos." *Selected Prose*. Trans. Mary Hottinger, and Tania and James Stern. Kingsport, TN: Pantheon Books, 1952. 129-41.

Stierle, Karlheinz. "Werk und Intertextualität." *Das Gespräch*. Eds. Karlheinz Stierle, and Rainer Warning. Poetik und Hermeneutik 11. Munich: Fink, 1984. 139-50.

Walser, Martin. *Selbstbewußtsein und Ironie. Frankfurter Vorlesungen.* Frankfurt/M.: Suhrkamp, 1981.

Wiethölter, Waltraut. "Der 'Fall' des Lord Chandos." *Hofmannsthal oder die Geometrie des Subjekts: Psychostrukturelle und ikonographische Studien zum Prosawerk.* Tübingen: Niemeyer, 1990. 57-85.

8

German Unification as Utopia: Martin Walser's Schiller

Alexander Mathäs

IN HIS NOVELLA *Dorle und Wolf* (1987; *No Man's Land*, 1988), Martin Walser uses Friedrich Schiller's *Die Jungfrau von Orleans* (1801; *The Maiden of Orleans*, 1959 [1824]) to promote the ideal of German unity. Like almost all other publications by the established author, *No Man's Land* was reviewed extensively in every major German newspaper or magazine. The novella's initial popularity is hardly surprising, since it had appeared as a series in the popular German magazine *Stern* even before it could be acquired in the bookstores. To this day, however, the novella has drawn little attention from literary scholars when compared to Walser's numerous other publications — not to mention his only other text of the same genre, *Runaway Horse* (1978).[1] In view of all the academic consideration that Walser received for his political outspokenness in support of German unification, scholarly disregard for the novella appears more than a coincidence. After the wave of revelations concerning the Stasi files, which have caused an abundance of reactions, both academic and nonacademic, *No Man's Land* has lost nothing of its timely significance and deserves renewed interest.

Many German critics have based their arguments against the novella on the foregone conclusion that spy novels do not belong to the realm of serious literature and that any attempt to combine the banal with the sublime must be viewed as a transgression of good taste. These critics failed to recognize

[1]The October 1992 MLA Bibliography database lists only one entry under *Dorle und Wolf:* Isabel Garcia-Wetzler, "Zwischen Faszination und Irritation: Der Übersetzer als Seiltänzer," *Proceedings of the XIIth Congress of the International Comparative Literature Association*, vol. V, ed. Roger Bauer, et al. (Munich: iudicium, 1990) 375-81.

the artistic qualities of *No Man's Land* because they grounded their judgment on inadequate aesthetic premises. This analysis of Walser's use of Schiller will clarify how he problematizes the conflict of the real and the ideal to reveal the hypocrisy of ideological dogmatism. Thus, Walser's transgression of genre expectations must be viewed as integral to the theme of his novella.

Walser uses Schiller to illustrate how the political goals of socialism have grown widely apart from socialist reality. Thus, *No Man's Land* can be read as a metaphorical rendition of Walser's own political development from the socialist of the late sixties and the seventies, who condemned the capitalist perversion of democratic principles, to the critic of socialist reality who has become an outspoken advocate of German unification. In spite of his political metamorphosis, however, Walser has maintained his underlying skepticism toward the propagandistic use of ideology. What concerned him before, during, and after German unification was that many West German intellectuals, who once had been his comrades in arms against capitalism during the sixties and seventies, had embraced Marxism with religious fervor and become insensitive to the historical changes that had widened the gap between the promise of socialist ideology and the fact of socialist reality in East Germany. In other words, Walser contended that these intellectuals and staunch defenders of socialism did not realize that they had dug themselves into the trenches of Cold War rhetoric and inevitably supported the status quo of Germany's division:

> There is nothing more meaningless than to point out once again that the division of Germany is not a consequence of the Second World War but a product of the Cold War ... that the war was a war of religion, a forty-year-long one ... Western Christianity against communist world revolution. Marxism as a monotheistic doctrine of truth kindled once again religious fire in the West, in areas that had long been regarded as secular; orthodox believers on both sides.[2]

However, Walser's disappointment with the promise of ideologies did not cause him to turn his back on politics. One could argue to the contrary that the author's increasing frustration over the apparent hypocrisy of Cold War

[2]Walser, "Vormittag eines Schriftstellers," *Die Zeit* 21 Dec. 1990: "Nichts Sinnloseres, als ein weiteres Mal darauf hinzuweisen, daß die deutsche Teilung nicht eine Folge des Zweiten Weltkriegs ist, sondern ein Produkt des Kalten Kriegs ... daß der Krieg ein Religionskrieg gewesen ist, ein vierzigjähriger ... [C]hristliches Abendland gegen kommunistische Weltrevolution, der Marxismus als monotheistische Wahrheitslehre hat im Westen noch einmal religiöses Feuer geweckt in längst säkularisiert geglaubtem Gelände; Orthodoxe hier und dort."

rhetoric initiated his wish to overcome the temporary solution of Germany's division ["Bedürfnis nach geschichtlicher Überwindung des Zustands Bundesrepublik"][3]. Walser's political desire for a unified Germany was in 1978 — when he first expressed it — according to his own words, pure utopia ["Reine Utopie"], or wishful thinking ["Wunschdenken"].[4] One year later the author accused the mass media in both German states of manipulating public opinion to accept the status quo of German separation as inevitable.[5] Walser maintained his confrontational stance toward the press with regard to German unity throughout the eighties. Even towards the end of the decade, when the author became very active in promoting German unity, the majority of Germans believed that there was not even the slightest chance of overcoming German division.[6] In view of these circumstances it is not surprising that many German critics were puzzled by Walser's treatment of German unification. One critic characterized his topic as most unlikely[7] and another as a slip into the abnormal.[8]

By evoking Friedrich Schiller, Walser appeals to the reader's historical awareness and stresses that the desire for German unity existed long *before* the Cold War and the political reasons that may have caused it. But Schiller is more than a cultural symbol to legitimate both the author's and his protagonist's desire for German unity: he serves also as a catalyst which enables the author to combine the political and personal spheres. Like Wolf, who becomes fascinated with Schiller's play because he feels it applies to his own situation, young Walser's first encounter with the Swabian poet develops into an intimate fascination with the Schillerian pathos, which teaches the adolescent the moral function of an idealist utopia. In his essay entitled

[3]Walser, "Händedruck mit Gespenstern," *Über Deutschland reden* (Frankfurt/M.: Suhrkamp, 1988) 23.

[4]Walser, "Über den Leser — soviel man in einem Festzelt darüber sagen soll," *Wer ist ein Schriftsteller? Aufsätze und Reden* (Frankfurt/M.: Suhrkamp, 1979) 101.

[5]Walser, "Händedruck mit Gespenstern," p. 11: "Und eine aus lauter monochromen Parteien bestehende öffentliche Meinung täuscht Vielfalt vor, wie die östliche veröffentlichte Meinung Öffentlichkeit vortäuscht."

[6]Walser, "Über Deutschland reden. Ein Bericht," *Über Deutschland reden*, p. 100.

[7]Jürgen Manthey, "Ehebruch mit Deutschland-Kummer," *Frankfurter Rundschau* 11 Apr. 1987.

[8]Heinrich Vormweg, "Ausrutscher ins Absonderliche," *Süddeutsche Zeitung* 14 Apr. 1987.

"Mein Schiller" [My Schiller] the author describes his first encounter with the Swabian poet:

> Schiller's poems were all relived and rewritten and turned into bombast and illusion. A hypocrisy tending toward the grandiose ran amok. But how else should one [the youngster] understand the moral message than through pretending it is real. Practicing is for the pianist what hypocrisy is for the moralist. Especially when he notices that it is hypocrisy. And Schiller let the boy notice it. The Schiller rays kept singing away the continuously growing flower of hypocrisy. What's better now: to fight against all odds and pretend as if one could win or wallow around right away in the warm morass of pessimism and call everything by its given name? To behave tautologically? For a Schiller boy this question does not exist. He has made the choice: for production, illusion, meaning, history, utopia.[9]

In *No Man's Land* the Schiller motif has two main functions. On one level it describes the reason for Walser's own artistic production. Like Schiller the author considers himself a moralist. The literary impulse arises from his defiance in accepting an unwanted reality. The result is a utopian ideal which probably will never be attained but serves as a moral guide. On a different level, the exaggerated style of Schiller's idealism helps the protagonist in *No Man's Land* become aware of his professional hypocrisy and teaches him to cling to his ideals by refusing to let them be corrupted by political reality. By adhering to Schiller's dualism, Walser is careful to emphasize the utopian character of his ideal of a unified Germany.

Walser's idealism has been misread by many reviewers as an artistic flaw. The critics' initial reactions to *No Man's Land* were so unfavorable that they reminded Martin Lüdke of the hitherto unparalleled harshness with which critics had responded to the appearance of Walser's *Beyond All Love*

[9]Walser, "Mein Schiller," *Liebeserklärungen*, p. 162: "Das [Schillers Gedichte] wurde alles nachgelebt und nachgedichtet und führte zu lauter Schwulst und Schein. Eine ins Grandiose zielende Heuchelei tobte sich aus. Aber wie anders als durch So-tun-als-ob soll einer die Moral-Lektion denn üben. Was dem Klavierspieler die Fingerübung ist dem Moralisten die Heuchelei. Vor allem wenn er merkt, daß es eine ist. Und Schiller ließ es den Knaben merken. Die Schiller-Strahlen sengten den andauernd nachwachsenden Heuchelflor andauernd weg. Was ist jetzt besser: aussichtslos kämpfen und doch so tun, als könne man gewinnen, oder gleich im warmen Morast des Pessimismus sich realistisch sielen und alles so taufen, wie es auch ungetauft schon heißt? Sich also tautologisch verhalten? Für einen Schiller-Knaben stellt sich die Frage nicht. Er hat gewählt. Die Produktion. Den Schein. Den Sinn. Die Geschichte. Die Utopie."

in 1976.[10] Heinrich Vormweg, for example, claimed that Walser's contribution to German unification had failed utterly ["völlig schiefgegangen"], and Werner Fuld characterized the novella as uninspired and full of clichés ["geistlos und klischeebeladen"].[11] Most of the reviewers aimed their attacks at the novella's content. Perhaps the greatest misjudgment among these was Martin Lüdke's assumption that the division of Germany had been accepted by all Germans and therefore was no longer of interest as a literary topic.

These critics were concerned with the lack of realism of both plot and characters.[12] And indeed, the motivation of the novella's action does appear unrealistic. The main character, Wolf Zieger, has a rather contrived reason for being a spy. A former music student, he joined the East German secret service in order to escape legal prosecution after hitting his piano teacher, who had not acknowledged his musical talent. Yet he maintains that the real reason for becoming a spy was neither his failed career as a pianist nor the immunity granted by the *Staatssicherheitsdienst* but his goal of assisting the GDR in achieving technological parity with West Germany. Ironically, technological parity is for Zieger a necessary precondition for a German unification of equals. It is therefore in the name of the political ideal of a unified Germany that Wolf takes advantage of his wife's position as a secretary in the ministry of defense. He does not want to involve her directly, however, and instead receives secret documents from one of her colleagues — named Sylvia — in return for sexual favors. The protagonist's behavior toward his wife, Dorle, can hardly be called considerate, even when he justifies the exploitation of both his wife's emotional and her colleague's sexual dependency in the name of patriotism. It seems that the author stretches the readers' suspension of disbelief to its limits when he asks them not only to believe his protagonist's story but also to sympathize with him.

The discrepancy between the protagonist's high ethical ideals in terms of political justice and his disrespectful behavior toward his fellow human beings in real life becomes even more apparent when he identifies himself

[10]Martin Lüdke, "Nichts Halbes, nichts Ganzes," *Die Zeit* 20 March 1987.

[11]Werner Fuld, "Ein Spion mit Sehstörungen," *Frankfurter Allgemeine Zeitung* 14 March 1987.

[12]For example, Werner Fuld characterized the protagonist as "lächerlich unglaubwürdigen Helden"; Heinrich Vormweg disqualified Walser's prose as "schlieriges Gerede" because of its disregard for historical facts; Jürgen Manthey maintained that Walser had left "den Boden der Realität zugunsten eines gekünstelten Motivgeflechts"; Martin Lüdke argued that the protagonist's suffering from German separation appears "etwas überstrapaziert."

with Friedrich Schiller's Joan of Arc figure. In contrast to the French heroine, Wolf Zieger's professional success is based not on celibacy but on sex appeal. It is, therefore, not surprising that a large number of German reviewers considered it inappropriate to compare Schiller's morally impeccable Joan to an adulterous opportunist like Wolf. They argued that the banalities of a spy thriller and the sublime pathos of Schiller's *Maiden of Orleans* were stylistically incompatible (Vormweg, Fuld). On the one hand, critics maintained that the author's ostentatious use of romantic symbolism is responsible for the ridiculously unbelievable plot (Manthey, Lüdke, Schwilk); on the other, they disapproved of the description of sexual and other profanities in the protagonist's everyday life (Lüdke, Fuld).

According to Goethe's widely accepted definition, the novella revolves around a most unusual event, an *unerhörte Begebenheit*. To judge Walser's novella merely on the basis of its true-to-life quality is, therefore, no less absurd than to conclude that Goethe's or Storm's novellas are worthless because they are unrealistic. No author would choose this literary genre in order to give a detailed account of empirical reality. That the German magazine *Der Spiegel* left it to Günter Nollau, the former head of the German secret service, to review Walser's novella shows how grotesque the search for truthfulness became. Nollau, hardly an expert in literary matters, examined the text exclusively under the aspect of its probability as a real spy story.[13]

There are several possible explanations for the critics' disregard for the autonomy of poetic truth. For one, it permitted them to express their own ideological points of view on contemporary German society and appear objective at the same time. Another reason why German critics may have ignored the interplay of fantasy and reality can be attributed to the topic's sincerity. German unity was for many reviewers a politically much too serious issue to become the subject of risky speculation. Thus, many of them considered it inappropriate to mix literary motifs with contemporary politics. One critic regretted that Walser "misused" literary symbolism to express his political opinion.[14] The underlying separation of art and politics disregards, however, that two hundred years ago the "Idealist rund um die Uhr" [idealist around the clock] Schiller also made use of symbolism to advance the cause

[13]Günther Nollau, "Ein General beim A-3-Verkehr," *Der Spiegel* 23 March 1987: 228.

[14]Both Lüdke and Manthey found fault with the combination of personal and national themes. According to Lüdke, a love story is ill suited to present political issues. And Manthey criticized the author for using the "gesamtdeutsche Kummer als Resonanzboden für die traurige Erlösungssucht eines reuevollen Ehebrechers."

of German unity in defiance of the French occupation.[15] Thus reviewers berated the author for combining facts and fiction, a violation which they themselves could be accused of when they based their judgments on the category of truthful depiction of reality. In condemning its lack of realism, reviewers failed to recognize the novella's peculiar oscillation between the sublime and the trivial as a playful innuendo of the irreconcilable conflict between the real and the ideal in romantic literature. Walser plays with the tradition of the genre when he thematizes the discrepancy between the reality of German separation and the — at that time — most unlikely event of German unification.

Long before Schiller began work on *The Maiden of Orleans* in 1801, he had become repelled by the reign of terror pursuant to the French Revolution. In awe of the destructive forces of uncontrolled political fervor, he wanted to advance the cause of German nationalism and at the same time warn his compatriots not to abandon their compassion for their fellow humans in favor of political dogmatism.[16] Schiller's *Maiden of Orleans* is less concerned with historical accuracy than with the development of the heroine's character. His dramatization of the Joan of Arc legend allowed him, however, to use the nationalistic overtones as a general background for Joan's personal growth towards human grandeur.

Walser works along similar lines when he depicts Wolf Zieger's decision to abandon his secret existence as a spy and surrender to the authorities as a victory of ethical behavior over abstract political ideals. Both Joan and Wolf are successfully advocating a political cause when they are confronted with the emotion of love and become aware of the dichotomy between their avowed public duty and their potential as human individuals. Both characters owe their political success to the total devotion to their cause, which implies the neglect of their personal ties. When Joan experiences love, this uncontrollable force from within takes complete possession of her and replaces her internalized political fervor, preventing her from carrying out her political mission. Afflicted with feelings of guilt over violating her oath to forswear

[15]Martin Walser, "Mein Schiller," *Liebeserklärungen*, p. 167.

[16]Schiller expresses his concern about the human tendency to exert power over fellow humans in the name of political dogma in a letter to Goethe of 17 September 1800: "Aber bei beiden Revolutionen sieht man die alte Unart der menschlichen Natur sich gleich wieder zu setzen, zu befangen und dogmatisch zu werden. Wo das nicht geschieht, da fließt man wieder zu sehr auseinander, nichts bleibt fest stehen und man endigt, so wie dort, die Welt aufzulösen, und sich eine brutale Herrschaft über alles anzumaßen." *Schillers Werke. Nationalausgabe*, vol. 30, eds. Lieselotte Blumenthal and Benno von Wiese (Weimar: Hermann Böhlhaus Nachfolger, 1961) 197.

earthly passion, she undergoes a painful development which makes her aware of her human capacities. Wolf matures in a similar way as Schiller's heroine when he realizes that his political activity as a spy causes the split of his personality. Reading Schiller's *Maiden of Orleans* works as a catalyst of change and helps Wolf confront his personal dilemma and eventually become aware of the reason for his self-alienation.

After once again exchanging sexual favors for information with his wife's colleague, Wolf notices that he has gained his professional success at the expense of his personal integrity. According to his own words, he has become a nobody living in a "no man's land," who has to lead a double existence and yet is at home in neither of his two lives: "The person he is, is the one he is not allowed to be, and the person he's allowed to be, he isn't" (NL 44). For Wolf the physical loss of home has become a loss of identity. Walser effectively uses the spy metaphor to illustrate how the split between the two Germanys affects the individual's psyche. It is in the context of the lost home that Zieger for the first time identifies himself with Schiller's Joan, quoting the fourth scene at the end of the prologue where Joan bids farewell to her hometown's garden of earthly delights in order to carry out her unearthly mission. In reading aloud passages of Schiller's drama, Wolf notices the humorous effect of Schiller's highfalutin style, which appears inappropriate for describing the banality of his daily life as a spy. And yet he recognizes a similarity between Joan's fate and his own: "He was aware of becoming declamatory, yet his delivery of certain passages implied that he knew he mustn't claim his declamatory tone as applying to himself. He would then drop back and lay claim to what he was reading aloud as a reference to himself" (NL 25). The wide gap between Joan's heroic pathos and the triviality of Zieger's own unheroic spy-existence reflects the discrepancy between his high political ideals and the profanity of his actual deeds. Schiller's stilted language helps the protagonist discover how grotesque the ideological justification of his professional career has become. Thus, Schiller's pathos serves as a metaphorical device revealing the deceptive rhetoric that justifies the rivalry between the two Germanys in the name of an illusory heroic idealism. Both the similarity and difference between Joan and Wolf initiate a process of self-recognition which ultimately leads Walser's protagonist to abandon his double existence as a spy. When Wolf discovers that Joan — as he — must decide between the pursuit of her private longing and service to her country, he becomes aware of the "relevance of the Schiller text to his own case" (NL 54). By turning himself in to West German authorities, the East German Wolf achieves a personal reconciliation with his West German wife and symbolically clears the path for East and West German unification.

The following examples will illustrate how Walser applies concepts of romantic irony by skillfully intertwining motifs and rhetoric from Schiller's play. The author plays with the notion of pathos even in the context of Wolf's undercover spy operations, where the narrator uses the word *pathetisch* [melodramatic] to describe Wolf's sexual encounter with Sylvia. Ironically, it is not Sylvia's language that reminds the protagonist of pathos but the silent mood in the room when she does not speak. Her choice of words, on the other hand, appears inappropriately matter-of-fact for the occasion of their romantic encounter: "But perhaps it was not even the choice of words. While their bodies were being aroused she spoke High German, almost like a schoolmarm. Maybe she simply had no luck with words. But even when she used the wrong words, she had the right feelings. Whereas he..." (NL 42). Sylvia's prosaic language calls attention to the semiprofessional reason for their get-together. Wolf, on the other hand, discovers pathos in the grotesquely affected mood, in the gaudy pretense of a romantic love affair, meant to conceal the commodified nature of their erotic encounter. Walser uses the romantic notion of wholeness as a metaphor for presenting the conflict between the real and ideal, between inclination and duty, between the public and the private, between spirituality and sensuality, between love and sex. Whereas Sylvia lacks the appropriate words, Wolf lacks the appropriate feelings. In contrast to Sylvia, however, who undresses "mit genausoviel Sachlichkeit wie Pathos" (DW 50) ["with an equal blend of casualness and melodrama" (NL 42)] and therefore does not feel the need to distinguish "zwischen Ernst und Spiel" (DW 98) ["between the real thing and pretense" (NL 87)], Wolf can no longer ignore his inner conflict: "He longed for feelings he could approve of. He couldn't live permanently in a state of self-rejection. Partitioned like Germany, he thought" (NL 36).

Schiller's pathos works as a mind-opener for Wolf, because it calls attention to the discrepancy between appealing illusions and sober reality. For Wolf this revealing experience is unpleasant and liberating at the same time. Like Joan, who feels that she has betrayed both her country and God by falling in love with an enemy, Wolf is plagued by feelings of guilt after deciding to abandon his shadow-existence as a spy and turn himself in. He quotes Joan's soliloquy in the fourth act in which she chastises herself for having given in to passion: "Unglückliche! Ein blindes Werkzeug fordert Gott,/ Mit blinden Augen mußtest Du's vollbringen! / Sobald du sahst, verließ dich Gottes Schild, / Ergriffen dich der Hölle Schlingen!" (DW 63) ["Unhappy one! A sightless instrument thy God demands,/ Blindly thou must accomplish his behest! / When thou didst see, God's shield / abandoned thee, / And dire snares of hell around thee pressed!" (NL 54)]. As in the story of Adam and Eve, human desire is the tool for obtaining knowledge but also the reason for despair. The twist in Walser's plea for passion arises, however, from Wolf's ability to satisfy his all too human needs in his adulterous relationship with Sylvia. It is a perversion of the Schillerian path to wisdom through love because Wolf exploits intimate feelings to obtain secret information. Ironically, Wolf realizes that he himself had become a blind tool in the grip of an ideology with which he can no longer identify.

The degradation of love parallels the corruption of the protagonist's political ideas. Just as love has become a commodity in exchange for secret information, his political ideals have been reduced to the mere question of technological and strategic parity. Thus, it is Joan's heroic idealism that causes Wolf's awareness of the difference between political rhetoric and its trivial perversion in everyday reality. Like Joan, who has to forsake her supernatural power to become a human being, Wolf has to give up his political aspirations to remain faithful to his political and moral ideals and preserve his identity. Both characters become individuals when they obey their inner voice in order to save their capacity for love and compassion. But whereas "Schiller takes pains to present Johanna's compassion not as an act of willful disobedience, or as a conscious surrender to temptation, but rather as an unreflected act, a spontaneous welling up of *Gefühl* [feeling],"[17] Wolf's decision to abandon his political mission arises from a process of reflection. However, both protagonists eventually arrive at the same conclusion: that their political ideals are incompatible with their human needs. Ideals that disregard these needs may be noble but, at the same time, inhumane. Like Schiller in *The Maiden of Orleans*, Walser favors the inner law over the starry heaven above in his discussion of Kant's categorical imperative. Both protagonists are faced with the insoluble dilemma that the uncompromising struggle for their political ideals deprives them of their freedom of choice and consequently prevents them from living the life of complete human beings. Schiller's text is applicable to Wolf's own fate, because — as it did for Joan — love makes him aware of the contradiction between his personal inclinations and the *no man's land* of his spy- existence. Both Joan and Wolf are eventually punished by the state for their decision to abandon their public duty in favor of their personal peace of mind. But to what extent does this attitude explain Walser's position on German unification?

Although the protagonist and the author have little in common as far as their biographies are concerned, one could read the text as Walser's attempt at coming to grips with the question of German unity, an issue that had held

[17]Donald H. Crosby, "Freedom through Disobedience: *Die Jungfrau von Orleans*, Heinrich von Kleist, and Richard Wagner," *Friedrich von Schiller and the Drama of Human Existence*, ed. Alexej Ugrinsky (New York: Greenwood, 1988) 39.

his attention since the 1970s.[18] From Walser's essays we know that the author shared his protagonist's dismay about the economic and technological disadvantages of the GDR. His sympathy and respect for the socialist Germany earned Walser the reputation of a leftist. In view of his more recent pleas for German unification some critics argue, however, that the once outspoken critic of capitalism had become a political conservative who wanted to turn the clock of history back in the name of an obsolete nineteenth-century nationalism. In opposition to these critics, it appears that Walser's former sympathy for socialism and his advocacy of a united Germany are only seemingly paradoxical, as his novella *No Man's Land* shows. Wolf Zieger's decision to sever his ties to the GDR does not mean he is giving up his ideals. On the contrary, he manages to preserve these ideals, because Schiller's *Maiden of Orleans* teaches him to recognize their corruption in political reality. When Wolf turns his back to the system of the GDR, he abstains from presenting himself as a victim of an oppressive system to the West German authorities and remains true to his moral principles. In light of these arguments *No Man's Land* can be regarded as a revealing analysis of the corruption of ideology in the name of patriotism.

Although from different ideological points of view, Walser has always been concerned with the exposure of political hypocrisy. In his essay entitled "Über Macht und Gegenmacht" (On Power and Antipower) the author sums up his political views of the mid-eighties, shortly before he wrote the novella. After it became obvious to Walser that the socialist promise had exhausted itself in empty rhetoric, he universalized his ingrained skepticism toward the abuse of power and applied it to *all* so-called "Wahrheitsbesitzer auf beiden Seiten" [purveyors of truth on both sides], including his former allies on the left.[19] Almost twenty years earlier, in a speech presented in 1967 to an audience of first-time voters, Walser quoted Marx to demonstrate how the term *democracy* had been exploited to serve the propaganda purposes of powerful interest groups:

> Karl Marx once said that "the 'idea' disgraced itself whenever it differed from 'interest.'" If a society vociferously supports the idea of democracy, but the interests of powerful groups in this society hinder the democratic process, then idea and reality will grow apart. The advocacy of the idea is constantly repeated, especially on Sun-

[18]Walser had already expressed his desire for a united Germany in his 1977 speech held in Bergen-Enkheim: "Über den Leser — soviel man in einem Festzelt darüber sagen soll," *Wer ist ein Schriftsteller? Aufsätze und Reden*, pp. 94-101.

[19]Martin Walser, "Über Macht und Gegenmacht," *Über Deutschland reden*, p. 59.

days and holidays, but interest reigns on workdays. And the idea disgraces itself.[20]

In *No Man's Land* Walser uses Schiller's utopian idealism as a metaphor for the discrepancy between the reality of German separation and the then utopian ideal of a single Germany. By contrasting the banalities of a spy's everyday reality to the stilted pathos in Schiller's *Maiden of Orleans*, he applies the Schillerian dichotomy of passion and its corruptibility by reason to the contemporary question of German unification. *No Man's Land* confirms that Walser had been disillusioned with GDR socialism long before the wall came down. Unlike many German leftist intellectuals, who — in view of the worldwide decline of socialism — had become defeatist, Walser in *No Man's Land* upholds a utopian perspective in order to illuminate the insufficiencies of reality.[21] This message becomes even more important after the demise of a socialist alternative.

[20]Martin Walser, "Die Parolen und die Wirklichkeit," *Heimatkunde. Aufsätze und Reden* (Frankfurt/M.: Suhrkamp, 1968) 63.

[21]Fritz Raddatz, for instance, argued shortly after German unification that it was time to forswear Marxist ideology altogether, not only because socialism had failed but also because many political crimes had been committed in its name: "Ehrlicherweise ist einzugestehen: Mit der linken Krücke Hoffnung ging es sich besser. Ehrlicherweise ist einzugestehen: Es war ein Blindenstock. Zu verabschieden ist ein Traum," "Die linke Krücke Hoffnung," *Die Zeit* 21 Sept. 1990.

Works Cited

Crosby, Donald H. "Freedom through Disobedience: *Die Jungfrau von Orleans*, Heinrich von Kleist, and Richard Wagner." *Friedrich von Schiller and the Drama of Human Existence*. Ed. Alexej Ugrinsky. New York: Greenwood, 1988. 37-42.

Fuld, Werner. "Ein Spion mit Sehstörungen." Rev. of *Dorle und Wolf*. *Frankfurter Allgemeine Zeitung* 14 March 1987.

Lüdke, Martin. "Nichts Halbes, nichts Ganzes." Rev. of *Dorle und Wolf*. *Die Zeit* 20 March 1987.

Manthey, Jürgen. "Ehebruch mit Deutschland-Kummer." Rev. of *Dorle und Wolf*. *Frankfurter Rundschau* 11 Apr. 1987.

Nollau, Günther. "Ein 'General' beim A-3-Verkehr." Rev. of *Dorle und Wolf*. *Der Spiegel* 23 March 1987: 228.

Raddatz, Fritz. "Die linke Krücke Hoffnung." *Die Zeit* 21 Sept. 1990.

Schiller, Friedrich. *Werke. Nationalausgabe*. Vol. 30. Ed. Lieselotte Blumenthal, and Benno von Wiese. Weimar: Hermann Böhlhaus Nachfolger, 1961.

Vormweg, Heinrich. "Ausrutscher ins Absonderliche." Rev. of *Dorle und Wolf*. *Süddeutsche Zeitung* 14 Apr. 1987.

Walser, Martin. "Die Parolen und die Wirklichkeit." *Heimatkunde. Aufsätze und Reden*. Frankfurt/M.: Suhrkamp, 1968. 58-70.

——. "Händedruck mit Gespenstern." *Über Deutschland reden*. Frankfurt/M.: Suhrkamp, 1988. 7-23.

——. "Mein Schiller." *Liebeserklärungen*. Frankfurt/M.: Suhrkamp, 1983. 157-71.

——. "Über den Leser — soviel man in einem Festzelt darüber sagen soll." *Wer ist ein Schriftsteller? Aufsätze und Reden*. Frankfurt/M.: Suhrkamp, 1979. 94-101.

——. "Über Deutschland reden. Ein Bericht." *Über Deutschland reden*. 76-100.

——. "Über Macht und Gegenmacht." *Über Deutschland reden*. 53-64.

——. "Vormittag eines Schriftstellers." *Die Zeit* 21 Dec. 1990.

9

A German Pragmatist: Martin Walser's Literary Essays

Steve Dowden

MARTIN WALSER'S NEAREST AMERICAN counterpart is probably John Updike. They belong to the same generation, the former having been born in 1927, the latter in 1932, and they both excel in the same prose forms: the novel and the literary essay. In addition, both writers are conspicuously interested in the riddles of postwar national life and identity in the contemporary middle classes. The neurotic perplexities of a Harry Angstrom or an Anselm Kristlein reflect the larger anxieties of the modern self — or at least the one that is white, male, and more or less affluent — as it floats freely on the unquiet seas of marriage and nation, religion and workplace, sex and the sundry bewilderments of just getting along in the conformist world of contemporary Germany and America.

Since a self always has to be born and raised somewhere, national identity inevitably emerges as a major theme for both novelists. Of course, neither of them advocates any kind of chauvinistic sense of nation or national destiny. Instead, each strives in his fiction to see his respective country with clarity and candor. In the interest of concrete specificity, they focus attention on the individual in society, rather than risk losing narrative momentum to abstraction and advocacy (moral ambiguity is always more interesting than moral certainty). In the psychosocial design of their novels, the public arena and private sphere are interlocked.[1] Nowhere is this more striking than in the realm of love and sex.

[1]The once-New Subjectivity of the 1970s and 80s did not necessarily signal a withdrawal into the "merely" private. Public and private can seldom be separated; Jonathan P. Clark, "A Subjective Confrontation with the German Past in Martin Walser's *Ein fliehendes Pferd*," *Martin Walser: International Perspectives*, eds. Jürgen E. Schlunk and Armand E. Singer, American University Studies: Series 1, Germanic Languages and Literature 64 (New York: Lang, 1987) 47-58.

Sexual misadventure and distress of varying degrees hold a special interest for both Updike and Walser. Of course, sex is, in and of itself, an arresting topic for most people, and it may be that it accrues no particular meaning other than itself. This is frequently enough true. Still, in this matched pair of writers, both plainly preoccupied with the American*ness* and German*ness* of their respective settings and characters, it is difficult not to assume that sex, too, has other, more self-transcendent meanings. Among them, it may be that the sexual self-doubts so troubling to Helmut Halm and Rabbit Angstrom tap some larger insecurity that is characteristic of the historical moment.

Larger insecurities are not hard to come by. In Updike's case the failure of American potency in Vietnam comes irrepressibly to mind. American military ventures in Grenada and the Persian Gulf, Somalia and Panama seem as linked to the restoration of national self-confidence as Rabbit Angstrom's endless search for self-affirmation in repeated erotic encounters with different women. Similarly, Helmut Halm's misgivings about his settled married life and his ebbing sexual prowess can be understood as a refracted image of German self-doubts about the firmness and fidelity of its commitment to liberal, Western values. A good wife, a good job, and a stable home leave Halm feeling unfulfilled. He yearns for something beyond the bourgeois average, something more dangerous, more Nietzschean. Exciting prospects beckon, especially in the hedonistic California of *Breakers* (1985). But ultimately Halm does not yield to his impulses — partly because he can never quite tell *his* impulses from the ones that his time and place have imposed upon him. Halm's self-doubt should be reassuring. In the current political climate of Germany and Central Europe, it is encouraging that Walser's would-be adventurers are inclined to return to their wives, the only stable characters in his world. In a Walser novel the reaffirmation of marriage seems oddly like a reaffirmation of Germany's postwar liberal order and the values that make it work: tolerance, self-acceptance, the commitment to living with and improving a fallible institution from within.

However, let us not get sidetracked into the interesting but complex issues of Walser's sexual themes. They are only one facet of the larger question of the literary correlation between individual and national self. Sex is merely an obvious example of how the public invades the private. The public saturates and governs the private when public standards of competition, performance, and domination become internalized in assumptions about sexual life. Helmut Halm is a typical example. He feels liberated in California, but in fact he surrenders his autonomy to a set of preestablished norms and expectations — a consumerist *Leistungsethik* — of exactly how the good life is to be led. The New Age myths that draw him to a narcissistic lifestyle, embodied in the allure of Fran Webb, liquidate his individuality as surely as the conformist myths that entrap Franz Horn in his German work life, or the ideological machinery that severs Alfred Dorn from the self of his past in *Die Verteidigung der Kindheit* (1991; In Defense of Childhood). What links ideology, work, politics, and sex here is the underlying issue of self-fulfillment, of true and authentic selfhood.

In novel after novel, authentic individuality (often expressed as the hunger for control over one's own life) emerges as Walser's guiding theme. It is not for nothing that Halm reads Kierkegaard and has written a book about Nietzsche, the two great masters of individualism. He clings to them like Huck Finn clings to his raft. Nor is it surprising that a novelist should take questions of individuality as his controlling theme. It has been with the novel at least since *Robinson Crusoe* (1719). In particular, there is something about the nature of the modernist novel — and both Walser and Updike have been shaped by modernism — that gives a special prominence to the actual and symbolic importance of the individual. According to Updike, fiction

> offers to enlarge our sense of possibilities, of potential freedom; and freedom is dangerous. The bourgeois, capitalist world, compared with the medieval hierarchies it supplanted and with the Communist hierarchies that would supplant it, *is* a dangerous one, where failure can be absolute and success may be short-lived. The novel and the short story rose with the bourgeoisie, as exercises in democratic feeling and in individual adventure. *Pamela*, *The Pilgrim's Progress*, *Robinson Crusoe* — what do they tell us but that our entrepreneurism, on one level or another, may succeed? If fiction is in decline, it is because we have lost faith in the capacity of the individual to venture forth and suffer the consequences of his dreams.[2]

Even though Walser, well known as a sharp critic of capitalism and its human costs, would presumably bridle at Updike's enthusiasm for capitalist metaphors, there is a sense in which Updike has described Walser personally and exactly.

Walser's protagonists have difficulty in asserting themselves and sustaining a sense of their own individuality. They lack what Updike, for better or for worse, calls "entrepreneurism." Updike goes on to point out that the entrepreneurial world is a dangerous one, that failure can be absolute, as it is for so many of Walser's protagonists who find themselves trapped in the web of capitalist competition and its social consequences. It is an insight that

[2]John Updike, "The Importance of Fiction," *Odd Jobs: Essays and Criticism* (New York: Knopf, 1991) 87.

Kafka expressed best of all, and which has not been wasted on Walser.[3] As surely as Josef K. is unable to break free of his trial, Franz Horn of *Beyond All Love* (1976) fails to overcome the mind-numbing job and way of life that oppress him. Such examples from Walser's fiction could be multiplied at length. Similarly, Updike's own protagonists are more likely to be defeated than not, even if the defeat is seldom absolute.

However, the entrepreneurism that Walser's characters lack is abundantly present in Walser himself. He labored in the ranks of broadcasting media during the 1950s before "venturing forth" on his own into that most uncertain and competitive of market-oriented livelihoods, free-lance writing. And even he, so he has said, was unable to make a living at it before he was fifty-one years old.[4] Still, Walser counts among the survivors. Where his protagonists mostly fail, i.e., in making their way independently, Walser has mostly succeeded. Moreover, he stands out in German literary and intellectual life as a plain-speaking individualist. His opponents are inclined to lump him together with the left, but the left has had hard words for him, too. For example, when Walser agreed to an interview to be published in the conservative daily *Die Welt*, left-wing observers claimed he had gone over to the other side. Walser's thinking is not ideologically bound to the agenda of one side or the other.

As a novelist he explores the failed lives of downtrodden and mystified middle- or lower-class men, combining sympathy and critique in fair measure. His allegiances as literary critic are similar, siding with the failures or, if not exactly failures, then at least the canonical outsiders of German literary history: Hölderlin and Kleist, Büchner, Kafka and Robert Walser. In this sphere, too, the ideal of autonomous individuality comes to the fore. It suggests that authentic selfhood may be the supreme virtue, or at least one of the chief virtues, in both the fiction and criticism that Walser writes.

Having begun as a critic in the late forties and early fifties with an academic dissertation on Kafka, which as a book subsequently became one of the more influential studies in academic Kafka criticism, Walser is no stranger to the claims of *Wissenschaft* on the study of literature in the academic setting. But the nonacademic Walser makes no pretense of impartiality or "scientific" standards of scholarship. As he sees it, the virtue of his criticism, and of literary criticism in general, is the spontaneity and personal

[3]Walser's protagonists are descendants of Kafka's K. and Josef K., concerning whom Walser has written with great insight; *Beschreibung einer Form: Versuch über Franz Kafka* (Munich: Hanser, 1961).

[4]*Auskunft: 22 Gespräche aus 28 Jahren*, ed. Klaus Siblewski (Frankfurt/M.: Suhrkamp, 1991) 140.

intensity of what he calls a *Lese-Erlebnis*.[5] Walser believes that criticism begins with our *experience* of the text.

Here we broach the task of his literary criticism, which is to understand the exploration of limitation and lack of freedom. In his best essays, which he has himself collected and published under the title *Liebeserklärungen* (1983; Declarations of Love), Walser examines the insecurities and deficiencies of great writers. He calls our attention to the ways in which a sense of inadequacy — *Mangel* is Walser's favorite word for it — can compel the writing of fiction and poetry. In Walser's literary essays the preoccupation with self and the fear of its entrapment are continuous with the same themes in his fictions. Walser sets his emphasis upon the *poverty* of the self, its precarious hold on life, and the need to escape into some wider realm.[6] Seen from a more positive point of view, writing is one way of establishing oneself in the world, of escaping from the narrowness of self that Walser has carefully described in his fiction and criticism.

In this sense the principal theme of Walser's literary criticism is freedom. He argues that the self is a small and airless place from which we must escape, and that fiction is one way of achieving a partial escape, and he strongly implies that literary criticism is similarly a way of escaping the limitations of mere self. Now, if literary criticism is to be an experimental way of freeing the self, what are the limits of its freedom? It is at this point that Walser runs afoul of the professional scholars. Subjectivity suggests arbitrariness.

It is obvious that a part of Walser's overall intention in his literary critical forays, which could also be described as raids, has been to attack and reinterpret the canon, casting Thomas Mann into the outer darkness,[7] and examining the received wisdom of German classicism with a skeptical eye, at least where Walser perceives that wisdom (especially its traditional place

[5]For a detailed look at his views see Thomas Nolden, "Der Schriftsteller als Literaturkritiker: Ein Porträt Martin Walsers," *Martin Walser: International Perspectives*, pp. 171-83; and Dirk Göttsche, "Liebeserklärungen und Verletzungen — Zur Literaturkritik von Martin Walser und Ingeborg Bachmann," *Literaturkritik: Anspruch und Wirklichkeit*, DFG Symposium 1989, ed. Wilfrid Barner (Stuttgart: Metzler, 1990) 197-212.

[6]Here, too, we ought to think of Updike's Rabbit character in his various novels, who is literally on the run: "The title [*Rabbit, Run*] is a piece of advice," writes Updike, "in the imperative mode..."; *Hugging the Shore: Essays and Criticism* (New York: Knopf, 1983) 851.

[7]"Ironie als höchstes Lebensmittel," *Die Zeit* 13 June 1975: 33-34; *Selbstbewußtsein und Ironie: Frankfurter Vorlesungen* (Frankfurt/M.: Suhrkamp, 1981) 115-52.

in German culture) to reaffirm the status quo of an oppressive social and political climate.

His detractors argue that his criticism is willfully slanted in the direction of his social and political prejudices and that this vested interest obliges him to misrepresent literary history. Walser's mode of critique is arguably antihistorical.[8] The charge, if true, aligns Walser with the advocates of postmodernist fiction. There are probably not many commentators who perceive Walser as a postmodernist. Still, the accusation that he is antihistorical, arbitrary in his dealing with literature, and given to making fun of the German preoccupation with high culture and cultural heros — from the dotty Goethe of *In Goethes Hand* (1982; In Goethe's Hand) to the Thomas Mann of his Frankfurt Lectures — seems to point in the direction of postmodern culture. *In Goethes Hand* can be seen as liberating, or disrespectful, or simply self-indulgent, depending on the interpreter's standpoint in the culture wars. From any point of view, Walser obviously intends to bring the exalted figure of Goethe back to earth.[9]

The leveling of cultural values has emerged as one of postmodernism's central and most pernicious features.[10] Walser is known as a champion of the marginal and traditionally uncanonical literary forms, from the dialect poetry, workers' literature, the writings of convicts and mental patients, to the odd films of Herbert Achternbusch. When asked about what he learned from his advocacy of all these forms of writing, Walser responded that he learned that anyone can become an author by virtue of what is missing from his life.[11] Anyone who writes out of some sense of lack or failure, as a reaction against it, is a writer as far as Walser is concerned. In an interview he clarified his view by way of a personal experience. During the late fifties he spent what for him was a liberating few weeks in the United States. When the visit was over he had no desire to return to West Germany, and when he did, the sense of entrapment that overcame him propelled a novel:

[8]Wolfgang Wittkowski, "Der Schriftsteller und die Tradition: Walser, Goethe und die Klassik," *Martin Walser: International Perspectives*, p. 167.

[9]Unlike his Thomas Mann, though, Walser returns his Goethe to the canon, arguing that Goethe's appeal lies in a personal vulnerability expressed as a literature in which evil and catastrophe are always overcome; "Goethes Anziehungskraft," *Liebeserklärungen* (Frankfurt/M.: Suhrkamp, 1981) 237-59.

[10]See esp. Alain Finkielkraut, *Die Niederlage des Denkens*, trans. Nicola Volland (Hamburg: Rowohlt, 1989) 115-40.

[11]*Auskunft*, p. 140.

> And then I sat down after about four weeks and wrote a novel. Out of pure rage, so to speak. I worked up everything, the whole decade of the fifties, for myself; I reacted to everything that had happened to me. The energy for it came out of the experience of entrapment: on a continent, in a country, in a language, in a family — this roped-off, bottled-up, packed-in feeling that goes with having a biography, that goes with the suspicion you are so-and-so who has to turn up with his passport at such and such an address. It seemed unbearable to me.[12]

His literary criticism, too, is driven by an inner need.[13] On these grounds Walser's criticism could be attacked as both too personal and partisan, too much bound to private experience. The dominant theme of his criticism is, indeed, the experience of insecurity, uncertainty, and 'unfreedom' common to the writers whom he favors. According to Walser, the experience of unfreedom is at the bottom of all literature. And to explore this unfreedom means an opportunity to overcome it, in a limited sense — or if not truly to banish it then at least to look it in the eye and challenge it.

Walser's essays, intellectually aggressive, subjective, and fallible, have something that criticism in its professional, institutional, academic form often lacks. This something is an appeal to actual aesthetic experience. What Walser offers, warts and all, ought to feel more reassuring to us than academic conventions allow.

First of all, Walser does not claim to have cornered the market on truth. In fact, he goes to considerable lengths to emphasize the subjectivity of his response. It is true that he is opinionated, makes effective rhetorical use of his prestige, and speaks with a command of text and language that implicitly lays claim to authority. But his voice is individual, not institutional, ideological but not binding. It should be a consolation to us that insight into literature is not in the keeping of a priestly caste. Walser presents it as a more democratic undertaking.

Second, criticism, like fiction in Updike's formulation, "offers to enlarge our sense of possibilities, of potential freedom; and freedom is dangerous." Subjectivity grades over into egotism all too easily. There is also a sense in which a one-sided critique of Walser's subjectivism undermines the liberating aspects of both reading literature and writing about it. When the professional

[12] *Auskunft*, p. 99.

[13] "Über den Umgang mit Literatur," *Martin Walser: International Perspectives*, pp. 202-03.

critic — Wolfgang Wittkowski, for example[14] — reproves Walser for shortcomings as a critic (in particular for what he denounces as a left-wing ideological bias), he also implies that only the expert is qualified to understand these matters properly. His posture is symptomatic of a wider problem. The right to speak about literature has been arrogated by a class of professionals. Current academic writing about literature sends the message that a *reading* cannot be successfully carried out without the legitimation of a rigorously elaborated critical apparatus.

The dangers of misunderstanding must be weighed against the freedom of independent reading. It is beyond dispute that literary scholarship — the existence of experts who have the time and inclination to study fiction and poetry in great depth — is a good thing. However, it is not such a good thing that intelligent nonexperts — ordinary theatergoers or readers of novels, for example — should feel obliged to defer to the experts. This may be especially true in the United States.

Whatever beneficial effects the rise of theory may have had in American departments of literature, it has also had the unfortunate side effect of repressing large numbers of actual and potential readers. What well-educated undergraduate is likely to care about or even remember the meaning of Lacanian analysis for good reading habits? More likely, undergraduates finishing college today leave the university with a certain feeling of inferiority in literary matters. Similarly, it seems likely that the well-educated German readers of today may experience a like feeling of exclusion when they pick up the most recent issue of *Merkur* and try to read a literary essay.

Third, the "subjectivity" of Walser's response is not closed and private. The distinction between subjectivity and introversion ought to be plainer now than it was in the discussion around the so-called New Subjectivity of the 1970s and 1980s. Individual experience merely serves as the self-evident point of departure into the political, social, historical, and other meanings a work may offer. He defines it concretely and pragmatically as experience, the way a book makes the reader think and feel, the world it opens up: "Erfahrungen sind im Gegensatz zu Meinungen nicht wählbar" [In contrast to opinions, experiences are ineluctable].[15]

[14]Wittkowski rebukes Walser as historically ill-informed, ideologically prejudiced, and fashionably subjective, even hedonistically egocentric (161).

[15]"Was ist ein Klassiker?," *Über Deutschland reden* (Frankfurt/M.: Suhrkamp, 1988) 40.

Subjective aesthetic experience, then, does not mark an abdication of intellectual responsibility.[16] Instead, it offers itself as a sensible place to begin serious thinking. But what should be the aim of "serious" literary criticism as practiced by a nonprofessional? The example of Martin Walser suggests this answer: Literary criticism aims, or ought to aim, to make us independent, to enable us to experience the world of poetry, drama, and fiction from the vantage of autonomous reflection. In the particular case of literary criticism, autonomy would mean freedom from the popular taste-makers, the setters of intellectual fashion, and preestablished schools of criticism. But is such a thing possible?

Commentators have noted an affinity between Walser's critical orientation and the reader-response theories of the Constance School. For his part, Walser has shown no particular interest in the theoretical edifice of his learned neighbors. When an eager questioner once tried to pin him down on the topic, Walser only said he was glad to hear that other people shared his point of view. We may reasonably suppose his lack of curiosity on this point to be a matter of principle. It points toward reservations about the immobility that can come of system-building, the entrapment within concepts that puts an end to the vitality of personal and public aesthetic experience.

These two features of his criticism are decisive: the primacy of aesthetic experience and the resistance to an institutionalized framework. The critical result of his way of thinking about literature is the notion of irony that he elaborates in his Frankfurt Lectures — but not only in his Frankfurt Lectures. The concept of irony turns up in all of his literary writings. What is most important and instructive from the perspective of writing about literature is not so much the particular concept of irony that he advocates. Instead, the way he arrives at it should arrest our attention. In Walser's criticism the emphasis falls on process, not product.

Walser is an advocate of the honest reading experience, which suggests that the discovery of fixed and permanent meanings is not his main interest. Aesthetic experience is infinitely renewable, which is another way of saying that meanings are variable. While the proximity of reader-response criticism is clear enough, it appears that Walser's views actually bring him closer to the aesthetics of American pragmatism. From the philosophical foundations in the writings of Ralph Waldo Emerson and William James, up through

[16]For a fuller account of contemporary views of subjectivism in a philosophical register see Charles Taylor, *The Ethics of Authenticity* (Cambridge: Harvard UP, 1992). Taylor offers strong arguments for maintaining confidence in autonomous subjectivity as a moral resource.

Dewey's *Art as Experience* (1934), to the recent literary criticism of Richard Poirier:[17] art is foremost and first of all experience.

There is no reason to believe that Walser has derived his views from the American pragmatist tradition. That does not mean, however, that the points at which they converge will not illuminate Walser's attitudes and practice as a writer of literary essays. Indeed, the very absence of imitation makes that convergence all the more interesting. He shares with the American pragmatists an antagonism to the professionalization of thinking about literature. In "What Pragmatism Means" William James describes the pragmatist as someone who

> turns his back resolutely once and for all upon a lot of inveterate habits dear to professional philosophers. He turns away from abstraction and insufficiency, from verbal solutions, from bad *a priori* reasons, from fixed principles, closed systems, and pretended absolutes and origins....[18]

The literary pragmatist could be described as one who turns away from the similar habits of the professional literary critics. Walser's turn of mind has less to do with Ingarden and Gadamer, the founding grandfathers of *Rezeptionstheorie*, than with the concrete reading experience of actual people. Obviously, Walser can only speak for himself, which shifts the center of gravity away from *what* he says toward the intellectual mobility that underlies his saying of it. The crisp precision of his criticism has the effect not of defining the normative response to a given work or writer but of challenging the reader to measure up to the sheer quality of imagination with reading experiences of his own. Walser's example invites us to explore our own reading experiences more fully and with a keener eye.

The emphasis on experience implies a liberal, democratic perception of literary meaning as something intrinsically subject to change. In this he is close to the preoccupation of American pragmatism with experiment, openness to new experience and change. Above all, the pragmatists have emphasized temporality and a certain skepticism about the permanence of things, including literary meanings. Emerson and his pragmatic followers, writes Poirier, "want to prevent words from coming to rest and want to dissuade us

[17]For example, *The Renewal of Literature: Emersonian Reflections* (New Haven: Yale UP, 1987). More than any other contemporary literary critic, Poirier is responsible for mining the vein of pragmatism for literary understanding.

[18]Cited in Richard Poirier, *The Renewal of Literature*, p. 17.

from hoping that they ever might."[19] In a similar spirit, Walser warns against the critics who have failed to understand that a book or a play is "a contribution to a process that is in continual motion."[20] Authoritative literary evaluations, he says, threaten to "bring the current to a standstill."[21] Walser is, for example, an opponent not of Goethe — whom he openly admires — but of the Goethe industry that has stylized and petrified the writer into the glorified image of a national monument.[22] The more liberating approach to Goethe, or any other tradition-encrusted national monument, is one of creative skepticism. Goethe ought to be challenged to renew himself over and over again.

The institutions of criticism resist this process of continual renewal. Theories of criticism, as Nietzsche repeatedly pointed out, always contain their own findings implicit within their system for producing them. The welter of competing critical discourses in current academic use is evidence enough. However, what is at issue here is not a clear-cut choice between "radical" theory and "traditional" reading that the contemporary cultural conservatives would like to force on us. The choice is a false one. After all, any utterance about literature is at some level always already informed by theory, or if not by a formal *theory* then at least by a set of more or less organized assumptions. There is nothing wrong with airing and exploring such assumptions. Instead of a choice between two mutually exclusive alternatives, we have only a question of proportion. Academic critics have a seldom-acknowledged vested interest in *difficulty*.

Difficulty is a value of literary modernism that has drifted into the critical establishment. In "The Metaphysical Poets" (1921) T. S. Eliot hailed difficulty as symptomatic of the age, and he went on to make it a literary virtue in his own poetry. The fiction of Joyce, Proust, Kafka, and Mann did their part, too, to establish difficulty as a component and virtue of modern prose. The challenge to readers may well have helped establish the academic critic as the master of complexity too arcane for the ordinary reader to fathom. It may also have helped establish complexity as a virtue of critical prose. The examples of Adorno and Benjamin are suggestive. Whatever historical assumptions may have shaped them, the technocratic idioms of literary

[19]Poirier, *The Renewal of Literature*, p. 16. The idea of that the passage of time means the continual renewal of literature is a piece of the pragmatist heritage that Poirier develops at length.

[20]*Wer ist ein Schriftsteller?*, p. 36.

[21]*Auskunft*, p. 102.

[22]*Liebeserklärungen*, pp. 237-59; *Auskunft*, pp. 113-14.

criticism are now a part of the intellectual landscape. The literary instrumentalization of figures as diverse as Lacan and Derrida, Foucault and Heidegger, Kristeva and Irigaray establishes the critic as master of a sectarian discourse that is pitched at a considerable remove from the unindoctrinated, usually nonacademic reader. Cliques and clerisies take shape and then struggle for turf in universities and in professional journals. The consequent professionalization of literary criticism, a system strictly policed by the academic publishing imperative and the tenure system, leaves a large gap between college-educated lay readers and the professors who taught their literature courses.

Walser's literary criticism suggests an alternative to the assumption that difficulty is a virtue of literature and criticism. His understanding of Kafka stands as a good example. No modern writer is more difficult than Kafka, yet this difficulty has not forced Walser into a defensive recourse to theoretical systems. Walser takes Kafka seriously as a writer, by which I mean he plainly believes that Kafka's writing seriously probes human nature and culture. The conventions of contemporary criticism take a writer such as Kafka less seriously. To scrutinize Kafka through the lens of New Historicism, for example, entails reducing Kafka to a case, the product of forces beyond his control. It entails taking Freud and Foucault more seriously than Kafka. It may be that we need a Kafkan reading of Foucault more earnestly than we need a Foucaultian reading of Kafka. It may be that Walser has offered something like that in *Breakers*, in which a major American literature department figures prominently.[23]

[23]Bernd Fischer deals with this question in his essay in reference to *Breakers*.

Works Cited

Finkielkraut, Alain. *Die Niederlage des Denkens*. Trans. Nicola Volland. Hamburg: Rowohlt, 1989.

Göttsche, Dirk. "Liebeserklärungen und Verletzungen — Zur Literaturkritik von Martin Walser und Ingeborg Bachmann." *Literaturkritik: Anspruch und Wirklichkeit*. DFG Symposium 1989. Ed. Wilfrid Barner. Stuttgart: Metzler, 1990. 197-212.

Nolden, Thomas. "Der Schriftsteller als Literaturkritiker: Ein Porträt Martin Walsers." *Martin Walser: International Perspectives*. Eds. Jürgen E. Schlunk, and Armand E. Singer. American University Studies: Series 1, Germanic Languages and Literature 64. New York: Peter Lang, 1987. 171-83.

Poirier, Richard. *The Renewal of Literature: Emersonian Reflections*. New Haven: Yale UP, 1987.

Taylor, Charles. *The Ethics of Authenticity*. Cambridge: Harvard UP, 1992.

Updike, John. *Hugging the Shore: Essays and Criticism*. New York: Knopf, 1983.

——. *Odd Jobs: Essays and Criticism*. New York: Knopf, 1991.

Walser, Martin. *Auskunft: 22 Gespräche aus 28 Jahren*. Ed. Klaus Siblewski. Frankfurt/M.: Suhrkamp, 1991.

——. "Goethes Anziehungskraft." *Liebeserklärungen*. Frankfurt/M.: Suhrkamp, 1981. 237-59.

——. "Ironie als höchstes Lebensmittel," *Die Zeit* 13 June 1975. 33-34.

——. *Selbstbewußtsein und Ironie. Frankfurter Vorlesungen*. Frankfurt/M.: Suhrkamp, 1981.

——. "Über den Umgang mit Literatur." *Martin Walser: International Perspectives*. 195-214.

——. *Über Deutschland reden*. Frankfurt/M.: Suhrkamp, 1988.

Wittkowski, Wolfgang. "Der Schriftsteller und die Tradition: Walser, Goethe und die Klassik." *Martin Walser: International Perspectives*. 157-69.

10

In Defense of the Past: The Life and Passion of Alfred Dorn in *Die Verteidigung der Kindheit*

Gertrud Bauer Pickar

WITH A PERSISTENCE AND ZEAL unmatched in earlier epochs, German authors since 1945 have documented and probed the enduring presence of the past in the contemporary world. They have sought to illuminate intellectual as well as economic, political, and social forces that led or contributed to the tumult, death, and destruction of the 1930s and 1940s and that at times have continued to be factors in the postwar era. Their writings emphasize the power of the past in the public arena and in the private lives of individuals, both as a conscious concern and as an unconscious yet powerful presence in the human psyche. Some authors, such as Günter Grass (from *Die Blechtrommel* [1957; *The Tin Drum*, 1962] to *Unkenrufe* [1992; Calls of the Toad]), have created works that encompass the broad fabric of the contemporary German scene; others have focused on the individual and reveal the significance of the past primarily in personal and psychological terms. Max Frisch, Heinrich Böll, Christa Wolf, Christoph Hein, Jurek Becker, and Martin Walser, to name but a few, portray the enduring and troubling presence of the past — societal, familial, and personal — in the lives of their protagonists and reveal the impact of past experiences, whether suppressed or acknowledged by their fictive characters. They explore the manner in which the perceived past affects internal thought processes, self-image, perception of others, and recognition of reality in general, and they trace the continuing ramifications of past experiences for the protagonists.

Walser has dealt with the painful years of the past in some of his dramas — *Eiche und Angora* (1962; *The Rabbit Race*, 1963) and *Der Schwarze Schwan* (1964; The Black Swan), works rich in literary allusion, focus on the Nazi and post-Nazi periods and the attempts of individuals to come to terms with the past[1] — and his novels are marked by overt as well as covert social criticism.[2] However, Walser's writings also reveal the long-term effects of personal past, particularly childhood. The recollection of the plight of his mother and the poverty of his early years become incentives that drive Hans Beumann in *Marriage in Philippsburg* (1957) to economic and social success; the childhood vision of a girl leaning against a chestnut tree haunts Anselm Kristlein in *Halbzeit* (1960; Half Time) propelling him from affair to affair in search of the promise of bliss and perfection he identifies with that memory-fragment; boyhood experiences leave Helmut Halm of *Runaway Horse* (1978) and *Breakers* (1985) with a sense of personal inadequacy; and memories of his mother and her chastising words when he overslept remain subliminal factors for Gottlieb Zürn in *The Swan Villa* (1980) in his obsessive but ineffectual efforts to gain durable financial security, in his feelings of guilt and failure, and in his bouts of inertia.[3] These works and others testify to the encroachment of the past into the present and to the life-shaping, sometimes crippling, and usually insidious influence of early experiences. Interestingly enough, they also indicate, albeit fleetingly, the lingering impact of the mother (mainly through her anxieties and her disapproval) upon the subsequent development of the protagonist. It is not surprising that with Alfred Dorn, the central figure of *Die Verteidigung der Kindheit* (1991; In Defense of Childhood), Walser has created another protagonist who is shaped by events of his childhood and whose life testifies to the continuing impact of the past — and to the dominating influence of his mother, who remains the most pervasive and persistent force in his life. With this novel, preoc-

[1]Cf. G.B. Pickar, "*Woyzeck* and *Hamlet* Recast: a study of two of Martin Walser's dramas," *University of Dayton Review* 7 (1971): 61-68.

[2]Cf. Heike Doane, *Gesellschaftspolitische Aspekte in Martin Walsers Kristlein-Trilogie* (Bonn: Bouvier, 1978), and Rainer Nägele, "Zwischen Erinnerung und Erwartung: Gesellschaftskritik und Utopie in Martin Walsers *Einhorn*," *Martin Walser*, ed. Klaus Siblewski (Frankfurt/M.: Suhrkamp, 1981) 114-31.

[3]While Dorn resembles many of Walser's male figures in his self-defeating behavior, he displays the greatest affinity to Gottlieb Zürn. Like Zürn in his efforts to save the Swan Villa, Dorn labors in vain to preserve the beauty of the past he venerates. Zürn and Dorn, as well as Halm of *Breakers*, are concerned with their clothing (in which they display questionable taste) and depend upon clothes for a feeling of assurance to meet the opportunities and challenges of the day. I am indebted to Heike Doane for the suggestion of the further parallel between Halm and Dorn, who both displayed remarkable ability and promise in their childhood (in Halm's case intellectual prowess), but whose later professional lives are rather mediocre.

cupation with the past as a thematic concern in Walser's writings reaches its zenith.

Alfred Dorn's literary ancestors, however, are to be found less in Walser's recent fiction than in the early stages of his literary career, a period marked by his indebtedness to Kafka,[4] a writer whose influence is again palpable in *Verteidigung*. Dorn, in his passion for collecting tangible remnants of his childhood, his veneration of the past and total absorption with it, and the attendant rejection of any meaningful or intimate involvement in a living present, is prefigured by the protagonists in two of Walser's short stories from the collection *Ein Flugzeug über dem Haus und andere Geschichten* (1955; An Airplane over the House and Other Stories): "Die Rückkehr eines Sammlers" (The Return of a Collector) and "Templones Ende" (Templone's End).[5] In the first, the protagonist Alexander Bonus, a strange E.T.A. Hoffmannesque figure, is a fanatic bird-feather collector, whose life revolves around his extensive assemblage of feathers. Consumed by the desire to preserve it intact but unable to obtain the requisite space in the postwar era, Bonus ultimately succeeds in housing his collection in its entirety, although the fragile feathers are already disintegrating. In "Templones Ende," the exclusive occupation of the protagonist is the study of outdated business reports in old newspapers; one day he is found dead under a pile of books and crumbling newspapers, suffocated by the dust — a fitting end to a life subsumed by events long past.

For Dorn, as for Bonus and Templone, the past is the exclusive focus of all interest and the central concern of life.[6] In Dorn's case, however, it is

[4]Cf. summarily Gabriele Schweikert, "'... weil das Selbstverständliche nie geschieht,' Martin Walsers frühe Prosa und ihre Beziehung zu Kafka," *Text + Kritik* 41/42 (1974): 31-37, and Pickar, "'Kalte Grotesken': Walser, Aichinger, and the Kafkan Legacy," *Crossings — Kreuzungen: A Festschrift for Helmut Kreuzer*, ed. Edward Haymes (Columbia, SC: Camden House, 1990) 115-43; furthermore, Frank Pilipp, "Zum letzten Mal Kafka? Martin Walsers Roman *Das Schwanenhaus* im ironischen Lichte der Verwandlung," *Colloquia Germanica* 22 (1989): 283-95.

[5]In another work of this collection, "Was wären wir ohne Belmonte" (What Would We Be without Belmonte), an all-consuming obsession with an unrealistic expectation (a career as concert pianist) leads the protagonists to endure a life of servility, which they accept while cherishing a very different dream. Incidentally, Dorn, too, had "fantasized a career as concert pianist" (VK 217), settling on law only because he believed himself not musically gifted enough to be a conductor and not strong-nerved enough to be a pianist (VK 58).

[6]All three — Bonus, Templone, and Dorn — are characterized by a single-minded pursuit, but the parallels between Bonus and Dorn are particularly striking. Like Dorn, Bonus lives as a bachelor and even in advanced years is described as having

his own individual past that becomes an all-consuming passion. Paralleling his increasing personal domination by his own past, Dorn consciously, and with ever increasing intensity, commits time and energy to his efforts to collect and preserve tangible evidence of that past. In fact, Dorn's adult life is dedicated to the relentless, even fanatic pursuit of his childhood and youth. His intent is less to relive those years than to secure that past; to serve the past by defending it against decay and destruction, and ultimately to protect it from obliteration and oblivion. Dorn is "insatiable when it came to the past"[7]; he "wanted to save what had been" (VK 13), "could not get enough of the past" (VK 14), and became agitated whenever he noticed that something of the past was threatened (VK 17).

Dorn's efforts are also directed less by the desire to learn more about his early years than to document his memory of them; to accumulate tangible evidence of their existence, particularly with regard to his role in them, and hence to re-create that past, at least for himself. Unlike Christa Wolf's fictive narrator-protagonist in *Kindheitsmuster* (1976; *A Model Childhood*, 1980) who returns as an adult to the scene of her childhood and in the process of remembering and relating experiences of her early years comes to a clearer understanding of herself, her past, and her present, Alfred Dorn stagnates,

a fleshy boy's face (the word *Jünglingsgesicht* is emphasized by repetition three times in the text). He, too, wages battle on the decay that attacked his collection of remnants of past life, fighting the inroads of mold, dust, and cobwebs, caring lovingly for these possessions, and attempting to resurrect their earlier luster. And like Dorn, he strives to make his collection complete. Furthermore both see their efforts as a preservation of "culture" and "traditional values," and both are inveterate letter writers, doggedly persistent, and successful in the pursuit of their objectives, which coincidentally involve acquiring more space during periods of housing shortage — in Dorn's case, a housing supplement, refugee status, and then the exit-permission for his mother requisite for obtaining the living space in the West he seeks.

[7]Specific words Walser employs, including *insatiable*, *indefatigable*, and *addicted*, are also reminiscent of Kafka's prose, as is the style of particular passages. Compare, for example, his professor's warning concerning Dorn's efforts to enter the legal profession: "when he considers that the second state examination is more difficult than the first and that afterwards there is the practice of the profession itself, then..." ["wenn er bedenke, daß die zweite Staatsprüfung schwerer sei als die erste und daß dann erst der Beruf komme, dann..."] (VK 145). Kafka, however, is not the only author evoked in this work so rich in literary reference and allusion. Of the others, Thomas Mann is by far the most prominent. Not only are he and his works discussed by the figures in the novel (one of Dorn's schoolmates, Detlev Krumpholz, even becomes a Mann specialist), but associations with Thomas Mann's fictive world permeate the text.

learning nothing from the past which he collects rather than investigates and never evaluates. Like Jurek Becker's Aron Blank in *Der Boxer* (1976; The Boxer) and Christoph Hein's first-person narrator in *Drachenblut* (1982; Dragonblood), Dorn remains a virtual prisoner of that past, entranced and encapsulated by it. His preoccupation with the past grows into an obsession, and as a consequence of his fanatic pursuit of the past, the potential for life and new experiences proffered by the present is forfeited. The significance of the present for Dorn lies solely in the opportunities it offers for protecting the past; the future, in turn, is seen exclusively as a threat both to the past and to the present as guardian of the past.

The tie to Kafka, tenuously drawn through the link to Walser's early works and furtively suggested through words and phrases reminiscent of Kafka, informs the entire novel. Not only does Dorn spend his last evening copying the signature of Kafka, but his own nature resembles a Kafkan protagonist. Cast in a world he finds alien, among colleagues and landladies he perceives as indifferent if not hostile to him and with whom he does not feel comfortable, Dorn seems constitutionally ill equipped to live in the present. He seems to move through the labyrinth of life, only half understanding the realities with which he is confronted yet doggedly pursuing his aims in the midst of partially imagined, partially real obstacles whose broader significance eludes him. His behavior, more than the course of his life itself, is affected by perceived but unverified suspicion of others, individuals whom he never seems able to fathom fully and whom he evidences no desire to understand. When he later becomes the victim of manipulative exploitation by a young man,[8] Dorn proves unable to cope with the phenomenon in any definitive manner. As with Kafka's figures, he is strangely incapable of dealing with the realities of his world and exhibits a blend of fascination with and aversion to sexual activity.

In the documentation of Dorn's existence, his tribulations and anxieties, Walser also rejects the highly subjective narrative style of his recent prose that features a point of view rigidly tied to the perceptions of the respective protagonist. He employs instead an impartial, descriptive mode reminiscent of Kafka, whose narrative style Walser had analyzed in his doctoral work, *Beschreibung einer Form* (1961; The Description of a Form), and adopted in his early prose. However, in a striking deviation from the early works — and Kafka — *Die Verteidigung der Kindheit* is also a meticulously detailed rendition of the real world. Not only is the setting historically and

[8]Richard Fasold, a con-artist and ne'er-do-well, holds a certain attraction for Alfred Dorn, an attraction he only partially recognizes. Fasold, a Felix Krull figure, who serves as a kind of Tadzio to Dorn's Aschenbach life, gains a hold over Dorn when he brings him a collection of pictures of old Dresden at a train station.

geographically accurate and rendered in great detail with undisguised care for accuracy, but the specifics of the protagonist and his life are drawn from an accumulation of actual documentation painstakingly amassed by an individual throughout a lifetime and made available to Walser. The dust jacket refers to the work as "historical writing of the everyday," noting "what is later called an epoch is at first just mundane everyday" and proclaiming that the novel tells of "the suffering and deeds of those, which historical writing ignores." In the midst of a compilation of detail and careful annotation of the inconsequential and the unnoteworthy, the protagonist, hardly noteworthy himself, lays claim to the status of an "everyman" by virtue of his utter lack of self-identity and self-awareness.

The novel thus presents the course of an ordinary life as registered by the individual himself with a narrative stance that avoids emotion or subjective hue and records the episodes and events of Dorn's life without illumination and with little or no commentary. Just as Dorn is able to achieve no distance from himself and the events of his life, so, too, the text only rarely provides insight and attempts no interpretation. It is a narrative mode appropriate for the depiction of the life of an individual who remains unaware of his own inner self; who is only subliminally aware of the shifting realities, familial and societal, about him; who reacts only when the changing reality impedes the execution of the routine he has established; and who expends his energies in the vain effort to create an island of stability, of resistance to the changes of the past and the attendant deterioration of the past.

While the novel covers Dorn's life after his move from the East — his study of law in West Berlin and his subsequent career in the West — the years prior to the novel's opening remain the focus of the narrative and of Dorn's adult life, for it is this period, particularly his early years, that preoccupy Dorn and are the target of his efforts in the novel's fictive present. They appear to have been happy years for him, although it should be noted that the reader has no access to that period except as it is recalled and re-created by Dorn himself.[9] Young Alfred apparently enjoyed the loving attention of his parents, and even though their views about his upbringing were often in conflict, he in turn gave every evidence of being excep-

[9]Not only are the informants whom Dorn ferrets out, contacts, and on occasion interviews selected by him, but the information they provide is also subject to the filter of his subjectivity and personal bias. As a result, the reader is presented only Dorn's view of his past, a feature easily overlooked in a work whose narrative stance is designed to imply objective reportage.

tional:[10] "He had been a successful child. Even a child prodigy" (VK 103). His talented piano playing, ability to compose, and skill at improvising, combined with the loving care and attention with which he was dressed, recall an earlier literary *Wunderkind*, Thomas Mann's Bibi Saccellaphylaccas ("The Infant Prodigy," 1914). Every opportunity was apparently lavished upon Alfred then and throughout his adolescence. Not only was he given private music lessons, but when he showed interest and skill in drawing, he was given instructions by a graphic artist (VK 20).[11] Dorn cherishes these early years and sees them as a lost Eden, even with regard to the relationship between his parents. His view is affirmed by a photograph he later receives depicting his mother, with laughing eyes, on a swing. His father is standing behind her, and both parents appear to him as beautiful and perfect as silent-movie stars. Even the setting, with flowering cherry-tree boughs and a forest indicated in the background, seems to corroborate a paradisiacal atmosphere.[12] These years came to an abrupt end when, in the course of one night, Alfred Dorn lost not only his maternal grandparents but all documentation of his early years, the latter being by far the greater loss for him. With these events, so traumatic for Dorn, his childhood suddenly ended, and Dorn never fully recovers. A fear of loss continues to haunt him — in trivial matters, such as a missing fountain-pen case or a lost plastic spoon, as well as those of cultural and historic significance, such as a Baroque church falling into ruin. Every loss "hit immediately at the very core of his being" (VK 78), and, he concludes, no loss was "as intense as the loss of the past" (VK 84-85).

[10]While both parents are presented as glorying in the accomplishments of their young child, there is a marked change in the father's stance, as evidenced by his denunciation of the mother's treatment of their son and repeated articulation of the dire consequences of that upbringing.

[11]There are other examples, as well. Thus, when as a school boy Alfred is embarrassed to shower with the others after gym class and wishes to avoid the embarrassment of uncontrolled erections, his mother swiftly arranges for him to have private orthopedic classes at the home of a woman instructor (VK 505). Dorn also receives a private tutor throughout his law studies.

[12]Ironically, this picture also spurs his realization that, until the birth of their children (particularly his own, following upon the death of his sister), the marriage of his parents had been a truly happy one. The thought that he had been the wedge between them appears as a new insight for the adult Dorn; yet it alerts the reader to the possibility of an earlier, subconscious perception that he was to blame for the end of their union, which, in turn, might have led to feelings of guilt and inadequacy.

The fire-bombing of Dresden destroyed not only much of the city but also the home he had known. In its aftermath, the conflicts over his upbringing deepened, and his parents separated. Nothing remained of the life that had been his, and Alfred himself appears unable to secure closure on this loss. In his own eyes he is marked for life by the destruction experienced that night, and he subsequently seems unable, or at least unwilling, to proceed into a life different and apart from the one he had known. The bond to his mother continues to be that of a young child and does not change with the passing years; he remains till death his mother's loyal and devoted son.[13] Concomitantly, his outward appearance, despite subsequent and progressive signs of deterioration which Dorn observes with alarm, remains boyish;[14] even his sexual nature remains pubescent. In fact, in many ways Dorn's later life gives evidence of an arrested development.[15]

The admission Dorn articulates in a rare and fleeting moment of self-recognition — "The first impression was always the most important for him" — followed by the confession that he could never free himself from the beginning ["Er kam vom Anfang nicht los"] (VK 15) proves to be an apt

[13]The bond is one recognized in death as well. Dr. de Bonnechose, Dorn's associate and friend, requests that the coffin be reopened to allow the cast of Martha Dorn's hands to be laid on her son's chest.

[14]Colleagues routinely assume Dorn to be much younger than his years; in law school he is given as nickname the diminutive "Dörnchen" [little thorn] and is teased about his soft and high voice (VK 82, 93). Only a classmate's wife speaks appreciatively of his possessing "eternal youth" (VK 102). Dorn retains his youthful appearance until death, though as with Detlev Spinell in *Tristan* (1902; 1930), Dorn has not only poor teeth — the sign of artistic inclination (Mann) or impotence — but also problems with thinning hair and warts. Spinell, for whom Mann coined the epithet "decayed infant" ["verwester Säugling"] as the nickname given him by another patient at the sanatorium "Einfried," and who possesses a "round, white, slightly bloated face that showed no sign of any facial hair" and "soft, blurred and boyish features" (Th. Mann, *Der Tod in Venedig und andere Erzählungen* [Frankfurt/M.: Fischer, 1977] 74), is a literary predecessor for Walser's Dorn.

[15]Although not a consciously willed decision, as was Oskar Matzerath's retention of his three-year-old body-size to avoid the expectations of adulthood in *The Tin Drum*, Alfred Dorn's reluctance to leave the state of childhood and his resistance to all efforts to "make a man of him" appear to have subsequently stultified his emotional growth. Other aspects of his life further indicate his continuing immaturity, such as his self-centeredness and lack of fiscal responsibility. Most telling is Dorn's wish "that his room had been much darker, then he would have dared to do what he never would have dared as long as could see himself: to sit down in the corner and suck his thumb" (VK 240).

description of his entire life. Thus, although the novel begins as the young Alfred Dorn leaves the GDR to take up his legal studies in West Berlin and hence to begin a life away from and independent of home and mother, he never really severs his tie with the past — or with his mother — but remains in steadfast and committed service to both. His father's often voiced anxiety about the nature of his wife's influence on their son and his continuing concern regarding Alfred's immaturity and possible lack of the requisite fortitude for academic success provide the note on which the story of Alfred Dorn's life begins. Waiting at the train station[16] with his estranged wife, Gustav Dorn warns: "Don't keep the boy from his work" (VK 9). His exhortation — the opening words of the novel — is validated by subsequent events. Dorn's frequent trips back to Dresden; his pursuit of photos, letters, clothes, and furniture corroborating his childhood years; and his obsession with moving mother and possessions into the West consume his time and energy. Just as these activities and his continuing immersion in them effectively jettison his plans to earn a doctorate in jurisprudence, they subsequently adversely affect evaluations of his job performance and thwart his chances for professional advancement.

Equally significant for the course of Alfred's years in the West is the letter from the elder Dorn which Alfred takes with him, the New Year's letter written after Alfred's failure to pass the examination for law school.[17] The message is unequivocal — the responsibility and the guilt for failing not only the first exam in Leipzig but also the makeup are Alfred's alone — and the cause for what can only be called a fiasco is Alfred's failure to heed his father's warnings and to change accordingly. These warnings can be reduced to a single prognosis: "Your softness will always keep you from succeeding" (VK 10). Alfred's efforts to defend himself from the thrust of this charge by recalling that Friedrich the Great's father had also called his son "an ef-

[16]The significance of the setting of the opening scene is not to be overlooked, since Dorn is always in transit — both physically and emotionally shuttling between Dresden and Berlin, between East and West, between mother and school or job, between the past and the present — and never comes to the end of his journeying.

[17]Gustav Dorn fails to take into consideration the political basis for the negative evaluation of Alfred's efforts. He did well in both the civil and criminal law parts of the examination but failed "to demonstrate the proper political consciousness" in the third part of the exam, that dealing with the official party line. Furthermore, there is indication that young Dorn was stigmatized by the fact that his father, a dentist, was a professional (VK 57).

feminate chap" provide but small comfort, and Alfred finds himself congenitally "unable to come to terms with the letter" (VK 11).[18]

By assuming the role of the "prophet of doom," Gustav Dorn, at least in Alfred's eyes, has a debilitating effect on him. It is a role which Alfred recognizes with more clarity than the presumably supportive role of his mother. Thus, he acknowledges the impact of his father's words and draws from them a rationalization for his own ineffectualness: "Alfred had no protection against prophecies. Prophecies lamed him. For him, prophesying something evoked its reality" ["Ihm etwas prophezeien hieß, es herbeireden"] (VK 11). Returning to his rooms at the close of a day, Alfred takes stock and determines once again that he has been found wanting: "he had not been able to assert himself." Placing himself squarely in front of the mirror, he recites his father's verdict: "That's how someone looks who's gone astray" (VK 77).[19] He knows that every day will bring new failure, new embarrassment, and he finds nothing easier than the listing of his inadequacies. In the world he enters, Dorn, like his fictional predecessors in Walser's works, finds himself unable to meet the demands of life — or even the expectations of others, whether articulated by his father, whose favorite word was *mastery*,[20] his professors, or his colleagues. Ultimately, Dorn concludes in words that echo the fears of his father: "Someday he would document himself as someone who could not hold his own" (VK 516). In Dorn's view, the secret of maturity is "becoming accustomed to being a failure" (VK 212), and this, too, is a factor which contributes to his reluctance to grow up. His fear of adulthood reverberates in his reference to it as the "worst of all choices" ["der falscheste aller Dampfer"] (VK 145), and, in response to his father's often reiterated exhortation, "Become a man," Dorn on one occasion asks himself: "After all ... why did everyone have to become a man?" (VK 90).

[18]The repeated charge of softness by his father (who views it not as an inherent characteristic but rather as attributable to Alfred's rearing) with its covert implications of effeminacy heralds Dorn's recurrent concern with possible homosexuality, a concern he is never able to lay to rest.

[19]The German idiom *unter die Räder kommen* used in the original text — "So sieht einer aus, der unter die Räder kommt" (VK 77) — is not only destructive and more violent in its imagery but also more decisive and irreversible than the English phrases *to lose one's way* or *to go astray*.

[20]The term Walser attributes to the father is *meistern*, "mastering" or "gaining mastery of something," but in its connotation of "successful exertion of effort undertaken to gain control" the one-word motto acquires the emphasis of an imperative.

Equally affecting his life is the strained relationship and power struggle between his estranged parents in which he is clearly a pawn. His own position in their continuing strife and his loyalty are never in question — he is unconditionally his mother's son. Already in the opening scene, the lines are sharply drawn:

> Alfred was allowed to show neither his father nor his mother that he was pleased by his father's presence at the farewell. Perhaps he was even a bit sorry that he had to treat his father as his mother treated him. She always noticed even the slightest deviation and was then immediately so miserable that it was unbearable. (VK 9)

Alfred understands that the satisfaction his mother derives from Gustav Dorn's appearing at the train station is predicated upon the latter sensing "that he could expect nothing but contempt from both wife and son" (VK 9). By extrapolation, even the success his father seeks for him translates in Alfred's thinking as a form of betrayal of his mother, and he is determined to protect her from any defeat, particularly at the hands of her despised husband. Alfred's perhaps unconscious incorporation of this equation as a guiding principle in his behavior has further consequences for his life as well, as he tries to please his mother and achieve the recognition she desires for him without granting his father the success he demands.[21]

Without question the most important person in Alfred's life is his mother. The constancy in his relationship to her, his mother-fixation, which Walser prefers to call "a great love," "a love rich in strife and comedy, sorrow and

[21]Although Dorn himself remains oblivious to it, he also seeks and desires his father's approval — and love. Despite his mother's wishes, he maintains contact with his father, sends birthday packages, and after his mother's death even considers someday erecting a monument to his father as well. In a sense he is caught in a double bind, for he believes his father's negative judgments — assessments that gain in reality through his father's articulation of them — yet he also wishes to prove him wrong and so gain his father's approval. Perhaps as a result of such preconditioning, Dorn suffers from a negative self-image and even takes comfort in his failures — "Always when his misfortune took a specific, concrete form, he had a sense of satisfaction. Perhaps it was a form of his know-it-all attitude" ["eine Art innerster Rechthaberei"] (VK 224). In any case, it is a satisfaction born of self-fulfilling prophecy. It is also this certainty of failure that underlies his interest in studying the history of Saxony — "Reading Saxon history meant being prepared that it would not end well" (VK 224), Dorn affirms.

tragedy," is never in doubt.[22] A colleague in law school, accompanying Alfred with his mother, recalls a Jewish saying he had learned from a New York cousin: "When a young man marries, he divorces his mother. And some just don't like divorce" (VK 181).[23] His comment, at which neither Alfred nor his mother take offense, serves the reader as a covert confirmation of Gustav Dorn's fear and repeated charge that Alfred is a "mother's boy." For Alfred, Martha Dorn is his refuge, his support, his anchor in life, but, as the reader learns, she is also a regressive force in his life, a force that draws him back to his past, to his childhood, to her realm of influence and domination.[24] Alfred, unlike earlier Walser protagonists, is aware of the strong bond he has with his mother and recognizes the influence she exerts upon him, an influence he neither resents nor resists. Dorn is constantly aware of her desires, her aspirations for him, and her position on all topics, and her wishes remain a dominant factor throughout his life.[25] Indeed, even in the last months of his life Dorn defends his filial devotion, telling an old schoolmate: "It is impossible to honor a mother too much." Continuing, he confesses: "One cannot be against one's mother. To be against one's father is easy. But one cannot be against one's mother. That is the curse" (VK

[22]The citations are from Walser's comments printed on the inside cover of the prepublication reading copy of the novel.

[23]That Dorn himself on occasion sees their relationship as comparable to a romantic liaison is indicated, for example, in conversation with his colleague. Wishing to spend alone with his mother the evening after passing the legal examination, he discloses that it was his mother to whom he had written so mysteriously and suggestively on an earlier occasion. Later, when he seeks living space for himself and his mother, he applies for the housing supplement for *married* couples. Although the application was justified and, indeed, granted, Dorn appears not to notice the irony of the title in his case.

[24]Cf., for example, Dorn's remark: "Only with her was there a *place to stay*. *His* place to stay. *She* was his place to stay" (VK 166; emphasis added) ["Nur bei ihr war eine Bleibe. Seine Bleibe. Sie war seine Bleibe"]. The central concept, *Bleibe*, which literally means place to stay, projects a feeling of warmth and security, the idea of a safe harbor; yet it is linguistically related to the word *bleiben* [to stay] and as such is an antithesis to change, growth. A later passage, in which Dorn reiterates his preference for "staying" versus "progress" or "development," indicates the importance he attributes to a state of no change (VK 230).

[25]Not only is it Martha Dorn who determines the adversarial relationship to the father, highlighted already on the opening page of the novel, but as the novel records the progress of Alfred Dorn's life the reader learns of the taboos she had placed on sexual intimacy, masturbation (VK 174-78), his potential homosexual inclinations, and psychiatric care.

511). Later that night in the hotel room, he reviews his thoughts about his mother-relationship, perhaps for the first time in his life, certainly the first time in the novel:

> No one had ever been able to tell him, why he should have broken the bond with the one person who always and totally had only his best interests at heart, just to be able to bond with other people, who could have his best interests at heart only to the degree that their own personal self-interest allowed. Only in the case of his mother did he know that her interests and his interests were not only the same, but truly identical. (VK 509)

Perhaps as an extension of his efforts to please his mother, Dorn, like Walser's traditional protagonists, is other-directed (to use a term of David Riesman), driven by an assumed need to please, to accommodate, to fit in.[26] Consequently, he faces life and the future with fear and apprehension: "Every day he came into new situations, in which he did not know how he was supposed to act" (VK 87). Considering the purchase of a silk tie on one occasion, Dorn attempts to clarify his stance: "He did not want to be conspicuous. He only wanted to be elegant. For his own sake. Others should not find anything to be critical of" (VK 146). Dorn himself is apparently oblivious to the contradiction inherent in his position in the juxtaposition of "his own sake" and the desire to avoid the criticism of "others." Significantly, in reiterating his stance, Dorn alters the verb: "He only wanted *to appear* elegant, no more than that" (VK 146).[27] The perhaps unconscious shift from "being" to "appearing" not only accentuates the importance of appearance over reality in his thinking but also implies a discrepancy between them.

[26]Cf. Pickar, "Martin Walser: The Hero of Accommodation," *Monatshefte* 62 (1970): 357-66. It is ironic that his one success, passing the exam in West Berlin, is in fact attributable to this ability to accommodate. As one of the professors notes, it was most remarkable how quickly Dorn was able to fall into the mind-set of the tester (VK 180). Some aspects of Dorn's behavior also bear remarkable similarities to David Riesman's description of the anomic person — "a characterological nonconformist who is frequently neurotic, but … may outwardly conform most of the time, while paying so high a price for this behavioral conformity as to develop psychosomatic symptoms"; *The Lonely Crowd* (New Haven: Yale UP, 1950) 288.

[27]Emphasis added; the word in the original text, *fein*, also carries the connotations of "immaculate" and "beyond reproach," both of which have further significance for Dorn in terms of the appearance he seeks to achieve.

Dorn's emphasis on externals extends beyond dress alone and is applicable to his life as a whole, for he consistently appears to be concerned less with who he is, what he does, and how he conducts himself than with how he and his actions are perceived. His behavior is determined by its probable impact on others; his efforts are directed at becoming the person others see, the person he is viewed and assumed to be. Again and again he seeks if not approval then at least sanction for his behavior. On one occasion, for example, Dorn, after dining, asks the waiter whether it would annoy anyone if he sat a little longer to jot down a few notes. When the waiter answers in the affirmative, Dorn leaves immediately — indicating his displeasure by not leaving a tip. Yet, in assessing the incident, he sees himself as the loser. His conclusion that "this waiter, too, would flunk him" is cast in school vernacular, for, as he himself notes, he finds it easiest to describe the behavior of others toward him in such terms (VK 87) — terms that harken back to a time in his adolescence when he was clearly dominated by authority figures.

Caught between feelings of rejection (his earlier assessment, "He felt himself held in contempt" [VK 80], seems to have continuing validity) and the need to accommodate, Dorn sees only one solution: "To forgive everybody everything. Otherwise you just won't make it" (VK 145). Consequently, any social interaction or association with others is painful and burdensome. "A social affair is torture," Dorn confesses: "One says what the others want to hear. Pain occurs not from twisting one's limbs, but through twisting truth" (VK 512). As a result of his social ineptness and his fear of embarrassment, Dorn seeks to avoid social situations and to remain as inconspicuous as possible. Yet he continues to seek social approbation, and here, too, his childhood provides a continuing reference point — "he wanted to be able to make a good impression, like before, when he was a child" (VK 96).

Dorn's view that normalcy was "living between two impossibilities" (VK 73), that decisions meant choosing between two "equally impossible" alternatives (VK 229) explains, in part, his escapism — not only into the past, into the childhood he attempts to defend against the inroads of time and adulthood but also into the fictive reality of cinema, into the subjective world of music, and into the oblivion of migraines. Dorn is a habitual moviegoer, even though he recognizes that he, so critically short of both time and money, can ill afford to indulge this habit. Music, which is as much a total experience for him as for his predecessor Gottlieb Zürn, provides another escape, this time into another identity — "As long as he listened he was as great and powerful and fervent as the music itself." Yet here, too, his relief is not unmarred, for "even as he listened, he regretted that afterwards he would no longer be the person he was as long as he was listening" (VK 85).

With the passage of time, Dorn turns to yet another means, the barbiturates on which he becomes increasingly dependent to induce the sleep he desires and to fight the insomnia with which he is plagued, and to bring him relief from the daily existence he so abhors and from the problems he is so ill equipped to confront, let alone resolve.

In any comparison with the present, the past for Dorn is always more attractive. It is this realm that provides him the most dependable and continuing outlet for avoiding the present, even approximating an alternative existence. It is no wonder that he once describes himself as "a bungled ancestral portrait" (VK 113) and feels so clearly out of kilter with the present. Appropriately, Dorn's professional life is also focused on a "production of the past" (VK 324). After serving the necessary internships in various courts in Berlin, he finds a position first in a private law firm that specializes in restitution cases; then, when his work fails to meet the standards of his superiors, he secures employment as a civil servant charged with researching and documenting claims for restitution, work which appropriately involved the attempt to reestablish the claims of the past in the present. Subsequently, he moves to the Ministry of Culture in Wiesbaden, with responsibilities for theater, legal affairs, and later the preservation of historical monuments, where his efforts are often inhibited by the general climate of lethargy towards such artifacts in a society in which social and economic rather than aesthetic concerns are dominant. Ironically, it is a position he eventually loses to a new, more favored colleague when, in time, concern with preserving the past becomes the fashion of the day (VK 488).

In Dorn's eyes, the present represents both a threat to the treasures of the past — whether a Baroque church, a historical monument, or a park bench he remembers from his boyhood — and a force that seeks to propel him out of his personal past. For him, life is "a conglomerate of tasks for which he was not suited," and the future nothing but a continuation and intensification of the present heightened to a degree that is insufferable ["ins Unerträglich gesteigerte Fortsetzung"] (VK 198). He associates the future as well with further advances in decay, repeatedly registered in his "hair and teeth, skin and bones" and observed with attentiveness and ever greater fear.[28]

Despite his other-directed nature and his preoccupation with the perceptions others have of him, Dorn, in his essence, is remarkably impervious to the world about him. As a result, he exhibits a strange ignorance of the realities even of his own life. He appears insensitive to the extent of the personal and financial sacrifices his mother (in her role as enabler) makes

[28]Even with regard to his habitual concern with his body an association is drawn to his mother, for, as Dorn notes, he has inherited his troublesome physical attributes not from his father but from his mother.

that allow him to live a sheltered life far from the grim economic reality of their situation. His obliviousness extends beyond the personal sphere, encompassing external realities as well; he barely registers even significant events of public and international import and appears either uninterested in or unaware of the social and political ramifications of historical events occurring about him. They have significance for him only to the degree that they constitute obstacles or inconveniences for his own personal program, such as interfering with his travel plans or those of his mother or destroying pastry sent through the mail. Within the more immediate sphere, Dorn's skewed perspective is evidenced by his inability to determine "whether that which was being said at any given moment was essential or unessential" (VK 81), a weakness which also reflects a general inability on his part to differentiate or evaluate, to ascertain the relevance or intrinsic worth of any particular statement or item. Subsequently, a proliferation of detail and a preoccupation with the everyday, the mundane, characterize his life and, appropriately, dominate the novel.

In his frenetic attempts to document his past and hence to verify his existence, Dorn remains oblivious to the concomitant loss of self — a loss indicated by confessional statements whose significance and validity he seems not to grasp: "He never had written anything, had always just made notes." Even when he begins to collect sentences from the past, "he never recorded what he himself had said" (VK 13). Apparently his memory only retains what others said, he concludes. Although he is painfully aware of his external appearance and concerned with skin blemishes and other physical abnormalities, Dorn appears to have little interest in the internal realities of his being. Moments of insight, such as those concerning his pedantic love of detail and of preparation (VK 217) or his tendency to flee from the tasks he set himself (VK 227), are transitory and without effect, as is the recurrent fear that the extensive preparations he habitually undertakes before beginning any project might be only a form of self-inhibition (VK 516). Indeed, perhaps as a consequence of Dorn's focus on the external and the total neglect of the internal, a vacuity of self evolves. With the passage of time all traces of self seem to evaporate, leaving nothing but the shell of a man who nevertheless seeks to function, albeit clumsily, in the world about him. To the outside world Dorn, with the passage of years, becomes increasingly "a comical figure, an eccentric."[29]

Dorn's resolve to collect and preserve everything and anything that can evidence his personal past, which itself is buttressed by his mother-fixation, is intensified by the death of his mother. Yet with this loss, the task itself

[29]Walser's prepublication description of his protagonist also evokes that earlier literary *Sonderling* — the stylishly dressed but highly eccentric Detlev Spinell.

becomes immeasurably more difficult: "His mother had been the treasure chest of his past. The death of his mother made his past into an unattainable continent" (VK 337). On the other hand, his life, structured and partially — though only superficially — filled first by his efforts to gain a law degree and then by his professional duties as a lawyer, is infused with new purpose and almost revitalized by a burst of renewed activity provided by his determination to create a memorial suitable for the memory of his mother, a monument that would likewise serve as a testimonial of their mutual bond of love. With Richard Wagner's grave at the villa Wahnfried[30] as his model — and with the help of a landscape architect and an internationally acclaimed sculptor — Dorn actually achieves his goal: a large, striking, and expensive marble tombstone, complete with an inset bronze lamb, is erected in Berlin's prestigious cemetery, Waldfriedhof. The word *Mother* is hewn into the stone.

The monument proves, however, to be the only project that Dorn succeeds in executing. His life-long dream of establishing his own "Alfred Dorn Museum," a Pergamon Altar[31] dedicated to himself and his personal history, remains unrealized; his plan to author a definitive work on Count Brühl[32] never takes concrete form; and even his less-defined intent to commit his own life to paper proves ephemeral. Ultimately, all of Dorn's endeavors to defend and memorialize his lost childhood in the shifting realities of his day,

[30]The name literally means "freedom *from* insanity or delusion," as well as the "freedom *of* delusion."

[31]The Pergamon Altar, a 120-meter-long relief frieze from the second century B.C. and one of the Seven Wonders of the Ancient World, was erected by Eumenes II of Pergamon to celebrate a victory and portrays the battle of the Titans with the gods. Uncovered by German excavations in the late nineteenth century, it was put on display in Berlin in 1930 in the Pergamon Museum. (It was removed by the Russian forces during the war and displayed in Moscow from 1945 to 1958, when it was returned to East Berlin.) Dorn reasons that if the Pergamon Altar could be reconstructed after two thousand years, it should certainly be possible to reconstruct one's own childhood (VK 263).

[32]Dorn's fascination with Count Brühl, who was the prime minister of August II, the Strong, and his son, August III, began with an anecdote he had heard as a boy concerning an incident between the count and his tailor. He was particularly taken with the fate of the tailor and with the Meißen porcelain that depicted him riding a goat. Dorn was intent upon completing his project that would depict the fall of an individual whose aspirations exceeded his position or potential. It was a theme which he saw as typically Saxon and one with which he also identified. Dorn, in his interest in the themes of hubris and failure connected with these figures, also associates them with Greek mythology and the fate of Bellerophon and his steed Pegasus (cf. VK 212-15).

thereby to verify and confirm his existence through documentation, are shown to be as futile as the efforts of Max Frisch's protagonist in *Der Mensch erscheint im Holozän* (1979; *Man in the Holocene*, 1980) to stave off the onslaught of senility and to preserve the crumbling walls of his consciousness by surrounding himself with fragments of his accumulated knowledge on scraps of paper attached to the walls of his house. The dispassionate, often convoluted narrative of Dorn's life not only reveals the futility of his efforts to defend and memorialize his lost childhood but also brings into question the whole and hallowed world of his childhood itself. Recently acquired pictures from his childhood provide the impetus for both Dorn's reexamination of his image of himself as child and his reevaluation of the past he cherishes. Snapshots depicting him staring out aggressively from his position between his parents contrast sharply with the idyllic image of his parents as a young couple. Suddenly Dorn is confronted with the disruptive role he had played in their relationship, a role which troubles him and signals the precarious nature of the premises underlying his endeavors.

In the pictures that Dorn now studies with a more critical and perhaps more discerning eye, a different and disturbing image of him as a child begins to emerge; he appears grotesque, self-conscious, and self-righteous. It is an unattractive image, one to which he applies the description "Napoleon as a turtle," and, more significantly, it contradicts his interpretation of his favorite picture. That earlier snapshot, so central to his image of his childhood, was taken during a vacation with his mother and shows young Alfred with a group of other guests at a small resort hotel. His right knee is bent; his left leg, jauntily raised, hovers above the ground, as if he wanted "to hover" like the fresco figures in the Sistine Chapel.[33] Dorn for years took inordinate pleasure in that boyish stance, but now a gnawing suspicion that perhaps he has been misreading his role as a child challenges the premises of his self-assumed mission in life, threatening the very foundation of his existence. As if in concert with this attack on his perception of the past, the bronze lamb inset in his mother's marble monument — the lamb with which Dorn identifies and through which he seeks to make his identity eternal — falls victim to vandals.[34] The lamb is stolen from the memorial,

[33]The work is rife with references to art that deserve critical attention. Of special interest here are Dorn's childhood fascination with Raphael's *Madonna and Child* and subsequently his projected duplication of the Sistine Chapel depicting his mother and himself (VK 138-39).

[34]The vandals who defaced the memorial represent antisocial elements and products of the novel's fictive present, not unlike Richard Fasold, the young man who so blatantly and ruthlessly exploits Dorn.

leaving but three holes where it had stood with its playful stance, a stance that mimicked his own in that childhood photograph. Dorn the son, Dorn the secure and eager child, has been effaced; only the memorial to his mother remains.

A further blow to Dorn and his all-consuming preoccupation with documenting the past occurs in conjunction with his class reunion. Like Helmut Halm in *Runaway Horse*, Dorn is amazed at how much more others remember: "On that evening he had heard more about the earlier years than on any other evening ever, but it left him with nothing but a sense of poverty and loss. Everybody knew more about before than he" (VK 507). With this final recognition his ability to fulfill his life's project becomes suspect and his life robbed of purpose. Returning from the reunion, which proves to be his last trip to the East, Dorn is overwhelmed by feelings of desolation and isolation, feelings that culminate in a sense of futility that encompasses even his own time-consuming efforts at preserving the past. His diligence and conscientiousness in writing letters, sending packages, and pulling together fragments of the past suddenly appear ridiculous to him (VK 512). It is a realization that calls into question Dorn's entire being. Without the mission to validate his life and provide a means of blocking out the struggles and unpleasantness of the present, the burden of living and coping with everyday matters becomes nigh intolerable, and Dorn becomes increasingly reliant on barbiturates.

As if paralleling the collapse of his self-assumed life's mission, the present he sought to deny and the body he had in recent years increasingly abused take their revenge. Dorn, so fastidiously concerned with maintaining an immaculate external appearance, watches through the years with growing concern the recurrence of warts, moles, and dandruff, indications that his body was rebelling. Death, apparently from an excessive dose of sleeping pills, brings final peace to Dorn, who once noted: "One did not ask to be born, comes into the world and has to suffer one abomination after another" (VK 80). When authorities, reluctantly and belatedly reacting to the concern of his aunt, break into the apartment, they discover his body on the living room floor. Dorn is lying bent, in a fetal position — "as if he had sought to give himself an embryonic shape" (VK 518) — in the dark, oval medallion of the Persian carpet, as if resting in its womblike center.

Investigation of the scene reveals Dorn's activities on the final evening of his life. He had made his habitual phone calls at day's end — his way of confirming his existence and reestablishing his identity through conversation with others. Sheaves of papers indicate that Dorn, who always "found the signatures of others more interesting, more worthy of being written, than his own" (VK 516),[35] spent his last evening practicing the signature of Kafka he had seen that very day on a publisher's flyer, thus reiterating and bringing to the fore the tie to Kafka so subtly interwoven throughout the novel. Later he had been reading the biography of Kaspar Hauser, perhaps because he was drawn to this historic and literary figure who had felt uncomfortable and out of place in a world in which he had not grown up — an individual ultimately unable to survive in a world for which his childhood had not prepared him. Dorn's colleague Dr. de Bonnechose makes particular note of the word *Jünglingskind*[36] on the open page of the biography, apparently finding the description appropriate to Dorn himself. Later, describing to his wife Dorn's position on the floor, Bonnechose draws a further comparison to Hodler's paintings of youths (VK 518),[37] emphasizing the youthful appearance of Dorn even in death.

Although his colleagues are amazed that Dorn, a lawyer, had made no provision for the rooms of memorabilia he had collected and preserved so painstakingly and at such personal cost in money and time — he had in fact died intestate — the reader is not surprised. For Dorn, who considered the past "the most important dimension of time" and for whom the present existed only to the extent it could serve to document the past or be itself subsequently documented, the future held no reality of its own. Those who knew Dorn better, however, did know where he would have wished to be buried: in Berlin, "in the grave, where the lamb was missing" (VK 520). With these words that evoke one last time the remarkable bond of love between mother and son which had marked his life, the novel that records the life and death, the sufferings and the passion of Alfred Dorn closes.

Yet even from the grave, as it were, Alfred Dorn reaches out into the present, for Walser allows Dorn himself to foreshadow the publication of a

[35]As a boy Dorn had also copied signatures of his schoolmates' fathers on grade reports. Another reference to Kafka may be given in Dorn's lesions in his groin reminiscent of the patient's strange, undefined sore in Kafka's "A Country Doctor." Other passages also evoke comparison with other stories of Kafka, including "A Hunger Artist."

[36]*Jünglingskind*, or youth-child, was the term Anselm Feuerbach had used to describe Hauser (VK 518), whose strange fate was the subject of Jakob Wassermann's popular novel *Kaspar Hauser* (1922). A number of books about Hauser also appeared in the 1950s and 1960s.

[37]Ferdinand Hodler (1853-1918), a Swiss painter and lithographer, was not only a forerunner of the Expressionists but also, as a young man, an acknowledged art nouveau or *J..gendstil* artist, which provides the context for the comment of Dorn's colleague.

work that would document his life, allowing a final, cautiously articulated expectation of his protagonist to be realized after the fact. The act is appropriately heralded in the image of Dorn's body, described as reaching out from the beyond with an arm, clasping a book — "the book lay open, by the hand from which it had slipped" (VK 518). The key, however, lies earlier in the novel. Gustav Dorn, who was a witness to Dorn's mania for documenting his past, assumes the underlying purpose for his son's activity to be a book, in which he, the father, would not cut a particularly good figure. Dorn, in an effort to reassure his father, explains that it is the preservation itself that interests him; significantly, however, he also adds that "sometimes despite all odds he had the feeling that someday everything that he preserved would be published. For that reason he treated all his documentation of the past as sacred objects" (VK 366).

With *Die Verteidigung der Kindheit* Walser as author thus accomplishes for Dorn what Dorn as protagonist fails to do; he creates a testimony to the life of Alfred Dorn[38] — and ultimately grants him the immortality he sought.

[38]For further discussion of what motivated Walser to undertake this project see the following essay by Heike Doane.

Works Cited

Doane, Heike. *Gesellschaftspolitische Aspekte in Martin Walsers Kristlein-Trilogie*. Bonn: Bouvier, 1978.

Mann, Thomas. *Der Tod in Venedig und andere Erzählungen*. Frankfurt/M.: Fischer, 1977.

Nägele, Rainer. "Zwischen Erinnerung und Erwartung: Gesellschaftskritik und Utopie in Martin Walsers *Einhorn*." *Martin Walser*. Ed. Klaus Siblewski. Frankfurt/M.: Suhrkamp, 1981. 114-31.

Pickar, Gertrud B. "'Kalte Grotesken': Walser, Aichinger, and the Kafkan Legacy." *Crossings — Kreuzungen: A Festschrift for Helmut Kreuzer*. Ed. Edward Haymes. Studies in German Literature, Linguistics, and Culture 43. Columbia, SC: Camden House, 1990. 115-43.

——. "Martin Walser: The Hero of Accommodation." *Monatshefte* 62 (1970): 357-66.

——. "*Woyzeck* and *Hamlet* Recast: a study of two of Martin Walser's dramas." *University of Dayton Review* 7 (1971): 61-68.

Pilipp, Frank. "Zum letzten Mal Kafka? Martin Walsers Roman *Das Schwanenhaus* im ironischen Lichte der *Verwandlung*." *Colloquia Germanica* 22 (1989): 283-95.

Riesman, David. *The Lonely Crowd*. New Haven: Yale UP, 1950.

Schweickert, Gabriele. "'... weil das Selbstverständliche nie geschieht.' Martin Walsers frühe Prosa und ihre Beziehung zu Kafka." *Text + Kritik* 41/42 (1974): 31-37.

11

The Cultivation of Personal and Political Loss: *Die Verteidigung der Kindheit*

Heike A. Doane

ALFRED DORN, THE PROTAGONIST in *Die Verteidigung der Kindheit* (1991; In Defense of Childhood) is related to the clan of his literary predecessors in some respects: he determines the narrative perspective of the novel to a large extent,[1] and his development is portrayed as a conflict between self-perception and possibilities for self-realization. But he differs from them significantly in a number of ways. In contrast to the Zürns, Horns, and Halms, Alfred likes to talk, and, though a member of the lower middle class, he has a strong, albeit childlike, self-esteem. However, what distinguishes him most from other Walser heroes is that he has a real-life prototype.[2] Alfred is a fictionalization of reality in the truest and strictest sense of the word. It is obvious why Walser was prompted to let Alfred develop as a literary counterpart from the papers of a dead man: the sense of loss as a dominant feeling of life, documented in such detail in these papers, is akin to the perception of inadequacy that is the defining impulse for all of Walser's writing.[3] When this sense of loss drives Alfred to rescue his past from oblivion, he compensates for a reality that he perceives as flawed, just as Walser does when he writes.

Of course, this process occurs on different planes for the author and his character: the Walserian perception of inadequacy finds expression in a

[1]Walser expands the narrative perspective at crucial points by granting the narrator virtual omniscience.

[2]The author's source of inspiration was a collection of old letters and documents brought to him in 1988.

[3]"Wer ist ein Schriftsteller?," *Wer ist ein Schriftsteller? Aufsätze und Reden* (Frankfurt/M.: Suhrkamp, 1979) 36-45.

literary response to the irreconcilable discrepancy between expectation and experience. Alfred, on the other hand, believes that the losses he has suffered diminish a once-intact collection of emotional and material property and that he must do everything he can to stop this process. He ignores the passage of time in order to retrieve the happiness of his childhood into the present. Alfred's guide in this undertaking is his unshakable self-esteem, which allows him to believe in the salvageability of a world reduced to rubble and ashes. His planned "Pergamon project,"[4] his insistence on crossing the East-West border despite increasing obstacles, and his Wiesbaden apartment modeled after the one in Dresden all signify his denial of the finality of his losses. Nevertheless, his career and development get trapped in the quagmire of losses and failures, both present and past, which he hopes to overcome by ignoring the irretrievability of time.

Even in his youthful prime, an age when most men strive to realize life's promise, he sets out to secure the past and recapture his childhood. Born and raised in Dresden as the sheltered only son of a dentist and his wife, Alfred has completed law school in Leipzig, only to fail his final examinations. He is almost twenty-four years old as he arrives in 1953 in West Berlin, where he hopes to bring his thwarted efforts to a successful conclusion after all. His relationship with his mother in Dresden is one of fervent admiration. He feels that for his mother's sake he must hate his father, who left the family three years earlier for a colleague twenty years his junior. An important pawn in the feud between his parents, the former honor student pursues his remedial studies conscientiously in order to secure a future for himself and his mother. But then his plans are totally dashed by the worsening of political relations between East and West and by his mother's illness. Because reentry into the GDR has become almost impossible for refugees and his mother is in need of care, he finally brings her to his small room in West Berlin, where she languishes for another two years. After her death, Alfred resolves to recover from across the border everything having to do with his and her life in Dresden. No sooner is his father dead than he also discerns a need for every reminder of him. His desire to secure the past finds further outlet in his profession. As a lawyer he works for seven years in an office in West Berlin that compensates victims of National Socialism for their losses. Then he takes a position with the Ministry of Culture in Wiesbaden, where he is responsible for the preservation of historic monuments. Having observed from afar the Communist regime's virtual vandalism of the few remnants of the Dresden Baroque, he intercedes in an effort to save the city of his childhood from further destruction, remaining undaunted when his continual pleas fall on

[4]Quotes given in English are my own translations.

deaf ears. At the age of fifty-eight he dies alone of an "accidental" overdose of pills (VK 517), without ever realizing any of his preservation projects.

By ordinary standards, Alfred's exterior life is not totally unsuccessful.[5] But in regard to his goal of saving the world with which he identifies, he fails utterly. The novel focuses on the relentlessness of his involuntary decline from self-assuredness to despair, from his resolve to preserve all he holds dear to a feeling of immeasurable loss. When, as a sixteen-year-old, Alfred begins to collect old photographs, he does not know yet that his obsession with the past can be satisfied only with the restoration of all that was. This Sisyphean work was triggered by an historic event. In the night of 13-14 February 1945 everything in Dresden that could have documented his childhood went up in flames: a cabinet full of photo albums, a wax record of his piano playing, and three home movies entitled "First Day of School," "Silver Wedding Anniversary," and "Confirmation," which documented the extraordinarily gifted child's leading role in the family (VK 14). His maternal grandparents also perished in the firestorm. Thus important witnesses and evidence of a unique childhood were lost. Until then, Alfred had flourished, and his awareness of his own uniqueness had made him an "enemy of all ordinariness" (VK 18). His mother had a way of further enhancing the picture of perfection with a camel's-hair coat, matching beret, and "milk-white" gloves (VK 172). At this early age Alfred also played a key role in ending his parents' quarrels. Recognizing the child's assertiveness, the father used to seal every reconciliation with the words: "Some day our boy is really going to be somebody" (VK 437).

The development of the child prodigy and family conciliator was interrupted when the father moved out and when Alfred failed the state examination in Leipzig two years later. Although there are sufficiently plausible reasons for both events — according to a female acquaintance the father had already realized his "dirty passions" (VK 356), and Alfred failed the examinations because of his political nonconformity — he believes he must still live up to the promise he embodied as a child (VK 409). From now on he fights on the side of the mother in his parents' marital war (VK 18), to make up for the wrong committed against her and to restore her lost happiness. He is not aware that his feeling of responsibility for her happiness is also rooted to some extent in her demands. For instance, after the divorce and before the Berlin exams the narrator relays the mother's claims: "Now it is entirely in Alfred's hands whether happiness will ultimately come to

[5]Alfred advances to *Regierungsdirektor* (VK 485) in the Ministry of Cultural Affairs of the State of Hesse. At the height of his career, he is not only responsible for the preservation of historical monuments but is also adviser to the state's theaters and legal counsel of the Ministry (VK 405).

them. She hopes this will penetrate her darling's little noggin" (VK 50).[6] Alfred finds nothing alarming about this remark, because in West Berlin, a city so alien to him, he lives only for the visits with his mother anyway. He declares his love for her in special-delivery letters almost daily, and she sacrifices as mothers do, in order to provide for her beloved son. While he "constantly searches for words and images with which he can celebrate his mother and himself in comic-pathetic exuberance" (VK 21), she sends him his laundry and cake packages. He gladly lets her manipulate him a little, because he would not want anything to cloud his enjoyment of her company (VK 38). Furthermore, his association with others has convinced him that he can never feel as much at home anywhere else as with her, that no one understands him as she does. Although he discovers negative things about her in later decades, he never doubts that she was the only human being whose interests were in complete harmony with his own and who unreservedly had his welfare at heart. His mother remains the only love in Alfred's life and his anchor in reality. The narrator comments:

> The tenderness between mother and son does not seem affected. They are quite open toward each other, as their letters show. She calls him every name from scum to prince in her letters to him. And he omits nothing from sheep to queen.[7] (VK 38)

The father regards Alfred's love for his mother as a sign of softness (VK 10, 55), and others simply label it *Affenliebe* (excessive and unnatural adoration) (VK 37). But in West Berlin it becomes his only means of self-preservation. Here he avoids every social contact, because he sees reminders of his father's "become-a-man propaganda" everywhere (VK 70, 90). The endless allusions to his sexual inexperience, his inability to win the acceptance of his fellow students, and the feeling of still being an outsider in the crowded, bustling city make returning home to his mother seem like the only chance of salvation from the threats of defeat and loss of identity. She must give him

[6]For similar incidents, see *Verteidigung*, pp. 71, 109.

[7]Here the author makes a direct reference to his sources. The question of whether this makes the depiction of Alfred's life a biography or a novel (which the narrator also addresses [VK 219-20]), must be decided in favor of the latter. Walser himself states that he has discovered in his character's "Sohn-Sein" [filial role], and especially in his fascination with the past, a universality that "makes everyone a poet, so to speak"; Walser in an interview with Christa von Bernuth, "Kindheit nach dem Tode: Ein Gespräch mit Martin Walser," *Die Zeit* 9 Aug. 1991. See also Volker Hage, "Walsers deutsches Requiem," *Die Zeit* 9 Aug. 1991, and Martin Lüdke, "Eine vom Leben zerriebene Geschichte," *Frankfurter Rundschau* 10 Aug. 1991.

"nourishment for the nerves and soul" (VK 65), for "she was his haven" (VK 166). Particularly since he recognizes himself to some extent in the gibes of his fellow students and accusations of his father, he wants to assert himself as the Alfred Dorn with whom he feels at one: who belongs, but as a top student; who succeeds magnificently in everything he does; who is unassailable despite his differentness. As in his youth, talent and recognition must complement each other. His classmates characterize him this way:

> A gentleman of finest form,
> his every act a super show,
> and popular with everyone,
> especially when he's on a roll. (VK 519)

Back when Alfred's talent for caricature guaranteed him the goodwill of his classmates, and his outstanding piano-playing the admiration of adults, he believed that his life would some day flower through his diverse talents. He was guided in this belief by a self-esteem molded by music: "As long as he listened, he became great and powerful and profound, just as the music was at the moment" (VK 85). In music he hears both a promise for the future and the essence of the past. It reminds him of the time when he performed his first composition, his "astounding and admirable Christopher Fantasy" (VK 103), and the great singer Kurt Böhme sent his compliments to the talented piano pupil (VK 218). He takes on the study of law only so that he can earn his bread and butter while training to be a pianist (VK 58). In Berlin he takes lessons from noted teachers for many years and then makes a record on which he plays Scarlatti, Bach, Chopin, Schumann, and Tchaikovsky, in order to communicate his true self to his acquaintances and coworkers (VK 372). Like music, the admiration of others is for him an echo of the old familiar self-esteem that cannot be tarnished by the wretchedness and ordinariness of reality.[8] Since childhood Alfred has used his other talent, drawing, to ward off any unpleasant demands on him. He answers the probing letters of his parents by signing his own with sketches of a frightened rabbit or proud giraffe; he breaks the tension of the classroom and lecture hall by circulating caricatures of his teachers on slips of paper. "*If nothing works out* [meaning his future success], *I'll jump into the Elbe*" (VK 103), he writes to his mother, followed by an inkblot figure below, with a little hat flying ahead of it. His distortion of reality and trivialization of himself, as well as his intuitive identification with famous personalities — his models

[8]Similarly, the praise from acquaintances in Dresden, after he has described to them the care he is giving his mother, produces a "self-perception almost like music" (VK 275).

include Chopin, Friedrich II, and Ludwig II — are attempts to minimize the pressures of daily life in favor of the past. He must rescue his childhood, the source of his talents, to protect himself from the present and to ensure that nothing stands in the way of the self-realization he envisions. In his literary work, a biography in which he plans to describe the rise and fall of the Saxon Count Brühl in order to prevent his own fall, his childlike certainty of being destined for greatness must therefore triumph over harsh reality (VK 213).

The hallmarks of Alfred's sense of self — the love between mother and son, and the abundance of artistic talents — can neither prevent the interference of mundane life nor assure him the recognition of his peers. In Leipzig it was hard enough to cultivate his childlike self and at the same time meet the demands of the present; in West Berlin he finds it even harder. Although he constantly tries, so that there will be nothing about him others could criticize (VK 146), he is regarded as a loner. In Leipzig his differentness still seemed to be the inevitable price of self-preservation, for which he then paid with his failure.[9] In Berlin he portrays an expected persona. Through self-training he wants to counteract the impression of softness that he leaves not only on his father; and when he is in danger of falling by the wayside in the pre-exam drills (VK 77) he applies himself with even more diligence to make up for his lack of assertiveness: "Alfred was more of the opinion that it was enough just to know how adults acted in this or that situation. But for that you didn't have to be an adult yourself" (VK 157).[10] In later years, when it becomes clear that mere role play is not sufficient for self-realization, he wants to slip *back* into his best and most comfortable role, that of perennial son, to distract from his loneliness and sexual indecisiveness (VK 331, 340).

As Alfred forgoes adult life in favor of childhood, he also forgoes sexual love in favor of filial love. The narrator, who in this instance reflects Walser's opinion,[11] warns against describing the closeness between mother and son in the "serviceable vocabulary" of the behavioral sciences. "It's better if not everything is clear," he says, "or nothing at all. Isn't it also possible to understand something that is not clear at all?" (VK 38). Assuming that love is a distinct rhythm of life, and that it is not tied to any particular configuration of participants, Walser describes the mother-son relationship

[9]Conversely, Alfred regards self-change as a breach of faith: "He had been like all others. He still was. The others were different now. Grown up" (VK 86).

[10]For more on self-portrayal, see *Verteidigung*, pp. 97, 274, 275, 341, 343.

[11]Walser, "Schreibend läßt sich fast alles ertragen," *Stern* 29 Aug. 1991: 123.

as incomparable, as the most important relationship in the world.[12] The novel demonstrates that other possibilities for happiness, including the erotic attractions of the adult world, can pale before the absoluteness of such a love. Therefore, his warning does more than shield his characters from prejudice: It points to the complexity of a mother-son symbiosis that ultimately determines the sexuality of the son.[13]

As a child, Alfred found the beauty of the Bavarian king (VK 107, 165) just as appealing as Giorgione's *Sleeping Venus* or the naked infants on the laps of various Madonnas in the Dresden Art Gallery. The goal of these joint museum excursions was routinely Raphael's Sistine Madonna, whose hovering maternal gaze, in Alfred's mind, mirrored that of his mother by his side (VK 138). He was particularly captivated by Parmigianino's *Madonna with the Rose*, because she seemed downright enchanted by her blond, naked, curly-headed lad. Alfred is struck by the sensuality the child seems to exude and the receptiveness of the mother. "And the rose above corresponds to his fully revealed organ below [on the mother's lap]" (VK 139). The adolescent interpretation of the Madonna enchanted by a little man lodges in Alfred's consciousness primarily because his parents' marriage was not a happy one and his mother lives celibate after the separation, like the famous paragon.[14] As strong in its aftereffect as the sexual connotation of Alfred's favorite art is his childhood impression that all sexual activity is bad. Particularly because the mother's admonitions on this subject were formulated vaguely and hence comprehensively, they resounded in the child's mind as inspiration from above. Although Alfred later gains additional knowledge about "the main subject" (VK 90, 91) from French and American films, from the remarks of his grandmotherly friend about feminine "beauty and wiles" (VK 67), and from her descriptions of his father's excesses (VK 356), the development of his sexuality continues to be repressed. Still burdened with his mother's taboos and his father's blatant encouragement to become sexually active, Alfred elects to cling to his juvenile ideas and practices for the

[12]"Das ist der Hauptmutterfluch," *profil* (Vienna) 21 Oct. 1991: 139.

[13]It would be instructive to compare the love for the mother with Eckermann's love for Goethe. In Walser's portrayal, the latter relationship also resembles such a symbiosis, where the internal world of a character is affected to a much greater extent than his counterpart realizes, or than external events suggest. See Heike A. Doane, "Love versus Life: Martin Walser Describes Johann Peter Eckermann's Development," *The Age of Goethe Today*, eds. Gertrud Bauer Pickar and Sabine Cramer, Houston German Studies 7 (Munich: Wilhelm Fink Verlag, 1990) 154-70.

[14]The mother calls the grown son "Männel" [little man] (VK 165), without realizing she is reinforcing his childlike sexual perception.

time being. As much as fellow student Pinkwart assures him that he makes an impression on women, and Mrs. Pinkwart "positively worship[s] him with her eyes" (VK 103), Alfred prefers to take his mother to the movies, whisper in her ear (VK 50), and call her names that he has heard his father bestow on his young wife (VK 136). True to his old childhood faith, he is still convinced during his university years that success and punishment depend on the same "divine watchdog" (VK 144) who created the connection between self-gratification and guilt. "He wanted to behave in such a way that the highest kindergartner in heaven would have nothing about him to find fault with and therefore would have to let him pass the examination" (VK 176). Naturally, the parents believe they can still exert influence on their adult son. The father advises him to do "what is manly" (VK 346); the mother thinks he should find a wife (VK 238). Both are concerned about Alfred's lack of interest in the opposite sex, but they fail to recognize his infatuation with his mother. "I love you terribly, send you lots of hugs and kisses, and remain the best you have, your dearly beloved little son..." (VK 73), he writes, without his mother's recognizing in these effusions anything more than childlike love.

After the mother's death, his sexual indecisiveness becomes tainted with the fear of becoming homosexual. Now in his thirties, he feels exposed to an "organized homosexual conspiracy" (VK 340) at his workplace, which he can fend off only by requesting a transfer to Wiesbaden. Not until he is about to leave does he learn that none of his coworkers consider him to be homosexual (VK 388), not even Rosellen, whose "girlish glances" (VK 332) have plagued him for years. Even though the suspicions of his own and others' homosexuality exist only in his imagination, they weigh upon him like real experiences. At the same time, the old association between desire and guilt remains so much a part of his fantasy that no female attraction can overcome it. Moreover, the type of femininity that he links with love is forever symbolized by the picture of a male child on the Madonna's lap, making it impossible for him to do with a woman "that which is generated by physical sympathy" (VK 389). Lingering childhood taboos, reinforced by his mother's admonition to ignore his body altogether, not only mar his vision of oedipal bliss, they also convince him that self-gratification is wrong and that intimate love with a person of the same sex would be "a horror" (VK 389). Over the years, Alfred's predicament becomes naturally more bearable, but not his awareness of having missed something important in life. As he looks at an old photograph of his parents, he suddenly recognizes a togetherness that surpasses the happy relationship between mother and son. His refusal to become an adult may have prevented him from falling prey to the temptations of the flesh, but it could not eliminate his conventional notions of emotional fulfillment and sexual love. His sexual abstinence epitomizes the inherent contradiction of his *modus vivendi*, i.e. his willingness to sacrifice all involvement in the present in order to recapture the intensity of emotions he felt as a child. Dr. Permoser, Alfred's psychotherapist, has the ultimate word. After Alfred has described himself as a nonpracticing homosexual and Permoser has added that Alfred is also a nonpracticing heterosexual, he remarks: "So you're the holy oxymoron personified" (VK 498).

Since the desire for self-determination is portrayed in this novel as a clash with an environment perceived to be hostile, parallels from Walser's earlier works come to mind. The most striking, perhaps, is that of Helmut Halm in *Runaway Horse* (1978), who seeks refuge in inwardness, just as Alfred seeks refuge in childhood. But unlike Halm, Alfred's flight is motivated not by years of experience but by the event of a single night in which his city and home went up in flames. He finds no consolation for this event. "No diffusion of the pain. No sense." Instead "a feeling of abandonment was forming. No loss is felt so clearly as the loss of the past" (VK 85). From this perception springs Alfred's compulsion to recover what he has lost, first and most tangibly, as he tries to collect all objects that played a part in his past (VK 195). In later years he also collects the figures of speech of those who were close to him as a child. He establishes a list of the sentences that his parents used, and even notes how they were articulated in an effort to authenticate them (VK 515). Only the exact wording is a suitable key to the past, because this is the only way the network of associations with the past can be perfectly restored. Mother and son had a way of enhancing the immediacy between words and situations through a kind of personal language (VK 123), thereby making the event a part of their exclusive experience. Ever since then, Alfred is no longer interested in the universality of language, but only in its ability to recall individual speech mannerisms and feelings.[15] Although he sees himself as a budding author and pianist, he attaches more value to that which can be documented than to artistic expression and invention. He views literature as a fallible tool when it comes to protecting the past from haziness or oblivion (VK 17). Walser has already discussed this concept in his novel *The Unicorn* (1966), and Alfred also knows that he cannot create a refuge for his childhood through art. To be sure, his lifelong desire to surmount all barriers separating him from his childhood cannot be fulfilled without abstract phenomena such as memory and language. But he tries to

[15]The function of such sentences, quotations and allusions within this novel are the subject of my paper "Zitat, Redensart und literarische Anspielung: Zur Funktion der gesprochenen Sprache in Martin Walsers Roman *Die Verteidigung der Kindheit*," *Colloquia Germanica* 25 (1992): 289-305.

restore to these phenomena the concreteness and reality that they once possessed.[16] By writing them down and "thinking about them" (VK 228) he aims to *reverse* his self-styled axiom: "If you forget something, it is as if it never was" (VK 278).

The more Alfred becomes convinced that the present brings harm rather than good, the more his obsession with his former life intensifies. His student days he regards as a coercion to leave the past behind; after his mother's death, the present continually brings threats of new losses. The resulting inner fear begins to overshadow his whole being. In the course of time, his Pergamon project, which is devoted to the reconstruction of his childhood (VK 263), becomes more and more clearly an attempt at survival of someone anticipating his own ruin. Although he clings for years to his hope of accomplishing "something significant one day" (VK 366), he also suspects that his projects could hinder rather than further his self-realization (VK 217). Eventually the future no longer appears to hold promise for great achievement but becomes a harbinger of ruin and decay (VK 198). As a young man, he set a goal for himself to "achieve great things for ten years, then end it all" (VK 237). Later he revises this plan, but he still does not want to admit that one can live with losses, and he is even less able to come to terms with his own mortality (VK 123). "Reality [for him] is a process of annihilation," which he counters with his "system of preservation" (VK 384), consisting of remembrance and the refutation of time.[17]

Under this omen, his life becomes a race against loss and decay. As acquaintances in Dresden and Berlin die off one by one, nothing intercedes to stop this downhill trend. Alfred becomes more and more lonely, because the witnesses to his fabulous childhood are dearer to him than the witnesses to his unfulfilled adult life. Early on, he dismisses the possibility of finding fulfillment through practicing law to foster his artistic talents. Later he discovers that neither music nor the planned historical novel can compete with the monumental task of conquering time, a task which he undertakes by immersing himself in his voluminous collection of letters, petitions, and facts. When, at age fifty-five, he feels forced to abandon the artistic route to

[16]Like his creator, Alfred is searching for the reality contained in language. Walser, in his essay "Märztage und Musik," explains how ordinary words and sentences relate to thousands of predecessors and how they derive their meaning from this relationship; *Geständnis auf Raten* (Frankfurt/M.: Suhrkamp, 1986) 77-79.

[17]Joseph von Westphalen and an anonymous critic for *Buch Aktuell* have pointed out that the novel from Alfred's perspective could be called "In Search of Lost Time," the translated title of Proust's *À la recherche du temps perdu* (1913-1927); "Ein deutsches Muttersöhnchen," *Der Spiegel* 12 Aug. 1991: 173; "Zu Besuch bei Martin Walser: Auf der Suche nach der verlorenen Zeit," *Buch Aktuell* Fall 1991: 75-77.

self-realization in favor of reconstructing the childhood self, he has long since become a "gray mouse" (VK 417). The sacrifices that he makes fail to revive the past and himself; they also put him in a morally dubious light. While he forgoes new friendships and new love, his suspicion of his own homosexuality closes in on him.[18] Of course, his hunger for life and yearning for companionship cannot be satisfied by his asceticism. Still, his deliberate withdrawal from life sustains his childlike credulity. In the end, he interprets the arrival of a homeless fellow Saxon as life calling him (VK 466), and he is positively overrun by the escapades of his young charge (VK 462). While he struggled against life all those years because it leads to death, his plans for self-preservation had an effect opposite to the intended one. An old, inexperienced child, he feels that his body failed him before he was ready to live the life he believed was his destiny.

Alfred is the first Walser hero to remain true to himself. Unlike other Walser characters, he is unwilling to adapt to his environment, because he regards any change in his self-perception as a concession to decay and death. He is unaware of being a victim of his conjuration of the past until it is too late for life. Instead of recovering what he has lost, the most he can do is continue to yearn for it. He is no more able to stop the destructiveness of reality than to consolidate his memories and realize their promise of greatness. After all, the reconstruction of his past also testifies to the destructive role of the "grotesquely precocious, know-it-all" child (VK 431) and thus betrays the illusion of an innocent, timeless, and perfect childhood. The annihilation he is fighting is more than resignation to time and death. It is also the darker side of himself which his fierce self-determination wants to deny.

It is conceivable that Alfred, with his aversion to compromise, would have become obsessed with the past under any circumstances; but it is Germany's history from 1945 to the 1980s that almost seems to compel him in his undertaking. The division of his homeland augments his perception of an all-encompassing precariousness, and at the same time it anchors his memory in the realm of objects and authenticity. He tries to transcend the German-German border by sheltering the things, sentences, and documents in his keeping from political reality. With countless packages and letters he builds a virtual bridge to Dresden, for his ties to the city and to the people involved in his past must not be broken. For him the border between East and West is merely a physical hindrance, not the expression of a political reality. He is very casual about traveling back and forth between the two parts of Berlin, and when the border becomes almost impassable he achieves his greatest

[18]The fact that Alfred remains celibate throughout his life refutes his self-accusations, in my opinion. Fantasies and fears alone do not substantiate a public sexual identity.

legal triumphs by managing to obtain a refugee identification card for himself and later an exit permit for his mother. He interprets day-to-day political events only in light of his personal needs and goals. When the workers demonstrate in East Berlin (1953), his main fear is that his visit to his mother will have to be postponed (VK 32); and while the barriers between East and West gradually mount, he goes to ever greater lengths to obtain free passage to Dresden. The Berlin Conference (1954), the Geneva talks (1955), the visit of Bulganin and Khrushchev to East Berlin (1955), and the Hungarian uprising (1956) prompt him to secure border passes. On the one hand, he interprets world history as a plot against himself and his mother; on the other, he associates the symptoms of the Cold War with the religious wars known from history.[19] He attributes his lifelong aversion to political parties to their claim that they represent everyone and are the answer to all problems (VK 419). Be it the slogans of the SED, of the students of 1968, or of the cultural politicians in red Hesse, in all of these it is the tendency to monopolize power that is disturbing to him (VK 498). Alfred experiences his era not as an arch-conservative, as a critic claims,[20] but rather as a political dropout, one whose early experiences prevent him from taking any further interest. Because the political fervor of others appears to him to serve only personal advantage (VK 62, 387), he sees no reason to gloss over his *own* analysis of current events with ideological slogans.

Unlike his literary predecessor Wolf Zieger in *No Man's Land* (1987), who also experiences the division of Germany as a rift in his own being and comes to similar conclusions,[21] Alfred does not broaden his personal viewpoint when it comes to politics. For example, that people in Dresden live without the conveniences he now enjoys is a source of "historic pain" to him (VK 93); and ever since his childhood he has seen the history of Saxony closely linked to his own destiny. He does not become a mediator between East and West like Zieger, because his understanding of history and his

[19]The sentence "Alfred gradually noticed that he was in the middle of a religious war" (VK 139) is presented as Alfred's thinking, but it is also clearly the opinion of the author, who has repeatedly drawn an analogy between ideology and religion in his essays. See, for example, "Religiöse Zeiten," *Geständnis auf Raten*, pp. 16-17, or "Zum Stand der Dinge," *FAZ* 5 Dec. 1989.

[20]Joseph von Westphalen, "Ein deutsches Muttersöhnchen," *Der Spiegel* 12 Aug. 1991: 173.

[21]Both know that neither part is complete without the other, and despite their very different perceptions of current events they are convinced that they lead only a very temporary existence in one part of the country, and, therefore, their self-realization depends on the restoration of the whole.

political sensibility are an expression of his preoccupation with self.[22] In Leipzig he was forced to adopt political viewpoints that struck him as absurd. In West Berlin, where his former Leipzig classmates quickly join the ruling SPD, he refuses to declare his support for the western half of the country.[23] He remains a "permanent emigrant" (VK 75) because he can no more give up his claim to his homeland than he can give up his claim to self-realization. Dresden, "home of everything green" (VK 30), becomes his universal yardstick. In Dresden he participates in everything; in Berlin he is excluded from everything. From Dresden, where the irrefutable conviction of his uniqueness formed, come financial and emotional support, practical advice, and study tips. Everything he accomplishes and would still like to accomplish must therefore be able to measure up to the expectations of his Dresden audience. To please them, he has to pass the exams in Berlin with honors (VK 171, 180), and only when the last of them has faded in the "gloominess of the GDR" does he give up the idea of earning a doctorate (VK 409). Everything worth knowing comes from Dresden — be it about the marriage of his parents or the political past of old friends — and sentences that Alfred carries with him throughout his life were first uttered in Dresden. Ever since the destruction of the city left Alfred with an all-encompassing feeling of loss, his every attempt at self-realization is foiled by the notion that only that which is lost contained life. Dresden becomes an emblem representing his hopes for rebuilding the past: "The more wretched the real Dresden was, the more vibrant his inner Dresden had to become" (VK 185). Still, this inner Dresden is not totally subject to Alfred's will, because it evokes more than the impression of vitality so dear to him. Aside from the discovery of hidden facts and ulterior motives, it also shows the relentlessness with which immediacy slips into the remoteness of time.

Yet it is the inner Dresden, with all its precariousness, that Alfred wants restored: a Dresden in which a young, arrogant Alfred pesters a Jew doing forced labor and at this moment comprehends the power of propaganda; a Dresden in which the family tries to protect Jewish acquaintances while

[22]Zieger sees his espionage as "mediation work." If he can break down the "superiority of one side," it will make it possible for the two parts to approach each other. Alfred, on the other hand, plans a historical novel about Saxony's past, because he sees the history of his homeland as a model for his own development and thus a source for self-help. See *No Man's Land*, pp. 140, 142; *Die Verteidigung der Kindheit*, pp. 213-17.

[23]Like Zieger, he does not develop a hostile attitude toward the West. Alfred shies away from paying mere lip service to any ideology; and Wolf knows that his prospects for personal happiness depend on whether he can feel at home in his wife's part of the country.

Alfred's godmother presses for their arrest; a Dresden where the survivors of the firestorm and persecution find their way back into their daily routine; a city of memories, in which the war and postwar periods live on and the behavior of the inhabitants can be traced back to the innermost depths of their souls. Unlike the author, Alfred does not realize that home is more than a place, that it is above all a feeling out of the past and, as such, "a dimension of time."[24] However, he knows that the history of Dresden and his own history have become one, and he therefore develops a "one-man campaign to rescue what is left of Dresden" (VK 489). At second-hand bookshops and auctions he buys up documents, pictures, and historical letters, which he hopes will one day diminish the city's loss. From the Communist authorities he demands an account of the whereabouts of other landmarks, be it a metal bench that has vanished since his last visit or a dilapidated Pöppelmann church (VK 487).[25] The hopelessness of these demands apparently makes no difference. On 14 February 1945 a school friend wanted to collect "the intellectual wealth of the fatherland" in a handcart (VK 506). Forty years later, Alfred is still trying to fulfill a similar task under similar conditions.

The author succeeds in the very restoration that defeats his character. By reassembling the countless individual components of Alfred's life, he creates a literary mosaic of the past, which, like *Halbzeit* (1960; Half Time), conjures up the image of an epoch.[26] By portraying his character as totally embracing the past, Walser has disproved his own and Alfred's theory of the irretrievability of the past through literature. As Walser makes his case against forgetting and entrusts us with this oddball Alfred, the premise of the novel as the historiography of everyday life,[27] as participation in inner com-

[24]Martin Walser, "Zu Besuch bei Martin Walser," p. 77.

[25]Mathäus Daniel Pöppelmann (1662-1736) was the builder of the Dresden *Zwinger* (completed in 1728).

[26]Joseph von Westphalen calls this novel an important piece of postwar literature that belies Schirrmacher's hypothesis that this literary phase is over ("Ein deutsches Muttersöhnchen," p. 174). Renate Braunschweig-Ullmann speaks of documentation inserted in a life story ("Spurensicherung der Vergangenheit als Schutz gegen die Angst," *Badische Neueste Nachrichten* 14 Aug. 1991), and Manfred Stuber speaks of an almost encyclopedic panorama of the time ("Mutters unerreichte Marmelade," *Mittelbayerische Zeitung* 7 June 1991).

[27]The original use of the expression "Geschichtsschreibung des Alltags" is found in Walser's essay "Wie geht es Ihnen, Jury Trifonow?," *Wer ist ein Schriftsteller?* (Frankfurt/M.: Suhrkamp, 1979) 25.

pulsions, doubts, and expectations, gains new credibility. Alfred's limited existence demonstrates how from ordinary and catastrophic personal experiences there arises a sense of being that can represent the collective consciousness of a whole generation. As Alfred defends his childhood and home against the passage of time, the passing times come to life again for the reader.

Die Verteidigung der Kindheit is Walser's second literary attempt to portray the suffering of a divided nation. In 1987 he stepped into the political limelight by arguing that the division of Germany had not resulted in the division of its people. Along with the protagonist of his novella *No Man's Land* he maintained that the German people still had an emotional need to unify the severed parts of their country. However, he doubted that he would ever be able to write a novel dealing with all of Germany.[28] Two years later, with unification still a political pipe dream, he was deeply involved in such a project. Apparently the discovery that the personal papers of Alfred's real-life prototype revealed feelings he shared — and had previously named his "Stuttgart-Leipzig-Gefühl"[29] — had eliminated his reservations about portraying life in a society he had not experienced first-hand. It seems that in the collection of countless photos, letters, and tickets, notations in calendars and on napkins, all testimony to the sensitivity and pedantry of a civil servant, Walser's own feeling of irreversible political loss had suddenly acquired a realistic quality. The novel succeeds in conveying and intensifying this quality. While critics of *No Man's Land* maintained that Walser could not convince readers that Germans were still suffering from the country's split,[30] most critics of *Die Verteidigung der Kindheit* conceded that it was an accurate portrayal of the psychological ramifications of the nation's fate.[31] Entrusting to someone else's life the proof of German indivisibility

[28]Martin Walser, "Ich hab' so ein Stuttgart-Leipzig-Gefühl," *Auskunft: 22 Gespräche aus 28 Jahren*, ed. Klaus Siblewski (Frankfurt/M.: Suhrkamp, 1991) 249.

[29]"Ich hab' so ein Stuttgart-Leipzig-Gefühl," p. 249.

[30]For example, Martin Lüdke, "Nichts Halbes, nichts Ganzes," *Die Zeit* 20 Mar. 1987; Jürgen Manthey, "Ehebruch mit Deutschlandkummer," *Frankfurter Rundschau* 11 Apr. 1987; Heinrich Vormweg, "Abrutscher ins Absonderliche," *Süddeutsche Zeitung* 14 Apr. 1987. In contrast, the American reception of the novella was favorable. See both Richard Eder's review of *No Man's Land* (*Los Angeles Times Book Review* 1 Jan. 1989) and Anthony Hyde's review (*New York Times Book Review* 22 Jan. 1989).

[31]Dieter Kief, "Anschreiben gegen die Entbehrungen der Gegenwart," *Eßlinger Zeitung* 5/6 Oct. 1991; Siegmund Kopitzki, "Ein Mann ohne Nimbus," *Südkurier*

is a breakthrough in Walser's narrative technique. In his effort to be true to his source, he manages to transcend the subjective, character-bound perspective in favor of a more realistic emphasis on the pluralistic influences that determine the course of everyday events.[32] In the past, Walser's ambition to free his protagonists from the constraints of their kinship with his own views and experiences at times seemed as paradoxical as squaring a circle. In creating Alfred Dorn, however, he no longer writes in the voice of a protagonist he invented as a partner in his own quest to understand the world around him; rather he strives to include and justify as many opposing viewpoints as Alfred and his prototype encountered.

Not surprisingly, the inclusion of multiple opinions has led some critics to surmise that Walser, in lending a stronger voice to his character's opponents, has turned from being a leftist critic of society to being its conservative apologist. Underlying this argument are three untenable assumptions: that the narrator's voice is always that of the author; that by offering a wider array of perspectives, Walser admits to being in agreement with these views; and that by tempering his critical stance with sympathy and understanding, he in fact affirms the way things are. This reasoning resembles that of Thomas Beckermann, the first critic to call Walser's fiction an affirmation of the status quo. Beckermann felt that Walser had failed at depicting practicable alternatives to a stagnant society.[33] His latest critics feel that Walser can no longer deny that he is resigned to — even content with — living in such a society.[34] Walser has answered the earliest criticism with an ar-

9 Oct. 1991; Lüdke, "Eine vom Leben zerriebene Geschichte" (see note 7); Jürgen Manthey, "Martin Walser: *Die Verteidigung der Kindheit*," *Deutschlandfunk* 18 Aug. 1991 (transcript, p. 3); Sabine Neubert, "Am Ende bleibt das Grabmonument," *Neue Zeit* 9 Oct. 1991; Stephan Reinhardt, "Das sächsische Muster," *Süddeutsche Zeitung* 3/4 Aug. 1991; Erich Wolfgang Skwara, "Ein Parzival-Roman der deutschen Teilung," *Neue Deutsche Literatur* Nov. 1991: 130-36.

[32]Ulrike Hick, "Interview mit Martin Walser," *Martin Walsers Prosa: Möglichkeiten des zeitgenössischen Romans unter Berücksichtigung des Realismusanspruchs* (Stuttgart: Akademischer Verlag Hans-Dieter Heinz, 1983) 294-95.

[33]Beckermann, *Martin Walser oder die Zerstörung eines Musters: Literatursoziologischer Versuch über "Halbzeit,"* Abhandlungen zur Kunst-, Musik- und Literaturwissenschaft 114 (Bonn: Bouvier, 1972) 206-10.

[34]These critics felt that Walser's development from a "leftist Saul to a rightist Paul" was exemplified by his attendance at a CSU party caucus in January 1989. See Thomas Thieringer, "Martin Walser: Politischer Schriftsteller, Romanautor, Dramatiker," *Süddeutsche Zeitung* 11 Jan. 1989; Roman Arens, "Der Nimbus von Kreuth und das neue Tandem der CSU," *Frankfurter Rundschau* 16 Jan. 1989.

gument that by extension can also be used to diffuse the latest, namely, that his fiction serves as a literary experiment with reality. All his fictional characters and events are invented to reveal this reality, not to alter it. Neither utopian sociological models nor imaginary political alternatives should, therefore, be affixed to the fictional image of the real world.[35] Nor, one must add, should the experiment be limited to the confines of one central narrative voice. Of course, any literary image of reality can only be a fragment of the whole, and the protagonists' thinking will always reflect that of their inventor to a degree. Alfred, too, remains a fictional character who embodies the author's experiences and sentiments. But to an even greater extent he represents his real-life prototype, whose philosophical and political opinions he voices. It is, therefore, predominately the prototype's view of the world, not the author's, that emerges through Alfred. By transferring the responsibility of narrating to a figure with a real past in *Die Verteidigung der Kindheit*, Walser minimizes the limitations of mediating reality and consciousness through literature. In relying on the testimony of a man he never met and adopting his cast of characters, Walser makes a case for Alfred's obsession with things past. The book validates Alfred's conviction that every person deserves a monument. While Walser relates events and emotions to flesh out the notations of the anonymous collector, Alfred emerges as a character who registers with seismographic sensitivity not only the losses that shaped his life but also a sense of being that is part of the German identity. The literary re-creation of this life stirs us to confront the losses imposed on everyone by the irreversibility of time. Thus, the writer has fulfilled his most important role, that of elucidating what we cannot easily accept or comprehend.

[35]Martin Walser, *Erfahrungen und Leseerfahrungen* (Frankfurt/M.: Suhrkamp, 1965) 92; *Heimatkunde* (Frankfurt/M.: Suhrkamp, 1968) 81, 84-85.

Works Cited

Albig, Jörg-Uwe, and Sven Michaelsen. "Schreibend läßt sich fast alles ertragen." Interview with Martin Walser. *Stern* 29 Aug. 1991: 121-30.

Arens, Roman. "Der Nimbus von Kreuth und das neue Tandem der CSU." *Frankfurter Rundschau* 16 Jan. 1989.

Beckermann, Thomas. *Martin Walser oder die Zerstörung eines Musters: Literatursoziologischer Versuch über "Halbzeit."* Abhandlungen zur Kunst-, Musik- und Literaturwissenschaft 114. Bonn: Bouvier, 1972.

Bernuth, Christa von. "Kindheit nach dem Tode: Ein Gespräch mit Martin Walser." *Die Zeit* 9 Aug. 1991.

Braunschweig-Ullmann, Renate. "Spurensicherung der Vergangenheit als Schutz gegen die Angst." Rev. of *Die Verteidigung der Kindheit. Badische Neueste Nachrichten* 14 Aug. 1991.

"Das ist der Hauptmutterfluch: Der Schriftsteller Martin Walser über sein Leben als Maulwurf, als Zuhörer, als Materialienverwandler und als Sohn seiner Mutter." *profil* (Vienna) 21 Oct. 1991: 138-40.

Doane, Heike A. "Love versus Life: Martin Walser Describes Johann Peter Eckermann's Development." *The Age of Goethe Today*. Eds. Gertrud Bauer Pickar, and Susanne Cramer. Houston German Studies 7. Munich: Fink, 1990. 154-70.

Eder, Richard. "Adultery for a Natural Cause." Rev. of *No Man's Land. Los Angeles Times Book Review* 1 Jan. 1989.

Hage, Volker. "Walsers deutsches Requiem." Rev. of *Die Verteidigung der Kindheit. Die Zeit* 9 Aug. 1991.

Hick, Ulrike. "Interview mit Martin Walser," *Martin Walsers Prosa: Möglichkeiten des zeitgenössischen Romans unter Berücksichtigung des Realismusanspruchs*. Stuttgarter Arbeiten zur Germanistik 126. Stuttgart: Akademischer Verlag Hans-Dieter Heinz, 1983. 291-303.

Hyde, Anthony. "The Crack in Wolf's Mirror." Rev. of *No Man's Land*. *New York Times Book Review* 22 Jan. 1989.

Kief, Dieter. "Anschreiben gegen die Entbehrungen der Gegenwart." Rev. of *Die Verteidigung der Kindheit*. *Eßlinger Zeitung* 5/6 Oct. 1991.

Kopitzki, Siegmund. "Ein Mann ohne Nimbus." Rev. of *Die Verteidigung der Kindheit*. *Südkurier* 9 Oct. 1991.

Lüdke, Martin. "Eine vom Leben zerriebene Geschichte." Rev. of *Die Verteidigung der Kindheit*. *Frankfurter Rundschau* 10 Aug. 1991.

——. "Nichts Halbes, nichts Ganzes." Rev. of *Dorle und Wolf*. *Die Zeit* 20 Mar. 1987.

Manthey, Jürgen. "Ehebruch mit Deutschlandkummer." Rev. of *Dorle und Wolf*. *Frankfurter Rundschau* 11 April 1987.

——. "Martin Walser: *Die Verteidigung der Kindheit*." *Deutschlandfunk*. 18 Aug. 1991 (Transcript, p.3).

Neubert, Sabine. "Am Ende bleibt das Grabmonument." Rev of *Die Verteidigung der Kindheit*. *Neue Zeit* 9 Oct. 1991.

Reinhardt, Stephan. "Das sächsische Muster." Rev. of *Die Verteidigung der Kindheit*. *Süddeutsche Zeitung* 3/4 Aug. 1991.

Skwara, Erich Wolfgang. "Ein Parzival-Roman der deutschen Teilung." Rev. of *Die Verteidigung der Kindheit*. *Neue Deutsche Literatur* 11 (1991): 130-36.

Stuber, Manfred. "Mutters unerreichte Marmelade." Rev. of *Die Verteidigung der Kindheit*. *Mittelbayerische Zeitung* 7 June 1991.

Thieringer, Thomas. "Martin Walser: Politischer Schriftsteller, Romanautor, Dramatiker." *Süddeutsche Zeitung* 11 Jan. 1989.

Vormweg, Heinrich. "Abrutscher ins Absonderliche." Rev. of *Dorle und Wolf*. *Süddeutsche Zeitung* 14 Apr. 1987.

Walser, Martin. *Auskunft: 22 Gespräche aus 28 Jahren*. Ed. Klaus Siblewski. Frankfurt: Suhrkamp, 1991.

——. *Erfahrungen und Leseerfahrungen.* Frankfurt/M.: Suhrkamp, 1965.

——. *Geständnis auf Raten.* Frankfurt/M.: Suhrkamp, 1986.

——. *Heimatkunde.* Frankfurt/M.: Suhrkamp, 1968.

——. *Wer ist ein Schriftsteller? Aufsätze und Reden.* Frankfurt/M.: Suhrkamp, 1979.

——. "Zum Stand der Dinge." *Frankfurter Allgemeine Zeitung* 5 Dec. 1989.

Westphalen, Joseph von. "Ein deutsches Muttersöhnchen." Rev. of *Die Verteidigung der Kindheit. Der Spiegel* 12 Aug. 1991: 171-74.

"Zu Besuch bei Martin Walser: Auf der Suche nach der verlorenen Zeit." *Buch Aktuell* Fall 1991: 75-77.

Selected Bibliography

I. Chronology of Walser's Prose Works:

——. *Ein Flugzeug über dem Haus und andere Geschichten* (1955).

——. *Ehen in Philippsburg* (1957).

——. *Halbzeit* (1960).

——. *Lügengeschichten* (1964).

——. *Das Einhorn* (1966).

——. *Fiction* (1970).

——. *Die Gallistl'sche Krankheit* (1972).

——. *Der Sturz* (1973).

——. *Jenseits der Liebe* (1976).

——. *Ein fliehendes Pferd* (1978).

——. *Seelenarbeit* (1979).

——. *Das Schwanenhaus* (1980).

——. *Brief an Lord Liszt* (1982).

——. *Meßmers Gedanken* (1985).

——. *Brandung* (1985).

——. *Dorle und Wolf* (1987).

——. *Jagd* (1988).

——. *Die Verteidigung der Kindheit* (1991).

——. *Ohne einander* (1993).

(All published by Suhrkamp Verlag, Frankfurt/M.)

II. Translations:

——. *Marriage in Philippsburg*. Trans. Eva Figes. Adapted by James Laughlin. Norfolk, CT: New Directions, 1961.

——. *The Unicorn*. Trans. Barrie Ellis-Jones. London: Calder & Boyars, 1971; New York: Boyars, 1981.

——. *Beyond All Love*. Trans. Judith L. Black. London: Calder, 1982; New York: Riverrun, 1983. First publication as separately paginated chapter of *New Writings and Writers 19*. London: Calder, 1981. New York: Riverrun, 1982.

——. *Runaway Horse*. Trans. Leila Vennewitz. New York: Holt, 1980.

——. *The Swan Villa*. Trans. Leila Vennewitz. New York: Holt, 1982.

——. *The Inner Man*. Trans. Leila Vennewitz. New York: Holt, 1984.

——. *Letter to Lord Liszt*. Trans. Leila Vennewitz. New York: Holt, 1985.

——. *Breakers*. Trans. Leila Vennewitz. New York: Holt, 1987.

——. *No Man's Land*. Trans. Leila Vennewitz. New York: Holt, 1988.

III. Dissertation, Selected Essays, Essay Collections:

——. *Beschreibung einer Form*. Munich: Hanser, 1961.

——. *Erfahrungen und Leseerfahrungen*. Frankfurt/M.: Suhrkamp, 1965.

——. *Heimatkunde. Aufsätze und Reden*. Frankfurt/M.: Suhrkamp, 1968.

——. "Mythen, Milch und Mut." *Christ und Welt* 18 Oct. 1968: 17.

——. "Berichte aus der Klassengesellschaft." Preface. *Bottroper Protokolle*. Compiled by Erika Runge. Frankfurt/M.: Suhrkamp, 1968. 7-10.

——. *Wie und wovon handelt Literatur? Aufsätze und Reden*. Frankfurt/M.: Suhrkamp, 1973.

——. *Wer ist ein Schriftsteller? Aufsätze und Reden*. Frankfurt/M.: Suhrkamp, 1979.

——. "Händedruck mit Gespenstern." 1979. *Versuch, ein Gefühl zu verstehen, und andere Versuche*. Stuttgart: Reclam, 1982. 91-104.

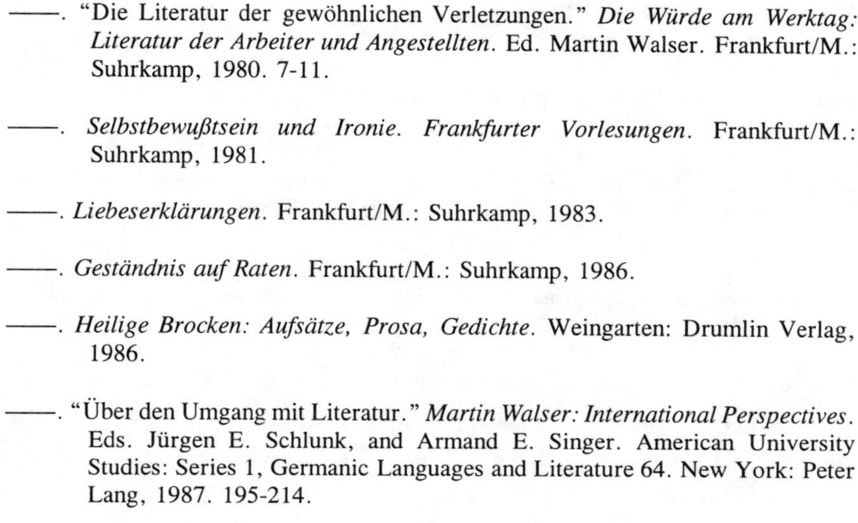

——. "Die Literatur der gewöhnlichen Verletzungen." *Die Würde am Werktag: Literatur der Arbeiter und Angestellten*. Ed. Martin Walser. Frankfurt/M.: Suhrkamp, 1980. 7-11.

——. *Selbstbewußtsein und Ironie. Frankfurter Vorlesungen*. Frankfurt/M.: Suhrkamp, 1981.

——. *Liebeserklärungen*. Frankfurt/M.: Suhrkamp, 1983.

——. *Geständnis auf Raten*. Frankfurt/M.: Suhrkamp, 1986.

——. *Heilige Brocken: Aufsätze, Prosa, Gedichte*. Weingarten: Drumlin Verlag, 1986.

——. "Über den Umgang mit Literatur." *Martin Walser: International Perspectives*. Eds. Jürgen E. Schlunk, and Armand E. Singer. American University Studies: Series 1, Germanic Languages and Literature 64. New York: Peter Lang, 1987. 195-214.

——. *Über Deutschland reden*. Frankfurt/M.: Suhrkamp, 1988.

IV. Interviews

Bloch, Peter André, et al. "Interview mit Martin Walser." *Gegenwartsliteratur: Mittel und Bedingungen ihrer Produktion*. Ed. P. A. Bloch. Bern, Munich: Francke, 1975. 257-71.

Brantl, Sybille. "Martin Walser: Sein Leben spricht Bände." *Cosmopolitan*. Oct. 1986. 32-37.

Frank, Niklas, and Joachim Köhler. "Ich hab' so ein Stuttgart-Leipzig-Gefühl." *Stern* 12 Mar. 1987: 220-24.

Hick, Ulrike. Interview with Martin Walser. *Martin Walsers Prosa: Möglichkeiten des zeitgenössischen Romans unter Berücksichtigung des Realisusanspruchs*. Stuttgarter Arbeiten zur Germanistik 126. Ed. Ulrich Müller, et al. Stuttgart: Akademischer Verlag Hans-Dieter Heinz, 1983. 291-303.

Hoffmeister, Donna L. "Interview mit Martin Walser am 31. August 1985." *Vertrauter Alltag, gemischte Gefühle: Gespräche mit Schriftstellern über Arbeit in der Literatur*. Bonn: Bouvier, 1989. 165-78.

Kaes, Anton. "Porträt Martin Walser: Ein Gespräch." *German Quarterly* 57 (1984): 432-49.

Karasek, and Rolf Becker. "Triumphieren nicht gelernt." *Der Spiegel* 8 Oct. 1990. 291-300.

Konjetzky, Klaus. "Gespräch mit Martin Walser." *Weimarer Beiträge* 21.7 (1975): 70-84.

Lang, Roland. "Wie tief sitzt der Tick, gegen die Bank zu spielen? Interview mit Martin Walser." *Martin Walser*. Ed. Klaus Siblewski. Frankfurt/M.: Suhrkamp, 1981. 45-56.

Martin Walser im Gespräch mit Günter Gaus. Television Interview. ARD. NDR. 2 Nov. 1985.

Michaelsen, Sven. "Wer lädt schon einen Skinhead ein...." *Stern* 29 July 1993: 107-11.

Olson, Michael P. "Interview mit Martin Walser." *New German Review: A Journal of Germanic Studies* 4 (1988): 41-55.

Osterle, Heinz D. "Wo viel Schatten ist, ist auch viel Licht. Eindrücke eines verhinderten Einwanderers." *Bilder von Amerika: Gespräche mit deutschen Schriftstellern*. Ed. Heinz D. Osterle. Münster: Englisch Amerikanische Studien, 1987. 219-30.

Reinhold, Ursula. "Gespräch." *Tendenzen und Autoren: Zur Literatur der siebziger Jahre in der BRD*. Berlin: Dietz, 1982. 284-95.

Reitze, Paul F. Interview with Martin Walser. *Die Welt* 29 Sept. 1986: 9; 30 Sept. 1986: 7.

——. "Mit kleinen Magneten auf Jagd nach Figuren." *Die Welt* 4 Oct. 1988: 21, 23.

Schneider, Irmela. "Ansprüche an die Romanform: Ein Gespräch mit Martin Walser." *Die Rolle des Autors: Analysen und Gespräche*. Ed. Irmela Schneider. Literaturwissenschaft—Gesellschaftswissenschaft 56. Stuttgart: Klett, 1981. 99-107.

Totten, Monika. "Ein Gespräch mit Martin Walser in Neuengland." *Basis* 10 (1980): 194-214, 264. Repr. in *Martin Walser*. Ed. Klaus Siblewski. Frankfurt/M.: Suhrkamp, 1981. 25-44.

Walser, Martin. *Auskunft: 22 Gespräche aus 28 Jahren*. Ed. Klaus Siblewski. Frankfurt/M.: Suhrkamp, 1991.

Zimmer, Dieter. "Die Überanstrengung, die das pure Existieren ist." *Die Zeit* 18 May 1973: 27.

V. Secondary Sources

Anz, Thomas. "Der Fall Franz Horn (in den Romanen Martin Walsers) und Tilman Mosers diagnostizistische Lektüre." *Gesund oder Krank? Medizin, Moral und Ästhetik in der deutschen Gegenwartsliteratur*. Stuttgart: Metzler, 1989. 88-95.

Batt, Kurt. "Fortschreibung der Krise: Martin Walser." *Martin Walser*. Ed. Klaus Siblewski. Frankfurt/M.: Suhrkamp, 1981. 132-38.

Bausinger, Hermann. "Realist Martin Walser." *Martin Walser*. Ed. Klaus Siblewski. 11-22.

Beckermann, Thomas. "Die neuen Freunde: Walsers Realismus der Hoffnung." *Text + Kritik* 41/42 (1974): 46-53.

——. "Epilog auf eine Romanform. Martin Walsers Roman *Halbzeit*: Mit einer kurzen Weiterführung, die Romane *Das Einhorn* und *Der Sturz* betreffend." *Martin Walser*. Ed. Klaus Siblewski. 74-113.

——. "'Ich bin sehr klein geworden': Versuch über Walsers 'Entblößungsverbergungssprache.'" *Martin Walser: International Perspectives*. Eds. Jürgen E. Schlunk, and Armand E. Singer. American University Studies: Series 1, Germanic Languages and Literature 64. New York: Peter Lang, 1987. 15-27.

——. *Martin Walser oder die Zerstörung eines Musters: Literatursoziologischer Versuch über "Halbzeit."* Abhandlungen zur Kunst-, Musik-, und Literaturwissenschaft 114. Bonn: Bouvier, 1972.

Behre, Maria. "Erzählen zwischen Kierkegaard- und Nietzsche-Lektüre in Martin Walsers Novelle *Ein fliehendes Pferd. Literatur in Wissenschaft und Unterricht* 23 (1990): 3-18.

Bessen, Ursula. "Martin Walser — *Jenseits der Liebe*. Anmerkungen zur Aufnahme des Romans bei der literarischen Kritik." *Martin Walser*. Ed. Klaus Siblewski. 169-83.

Blocher, Friedrich K. "Unter dem Diktat des Scheins: Zu Walsers *Ein fliehendes Pferd*." *Identitätserfahrung: Literarische Beiträge von Goethe bis zu Walser*. Pahl-Rugenstein Hochschulschriften. Gesellschafts- und Naturwissenschaften 157. Cologne: Pahl-Rugenstein, 1984. 85-96.

Blöcker, Günter. "Poetiken des Mangels. Zu Martin Walser und Peter Rühmkorf." *Poetik*. Ed. Horst Dieter Schlosser, and Hans Dieter Zimmermann. Frankfurt/M.: Athenäum, 1988. 161-70.

Bohn, Volker. "Ein genau geschlagener Zirkel: Über *Ein fliehendes Pferd*." *Martin Walser*. Ed. Klaus Siblewski. 150-68.

Borries, Mechthild, and Dagmar Ploetz (eds.). *Martin Walser*. Werkheft Literatur. Munich: iudicium, 1989.

Breier, Harald. "Brando Malvolio, ein Mann von (fünfund)fünfzig Jahren: Form und Funktion des Zitats in Martin Walsers Roman *Brandung*. *Literatur in Wissenschaft und Unterricht* 21 (1988): 191-201.

Bullivant, Keith. *Realism Today: Aspects of the Contemporary German Novel*. Leamington Spa, Hamburg, New York: Berg, 1987.

Clark, Jonathan P. "A Subjective Confrontation with the German Past in *Ein fliehendes Pferd*." *Martin Walser: International Perspectives*. 47-58.

Cory, Mark E. "Romancing America: Reflections of Pocahontas in Contemporary German Fiction." *German Quarterly* 62 (1989): 320-328.

Demetz, Peter. "Martin Walser: Analyzing Everyman." *After the Fires: Recent Writings in the Germanies, Austria, and Switzerland*. San Diego: Harcourt Brace Jovanovich, 1986. 349-61.

Dierks, Manfred. "'Nur durch Zustimmung kommst du weg': Martin Walsers Ironie-Konzept und *Ein fliehendes Pferd*." *Literatur für Leser* 7 (1984): 44-53.

Doane, Heike. "Der Ausweg nach innen: Zu Martin Walsers Roman *Seelenarbeit*." *Seminar* 18 (1982): 196-212.

——. *Gesellschaftspolitische Aspekte in Martin Walsers Kristlein-Trilogie*. Bonn: Bouvier, 1978.

——. "Martin Walsers Ironiebegriff: Definition und Spiegelung in drei späten Prosawerken." *Monatshefte* 77 (1985): 195-212.

——. "Martin Walsers *Seelenarbeit*: Versuche der Selbstverwirklichung." *Neophilologus* 67 (1983): 262-72.

——. "Die Anwesenheit der Macht: Horns Strategie im *Brief an Lord Liszt*." *Martin Walser: International Perspectives*. 81-102.

——. "Innen- und Außenwelt in Martin Walser's [sic] Novelle *Ein fliehendes Pferd*." *German Studies Review* 3 (1980): 69-83.

——. "Zitat, Redensart und literarische Anspielung: Zur Funktion der gesprochenen Sprache in Martin Walsers Roman *Die Verteidigung der Kindheit.*" *Colloquia Germanica* 25 (1992): 289-305.

——. "Zur Intensivierung der politischen Thematik in Martin Walsers Kristlein-Trilogie." *Weimarer Beiträge* 30 (1984): 1842-51.

Dutschke, Manfred. "Jenseits der Wellen könnte man schwimmen — einige Bemerkungen zu Martin Walsers *Brandung.*" *German Studies in India* 10 (1986): 1-8.

Figge, Udo L. "'DEATH, BOUND TO': Literatur in Martin Walsers *Brandung. Das fremde Wort: Studien zur Interpretation von Texten.* Festschrift für Karl Maurer zum 60. Geburtstag. Eds. Ilse Nölting-Hauff, and Joachim Schulze. Amsterdam: B.R. Grüner, 1988.

Fickert, Kurt. "A Literary Collage: Martin Walser's *Brandung. The International Fiction Review* 15.2 (1988): 96-102.

Fischer, Bernd. "Walser und die Möglichkeiten moderner Erzählliteratur: Beobachtungen zum *Brief an Lord Liszt.*" *Martin Walser: International Perspectives.* 103-10.

Göttsche, Dirk. "Liebeserklärungen und Verletzungen — Zur Literaturkritik von Martin Walser und Ingeborg Bachmann." *Literaturkritik: Anspruch und Wirklichkeit.* DFG Symposium 1989. Ed. Wilfrid Barner. Stuttgart: Metzler, 1990. 197-212.

Gossmann, Wilhelm. "Heimatkunde in den Romanen Martin Walsers." *Literatur und Provinz: Das Konzept Heimat in der "neueren" Literatur.* Ed. Hans-Georg Pott. Paderborn: Schöningh, 1986. 85-100.

Haase, Donald. "Martin Walser's *Ein fliehendes Pferd* and the Tradition of Repetitive Confession." *32nd Mountain Interstate Foreign Language Conference.* Ed. Gregorio C. Martín. Winston Salem, NC, 1984. 137-44.

Hamm, Peter. "Martin Walsers Tendenz." *Martin Walser: International Perspectives.* 1-14. Ext. vers. of "Walsers Tendenz. Laudatio auf Martin Walser." *Deutsche Akademie für Sprache und Dichtung Darmstadt. Jahrbuch (1981/82).* Heidelberg: L. Schneider, 1982. 82-90.

Hick, Ulrike. *Martin Walsers Prosa: Möglichkeiten des zeitgenössischen Romans unter Berücksichtigung des Realismusanspruchs.* Stuttgarter Arbeiten zur Germanistik 126. Ed. Ulrich Müller et al. Stuttgart: Akademischer Verlag Hans-Dieter Heinz, 1983.

Hillmann, R[oger]. "*Ein fliehendes Pferd* — A Reconsideration." *AUMLA* 65 (1986): 48-55.

Hoffmeister, Donna L. "Fantasies of Individualism: Work Reality in *Seelenarbeit*." *Martin Walser: International Perspectives*. 59-70.

Jansen, Angelika C. "Walser's *Ein fliehendes Pferd:* Reception and Position of the Work in Contemporary West German Society." Diss. New York University, 1982.

Keith-Smith, Brian. "The German Academic Novel of the 1980s, or a Tale of Four Hetero-Academic Novels." *Literature on the Threshold: The German Novel in the 1980s*. Eds. Arthur Williams, Stuart Parkes, and Roland Smith. New York, Oxford, Munich: Berg, 1990. 135-52.

Knorr, Herbert. "Gezähmter Löwe — fliehendes Pferd. Zu Novellen von Goethe und Martin Walser." *Literatur für Leser* 2 (1979): 139-57.

Laemmle, Peter. "'Lust am Untergang' oder radikale Gegen-Utopie? *Der Sturz* und seine Aufnahme in der Kritik." *Martin Walser*. Ed. Klaus Siblewski. 204-13.

Liewerscheidt, Dieter. "Die Anstrengung, ja zu sagen: Martin Walsers Ironie-Konzept und die Romane von *Jenseits der Liebe* bis *Brief an Lord Liszt*." *Literatur für Leser* 9 (1986): 74-88.

Mathäs, Alexander. *Der kalte Krieg in der Literaturkritik: Der Fall Martin Walser*. German Life and Civilization 12. New York: Peter Lang, 1992.

Mews, Siegfried. "Ein entpolitisierter Heine? Zur Rezeption Heines in Martin Walsers *Brandung*." *Heine-Jahrbuch* 27 (1988): 162-69.

——. "Martin Walsers *Brandung*: Ein deutscher Campusroman?" *German Quarterly* 60 (1987): 220-36.

Möhrmann, Renate. "Der neue Parvenue: Aufsteigermentalität in Martin Walsers *Ehen in Philippsburg*." *Basis* 6 (1976): 140-60.

Moser, Tilmann. "Selbsttherapie einer schweren narzißtischen Störung." *Romane als Krankengeschichten: Über Handke, Meckel und Martin Walser*. Frankfurt/M.: Suhrkamp, 1985. 77-141.

Nägele, Rainer. "Martin Walser. Die Gesellschaft im Spiegel des Subjekts." *Zeitkritische Romane des 20. Jahrhunderts. Die Gesellschaft in der Kritik der deutschen Literatur*. Ed. Hans Wagener. Stuttgart: Reclam, 1975. 318-41.

——. "Zwischen Erinnerung und Erwartung: Gesellschaftskritik und Utopie in Martin Walsers *Einhorn.*" *Martin Walser*. Ed. Klaus Siblewski. 114-31.

Nef, Ernst. "Das bürgerliche Bewußtsein: hilflos. Zu Martin Walser, *Das Schwanenhaus.*" *Schweizer Monatshefte* 60 (1980): 1044-45.

——. "Die alltägliche Deformation des bürgerlichen Heldenlebens: Zu Martin Walsers *Seelenarbeit.*" *Schweizer Monatshefte* 59 (1979): 565-69.

Nolden, Thomas. "Der Schriftsteller als Literaturkritiker: Ein Porträt Martin Walsers." *Martin Walser: International Perspectives*. 171-83.

Parkes, Stuart. "Martin Walser: Social Critic or 'Heimatkünstler': Some Notes on His Recent Development." *New German Studies* 10 (1982): 67-82.

Pezold, Klaus. "Martin Walser am Übergang zu den achtziger Jahren." *Weimarer Beiträge* 30 (1984): 1830-41.

Pfaff, Lucie. *The American and German Entrepreneur: Economic and Literary Interplay*. American University Studies 16. New York: Peter Lang, 1989.

Pilipp, Frank. "Martin Walser's *Jagd*: Portrait of the Artist As a Not So Angry Old Man?" *Postscript: Publication of the Philological Association of the Carolinas* 9 (1992): 41-47.

——. *The Novels of Martin Walser: A Critical Introduction*. Studies in German Literature, Linguistics, and Culture 64. Columbia, SC: Camden House, 1991.

——. "Von den Nöten des Kleinbürgers: Individueller und sozialer Determinismus in Martin Walsers Prosa." *Leseerfahrungen mit Martin Walser: Neue Beiträge zu seinen Texten*. Eds. Gertrud Bauer Pickar, and Heike Doane. Munich: Fink, due 1994.

——. "Zum letzten Mal Kafka? Martin Walsers Roman *Das Schwanenhaus* im ironischen Lichte der *Verwandlung.*" *Colloquia Germanica* 22.3/4 (1989): 283-95.

Reinhold, Ursula. "Erfahrung und Realismus: Über Martin Walser." *Weimarer Beiträge* 21.7 (1975): 85-104.

——. "Zu Walsers Romanen in den siebziger Jahren." *Tendenzen und Autoren: Zur Literatur der siebziger Jahre in der BRD*. Berlin: Dietz, 1982. 295-308.

——. "Zu Martin Walsers *Seelenarbeit.*" *Sinn und Form* 32 (1980): 901-05.

Rockwood, Heidi. "The Nature Dimension in Martin Walser's *Ein fliehendes Pferd*. *West Virginia University Philological Papers* 37 (1991): 194-201.

Schlunk, Jürgen E., and Armand E. Singer (eds.). *Martin Walser: International Perspectives*. American University Studies: Series 1, Germanic Languages and Literature 64. New York: Lang, 1987.

Scholz, Joachim J. "Der Kapitalist als Gegentyp: Stadien der Wirtschaftswunderkritik in Walsers Romanen." *Martin Walser: International Perspectives*. 71-80.

Seifert, Walter. "Martin Walser: *Seelenarbeit*. Bewußtsinsanalyse und Gesellschaftskritik." *Deutsche Romane von Grimmelshausen bis Walser*. Ed. Jakob Lehmann. Königstein/Ts.: Scriptor, 1982. 545-61.

Siblewski, Klaus. "Die Selbstanklage als Versteck. Zu Xaver und Gottlieb Zürn." *Martin Walser*. Ed. Klaus Siblewski. 169-83.

——. "Eine Trennung von sich selbst. Zur *Gallistl'schen Krankheit*." *Martin Walser*. Ed. Klaus Siblewski. 139-49.

——. "Martin Walser." *Kritisches Lexikon zur deutschsprachigen Gegenwartsliteratur*. Ed. Heinz Ludwig Arnold. Munich: Text + Kritik, 1980.

Sinka, Margit M. "The Flight Motif in Martin Walser's *Ein fliehendes Pferd*." *Monatshefte* 74 (1982): 47-58.

Thomas, R. Hinton. "Martin Walser — The Nietzsche Connection." *German Life and Letters* 35 (1981/82): 319-28.

Töteberg, Michael. "Martin Walser." *Kritisches Lexikon zur deutschsprachigen Gegenwartsliteratur*. Ed. Heinz Ludwig Arnold. Munich: Text + Kritik, 1992.

Wagner-Egelhaaf, Martina. "Franz antwortet: Martin Walsers 'Brief an Lord Liszt' (1982) und Hugo von Hofmannsthals 'Ein Brief' (1902) oder Über das Vergleichen literarischer Texte." *Germanisch-Romanische Monatsschrift* 39.1 (1989): 58-72.

Waine, Anthony. *Martin Walser*. Munich: Text + Kritik, 1980.

——. "Martin Walser." *The Modern German Novel*. Ed. Keith Bullivant. Leamington Spa, Hamburg, New York: Berg, 1987. 259-75.

——. "Productive Paradoxes and Parallels in Martin Walser's *Seelenarbeit*." *German Life and Letters* 34 (1980/81): 297-305.

Weing, Siegfried. "Kierkegaardian Reflections in Martin Walser's *Ein fliehendes Pferd.*" *Colloquia Germanica* 25 (1992): 275-88.

Wiethölter, Waltraud. "'Otto' — oder sind Goethes Wahlverwandtschaften auf den Hund gekommen? Anmerkungen zu Martin Walsers Novelle *Ein fliehendes Pferd.*" *Zeitschrift für deutsche Philologie* 102 (1983): 240-59.

Winkler, Michael. "Martin Walser." *Dictionary of Literary Biography 75: Contemporary German Fiction Writers Second Series*. Eds. Wolfgang D. Elfe, and James Hardin. Detroit: Gale, 1988. 241-48.

VI. Selected Reviews:

Ayren, Armin. "Spion für die deutsche Einheit." Rev. of *Dorle und Wolf. Badische Zeitung* 4/5 Apr. 1987.

Baumgart, Reinhard. "Überlebensspiel mit zwei Opfern." Rev. of *Ein fliehendes Pferd. Der Spiegel* 27 Feb. 1978: 198-99.

Becker, Rolf. "Der Sturz des Franz Horn." Rev. of *Jenseits der Liebe. Der Spiegel* 5 Apr. 1976: 204-06.

——. "Martin Walsers Groteske ohne Ende." Rev. of *Brief an Lord Liszt. Frankfurter Allgemeine Zeitung* 11 Sept. 1982.

Braunschweig-Ullmann, Renate. "Spurensicherung der Vergangenheit als Schutz gegen die Angst." Rev. of *Die Verteidigung der Kindheit. Badische Neueste Nachrichten* 14 Aug. 1991.

Fuld, Werner. "Ein Spion mit Sehstörungen." Rev. of *Dorle und Wolf. Frankfurter Allgemeine Zeitung* 14 Mar. 1987.

Greiner, Ulrich. "Der gute Hirte Martin Walser." Rev. of *Seelenarbeit. Frankfurter Allgemeine Zeitung* 17 Mar. 1979.

——. "Der Selbstverhinderungskünstler." Rev. of *Brandung. Die Zeit* 30 Aug. 1985.

Grössel, Hanns. "Herr Dr. Gleitze und sein Knecht Xaver." Rev. of *Seelenarbeit. Neue Rundschau* 90 (1979): 284-87.

Halter, Martin. "Der alte Mann und das Mädchen." Rev. of *Brandung. Badische Zeitung* 11 Sept. 1985: 8.

——. "Das Dasein als fortgesetztes Weder-Noch." Rev. of *Dorle und Wolf. Basler Zeitung* 24 Mar. 1987: 33.

Hamm, Peter. "Das Prinzip Heimat." Rev. of *Seelenarbeit. Die Zeit* 16 Mar. 1979: 13.

Haubrich, Joachim. "Menschlicher Schwächeanfall." Rev. of *Dorle und Wolf. Allgemeine Zeitung Mainz* 2 May 1987.

Hendscheid, Eckhard. "Geld macht dumm und immer dümmer." Rev. of *Das Schwanenhaus. Frankfurter Rundschau* 23 Aug. 1980.

Hyde, Anthony. "The Crack in Wolf's Mirror." Rev. of *No Man's Land. New York Times Book Review* 22 Jan. 1989.

Karasek, Hellmuth. "Gott oder doch nur Gottlieb?" Rev. of *Das Schwanenhaus. Der Spiegel* 11 Aug. 1980: 131-33.

——. "Malvolio in Kalifornien." Rev. of *Brandung. Der Spiegel* 26 Aug. 1985: 158-59.

——. "Schattenwelt der Angestellten." Rev. of *Brief an Lord Liszt. Der Spiegel* 18 Oct. 1982: 244.

Kief, Dieter. "Anschreiben gegen die Entbehrungen der Gegenwart." Rev. of *Die Verteidigung der Kindheit. Eßlinger Zeitung* 5/6 Oct. 1991.

Kopitzki, Siegmund. "Ein Mann ohne Nimbus." Rev. of *Die Verteidigung der Kindheit. Südkurier* 9 Oct. 1991.

Kurz, Paul Konrad. "Wer hat Angst vor Martin Walser?: I. Der ironische Stil" Rev. of *Brief an Lord Liszt. Frankfurter Hefte* 38.1 (1983): 65-66.

Lüdke, Martin. "Eine vom Leben zerriebene Geschichte." Rev. of *Die Verteidigung der Kindheit. Frankfurter Rundschau* 10 Aug. 1991.

——. "Nichts Halbes, nichts Ganzes." Rev. of *Dorle und Wolf. Die Zeit* 20 March 1987.

Manthey, Jürgen. "Ehebruch mit Deutschlandkummer." Rev. of *Dorle und Wolf. Frankfurter Rundschau* 11 April 1987.

Neubert, Sabine. "Am Ende bleibt das Grabmonument." Rev of *Die Verteidigung der Kindheit. Neue Zeit* 9 Oct. 1991.

Nollau, Günther. "Ein 'General' beim A-3-Verkehr." Rev. of *Dorle und Wolf. Der Spiegel* 23 Mar. 1987: 228-30.

Pawel, Ernst. "The Empty Success of Herr Zürn." Rev. of *The Swan Villa. The New York Times Book Review* 10 Oct. 1982.

Reinhardt, Stephan. "Das sächsische Muster." Rev. of *Die Verteidigung der Kindheit*. *Süddeutsche Zeitung* 3/4 Aug. 1991.

Skwara, Erich Wolfgang. "Ein Parzival Roman der deutschen Teilung." Rev. of *Die Verteidigung der Kindheit*. *Neue Deutsche Literatur* 11 (1991): 130-36.

Sokolov, Raymond. "German Fiction Without Fear." Rev. of *Breakers*. *The Wall Street Journal* 17 Nov. 1987: 36.

v[on] M[att], B[eatrice]. "'Als wäre es das Ganze': Martin Walser: *Dorle und Wolf*." *Neue Zürcher Zeitung* 27 Mar. 1987, overseas edition: 51.

von Matt, Peter. "In Nöten bis zum Hals." Rev. of *Meßmers Gedanken*. *Frankfurter Allgemeine Zeitung* 23 Mar. 1985.

——. "Schick wie Designer-Jeans." Rev. of *Ohne einander*. *Der Spiegel* 2 Aug. 1993: 138-40.

Vormweg, Heinrich. "Ausrutscher ins Absonderliche." Rev. of *Dorle und Wolf*. *Süddeutsche Zeitung* 14 Apr. 1987.

——. "Bittersüß die Schmerzen des Alterns." Rev. of *Brandung*. *Süddeutsche Zeitung* 31 Aug. 1985: 104.

——. "Franz Horn gibt auf." Rev. of *Jenseits der Liebe*. *Merkur* 30 (1976): 483-85.

Notes on Contributors

Keith Bullivant, formerly Professor of German at the University of Warwick, teaches at the University of Florida. He has published numerous articles in the field of nineteenth- and twentieth-century German literature and on cultural topics. Among his book publications are *Literature in Upheaval* (1974), *Between Chaos and Order: The Work of Gerd Gaiser* (1980), *Realism Today: Aspects of the Modern German Novel* (1987), and *The Future of German Literature* (1993).

Heike A. Doane received her doctorate from McGill University. Formerly an Associate Professor of German at the University of Vermont, she is currently an independent scholar. She is the author of *Gesellschaftspolitische Aspekte in Martin Walsers Kristlein-Trilogie* (1978), *Hans und Heinz Kirch: Erläuterungen und Dokumente* (1985), and a number of articles on Walser, Storm, Seghers, Hans Werner Richter, and Christoph Hein.

Steve Dowden is a Humboldt Fellow at the Universität Konstanz. He is the author of *Sympathy for the Abyss: A Study in the Novel of German Modernism* (1986) and *Understanding Thomas Bernhard* (1991), and the editor of *Hermann Broch: Literature, Philosophy, Politics* (1988). He is at work on a book about Goethe's fiction and its relationship to modernism.

Bernd Fischer is Professor of German at Ohio State University. He is the author of *Literatur und Politik: Die "Novellensammlung von 1812" und das "Landhausleben" von Achim von Arnim* (1983), *Kabale und Liebe: Skepsis und Melodrama in Schillers bürgerlichem Trauerspiel* (1987), *Ironische Metaphysik: Die Erzählungen Heinrich von Kleists* (1988), and *Christoph Hein: Drama und Prosa im letzten Jahrzehnt der DDR* (1990).

Wulf Koepke, Distinguished Professor of German at Texas A&M University, has published extensively on literature of the Age of Goethe and on twentieth-century writers. He has authored books on Jean Paul (1977), Lion Feuchtwanger (1987), Johann Gottfried Herder (1987), and Max Frisch (1990) and has edited other volumes on Herder and exile literature. Professor Koepke is the founding president of the International Herder Society.

Richard Lawson is Professor Emeritus of German at the University of North Carolina at Chapel Hill. He was formerly editor of the University of North Carolina Studies in the Germanic Languages and Literatures and presently is coeditor at Ariadne Press. He has written several books in the fields of twentieth-century German literature and American literature. His most recent is a study of Elias Canetti; he is currently preparing a book on Thomas Mann.

Alexander Mathäs completed the *Staatsexamen* at the University of Tübingen and received his Ph.D. from the University of Texas at Austin. He is currently Assistant Professor of German at Virginia Polytechnic Institute and State University in Blacksburg. Professor Mathäs is the author of *Der Kalte Krieg in der Literaturkritik: Der Fall Martin Walser* (1992) as well as articles on literary theory and various aspects of Walser's work.

Siegfried Mews is Professor of German and Chair of the Department of Germanic Languages at the University of North Carolina at Chapel Hill. From 1983 until 1989 he was the Executive Director of the South Atlantic Modern Language Association (SAMLA) and Editor of the association's journal, the *South Atlantic Review*. Professor Mews has published extensively in the area of German literature of the nineteenth and twentieth centuries as well as in comparative literature. Author and editor of numerous books, he recently edited *Critical Essays on Bertolt Brecht* (1989).

Gertrud Bauer Pickar is Professor of German at the University of Houston. She has published a number of articles on German authors of the nineteenth and twentieth centuries and is the author of *The Dramatic Works of Max Frisch*. In addition, she has edited or coedited volumes on Grass, Expressionism, and the Age of Goethe and is currently coediting a collection of essays on Martin Walser for Houston German Studies with Heike Doane.

Frank Pilipp received his Ph.D. from the University of North Carolina at Chapel Hill and is currently Assistant Professor of German at Lynchburg College in Virginia. He is the author of *The Novels of Martin Walser: A Critical Introduction* (Camden House, 1991) and a number of articles on Walser and other contemporary German and Austrian writers, as well as on film.

Martina Wagner-Egelhaaf received her doctorate from the Universität Tübingen and is currently *Wissenschaftliche Assistentin* in Modern German Literature at the Universität Konstanz. Her dissertation, *Mystik der Moderne: Die visionäre Ästhetik der deutschen Literatur im 20. Jahrhundert*, was published by Metzler Verlag in 1989. She has written essays on mysticism and deconstruction, as well as articles on Rilke, Musil, Handke, and others. She is currently finishing a book on melancholy and literature.